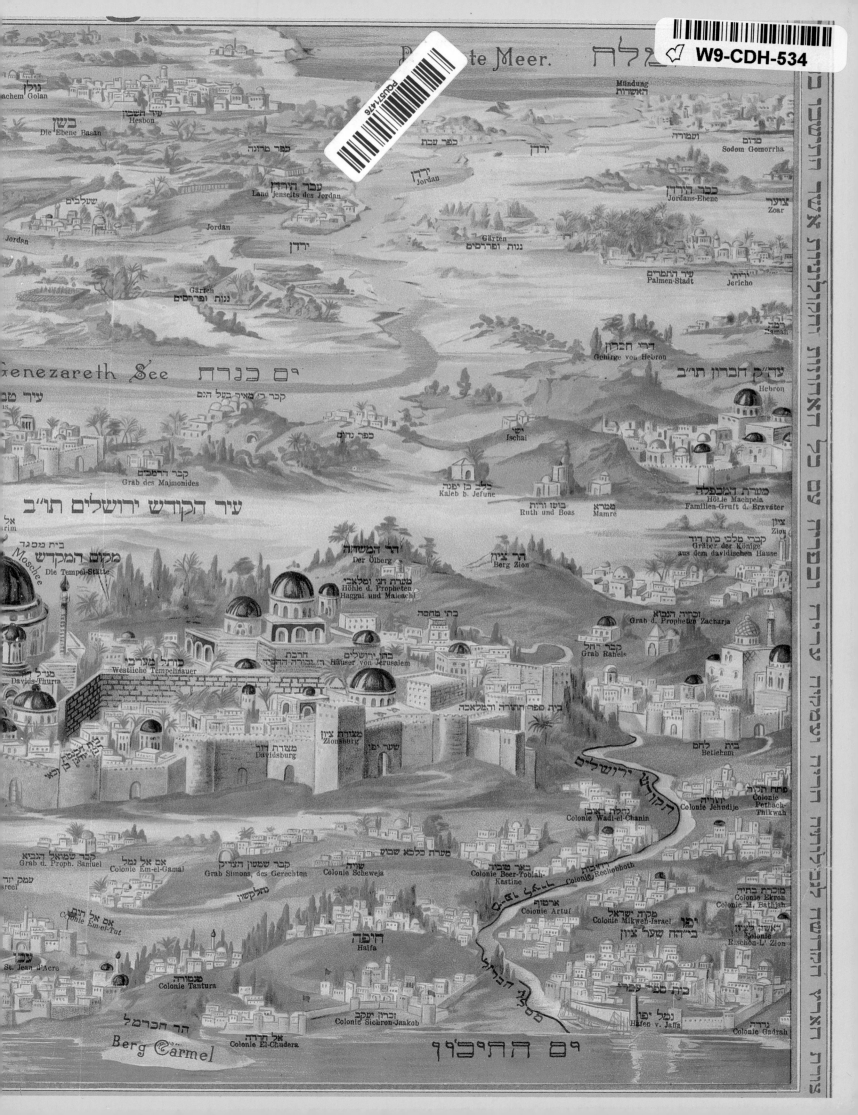

TO BE A FREE PEOPLE

The Saga of Israel

"LIBI" - THE FUND FOR STRENGTHENING ISRAEL'S DEFENCE

Dear SAR'EL Volunteer:

At the sixtieth anniversary of the State of Israel, LIBI and SAR'EL commend your devotion and contribution to the IDF, by personally participating in the endeavor of securing and defending our country.

LIBI is The Fund for Strengthening Israel's Defense. All contributions to LIBI are dedicated to the education, the medical and social services for the young and brave soldiers.

LIBI and SAR'EL are proud to present you with this book that narrates the saga of Israel, and reveals the spirit and the values that motivated us through the centuries - until we became, once again, a free people in our land.

LIBI salutes you and your friends, and is confident that your solidarity with Israel and your devotion to the IDF are a deep bond that will keep us together in the future.

For more information on Libi's activities, you can contact us through our web-site: **www.libi-fund.org.il**, or by E-mail: **libifund@netvision.net.il**.

SAR'EL
THE NATIONAL PROJECT
FOR VOLUNTEERS FOR
ISRAEL

General   Danny   Matt
Chairman of the LIBI Fund

General Aharon Davidi
Chairman of SAR'EL

Left: The Declaration of Independence

Nathan Alterman: " We shall pass over the land with ploughs."
Panoramic view of the Valley of Jezreel

TO BE A FREE PEOPLE

The Saga of Israel

*"...To be a free people in our land
The Land of Zion and Jerusalem..."*

from *Hatikvah* - "The Hope"
Israel's national anthem

Editor: MICHAEL BAR-ZOHAR

Magal Books

Tel Aviv

TO BE A FREE PEOPLE
The Saga of Israel

Edited by Dr. Michael Bar-Zohar

The English edition of this book was made possible with the help of:
The Emory Institute for the Study of Modern Israel, Dr. Kenneth W. Stein, Director
The Samueli Foundation, Orange County, California
Larry Thorpe and Barbara Williams, Atlanta, Georgia
We are deeply grateful for their support

Design:	**Yehuda Salomon**
English graphic adaptation:	**Studio Pini Hamou, Font-Art**
Special consultant to the editor:	**Dr. Mordechai Na'or**
Editorial coordinator:	**Nilly Lurie-Ovnat**
Research:	**Noga Cohen, Limor Vidas**
Editor and supervision of the English edition:	**Asher Weill**
Translations:	**Mordechai Beck, Chaya Galai, Asher Weill**
Production:	**Teper Ltd.**

ISBN 965-7226-11-2

The editor expresses his thanks and appreciation to all the writers, illustrators, photographers and copyright owners who gave permission for their work to be published in this book. Every attempt has been made to trace copyright owners: any omissions will be corrected in subsequent editions

Poems and works in copyright by writers not cited below ©Akum, the Society of Authors and Composers in Israel

Yaakov Orland, p.107, ©Triola Publishers and Akum; Avigdor HaMeiri, p.56, ©Nagan Music Publishers and Akum; Hadag Nahash and Sha'anan Street p.202 ©Anana Ltd. and Akum; Israel Rashal, p.108 ©Sharon Music Publishers and Akum; Yaakov Orland, p.175, Nathan Alterman p.121, Yehiel Mohar, p.158, Alexander Penn, p.81, Zerubavel Gilad, p.111, all ©Culture and Educational Enterprises and Akum; Yehuda Amichai, p.151 "From Man you came and from Man you will return" and S.Agnon p.33,129 "From Myself to Myself" ©Schocken Publishers; Naomi Shemer, p.159, ©Estate of Naomi Shemer; Mordechi Naor, p.107, Ben-Zvi Institute, Jerusalem; Amos Oz, p.200, ©Amos Oz, 1972; Uri Zvi Greenberg, p.26, ©"Collected Works of Uri Zvi Greenberg", volume 3, Bialik Institute, Jerusalem; Talma Alyagon-Roz ,p.234, words and music, ©Talma Alyagon-Rose. p. 20, 88. Haim Nachman Bialik: "In the City of Slaughter" and "The Dead of the Desert" from "Shirot Bialik." Alpha Publishing Company, Columbus, Ohio, 1987. p.26. Uri Zvi Greenberg: "Truth is One and not Two," from "Modern Hebrew Poetry: an Anthology," Federation of Zionist Youth, London, 1940. p.41. Yigael Yadin: "Bar-Kokhba." Weidenfeld and Nicholson, London and Jerusalem, 1971. p.43. Michael Bar-Zohar: "Yaacov Herzog – A Biography," Halban Publishers, London, 2004. p.48. Moshe Dayan: "Story of My Life," Weidenfeld and Nicholson, London, 1976. p.63. Haim Nachman Bialik: "To a Bird" from "Selected Poems of Hayyim Nahman Bialik," Bloch Publishing Company, New York. p.88. Dan Pagis: "Written in the Sealed Railway-Car" from "Points of Departure" ©Jewish Publication Society of America, 1981. p.90. Gideon Hausner: "Justice in Jerusalem," Schocken Publishers, New York, 1968. p.102. Hanoch Bartov: "The Brigade," Holt, Rinehart and Winston, New York. p.117. Geula Cohen: "The Voice of Valor 1943-48," Holt, Rinehart and Winston, New York, 1966. p.146. Moshe Shamir: "With his Own Hands," Israel Universities Press, Jerusalem and the Institute for the Translation of Hebrew Literature, 1970. p. 151. Yehuda Amichai: "Yitzhak's Last Kit Bag" from "Yehuda Amichai: A Life in Poetry 1948-1994," HarperCollins (Perennial Books), New York. p.163. Michael Bar-Zohar: "Facing a Cruel Mirror" MacMillan, New York. p.167. Meir Wieseltier: "To be Continued," from "The Flower of Anarchy," University of California Press, Los Angeles, 2003. p.179. Ronny Someck: "Poverty Line" from "The Fire Stays in Red," University of Wisconsin Press/Dryad Press". p.200. Amos Oz: "Under this Blazing Light," Cambridge University Press

Front endpapers: Land of Israel, Germany, 1890. Rear endpapers: Arthur Szyk, Scroll of Independence

Magal Books, P.O. Box 48031, Tel Aviv Israel
magalbooks@aol.com
Printed in Israel, 2008

The Declaration of Independence

ERETZ-ISRAEL was the birthplace of the Jewish people. Here their spiritual, religious and political identity was shaped. Here they first attained to statehood, created cultural values of national and universal significance and gave to the world the eternal Book of Books.

After being forcibly exiled from their †ditional attachment, Jews strove in every successive generation to re-establish themselves in their ancient homeland. In recent decades they returned in their masses. Pioneers, ma'apilim [(Hebrew - immigrants coming to Eretz-Israel in defiance of restrictive legislation] and defenders, they made deserts bloom, revived the Hebrew language, built villages and towns, and created a thriving community controlling its own economy and culture, loving peace but knowing how to defend itself, bringing the blessings of progress to all the country's inhabitants, and aspiring towards independent nationhood.

In the year 5657 (1897), at the summons of the spiritual father of the Jewish State, Theodore Herzl, the First Zionist Congress convened and proclaimed the right of the Jewish people to national rebirth in its own country.

This right was recognized in the Balfour Declaration of the 2nd November, 1917, and re-affirmed in the Mandate of the League of Nations which, in particular, gave international sanction to the historic connection between the Jewish people and Eretz-Israel and to the right of the Jewish people to rebuild its National Home.

The catastrophe which recently befell the Jewish people - the massacre of millions of Jews in Europe - was another clear demonstration of the urgency of solving the problem of its homelessness by re-establishing in Eretz-Israel the Jewish state, which would open the gates of the homeland wide to every Jew and confer upon the Jewish people the status of a fully privileged member of the comity of nations.

Survivors of the Nazi Holocaust in Europe, as well as Jews from other parts of the world, continued to migrate to Eretz-Israel, undaunted by difficulties, restrictions and dangers, and never ceased to assert their right to a life of dignity, freedom and honest toil in their national homeland.

In the Second World War, the Jewish community of this country contributed its full share to the struggle of the freedom- and peace-loving nations against the forces of Nazi wickedness and, by the blood of its soldiers and its war effort, gained the right to be reckoned among the peoples who founded the United Nations.

On the 29th November, 1947, the United Nations General Assembly passed a resolution calling for the establishment of a Jewish State in Eretz-Israel; the General Assembly required the inhabitants of Eretz-Israel to take such steps as were necessary on their part for the implementation of that resolution. This recognition by the United Nations of the right of the Jewish people to establish their state is irrevocable.

This right is the natural right of the Jewish people to be masters of their own fate, like all other nations, in their own sovereign State.

ACCORDINGLY WE, MEMBERS OF THE PEOPLE'S COUNCIL, REPRESENTATIVES OF THE JEWISH COMMUNITY OF ERETZ-ISRAEL AND OF THE ZIONIST MOVEMENT, ARE HERE ASSEMBLED ON THE DAY OF THE TERMINATION OF THE BRITISH MANDATE OVER ERETZ-ISRAEL AND, BY VIRTUE OF OUR NATURAL AND HISTORIC RIGHT AND ON THE STRENGTH OF THE RESOLUTION OF THE UNITED NATIONS GENERAL ASSEMBLY, HEREBY DECLARE THE ESTABLISHMENT OF A JEWISH STATE IN ERETZ-ISRAEL, TO BE KNOWN AS THE STATE OF ISRAEL.

WE DECLARE that, with effect from the moment of the termination of the Mandate being tonight, the eve of Sabbath, the 6th Iyar, 5708 (15th May, 1948), until the establishment of the elected, regular authorities of the state in accordance with the Constitution which shall be adopted by the Elected Constituent Assembly not later than the 1st October 1948, the People's Council shall act as a Provisional Council of State, and its executive organ, the People's Administration, shall be the provisional government of the Jewish state, to be called "Israel".

THE STATE OF ISRAEL will be open for Jewish immigration and for the Ingathering of the Exiles; it will foster the development of the country for the benefit of all its inhabitants; it will be based on freedom, justice and peace as envisaged by the prophets of Israel; it will ensure complete equality of social and political rights to all its inhabitants irrespective of religion, race or sex; it will guarantee freedom of religion, conscience, language, education and culture; it will safeguard the Holy Places of all religions; and it will be faithful to the principles of the Charter of the United Nations.

THE STATE OF ISRAEL is prepared to cooperate with the agencies and representatives of the United Nations in implementing the resolution of the General Assembly of the 29th November, 1947, and will take steps to bring about the economic union of the whole of Eretz-Israel.

WE APPEAL to the United Nations to assist the Jewish people in the building-up of its state and to receive the State of Israel into the comity of nations.

WE APPEAL - in the very midst of the onslaught launched against us now for months - to the Arab inhabitants of the State of Israel to preserve peace and participate in the upbuilding of the state on the basis of full and equal citizenship and due representation in all its provisional and permanent institutions.

WE EXTEND our hand to all neighboring states and their peoples in an offer of peace and good neighborliness, and appeal to them to establish bonds of cooperation and mutual help with the sovereign Jewish people settled in its own land. The State of Israel is prepared to do its share in a common effort for the advancement of the entire Middle East.

WE APPEAL to the Jewish people throughout the Diaspora to rally round the Jews of Eretz-Israel in the tasks of immigration and upbuilding and to stand by them in the great struggle for the realization of the age-old dream - the redemption of Israel.

PLACING OUR TRUST IN THE ALMIGHTY, WE AFFIX OUR SIGNATURES TO THIS PROCLAMATION AT THIS SESSION OF THE PROVISIONAL COUNCIL OF STATE, ON THE SOIL OF THE HOMELAND, IN THE CITY OF TEL-AVIV, ON THIS SABBATH EVE, THE 5TH DAY OF IYAR, 5708 (14TH MAY,1948).

David Ben-Gurion

Daniel Auster / Mordechai Bentov / Yitzhak Ben Zvi / Eliyahu Berligne / Fritz Bernstein / Rabbi Wolf Gold / Meir Grabovsky / Yitzhak Gruenbaum / Dr. Abraham Granovsky / Eliyahu Dobkin / Meir Wilner-Kovner / Zerach Wahrhaftig / Herzl Vardi / Rachel Cohen / Rabbi Kalman Kahana / Sa'adia Kobashi / Rabbi Yitzchak Meir Levin / Meir David Loewenstein / Zvi Luria / Golda Myerson / Nachum Nir / Zvi Segal / Rabbi Yehuda Leib Hacohen Fishman / David Zvi Pinkas / Aharon Zisling / Moshe Kolodny / Eliezer Kaplan / Abraham Katznelson / Felix Rosenbluth / David Remez / Berl Repetur / Mordechai Shattner / Ben Zion Sternberg / Bechor Shitreet / Moshe Shapira / Moshe Shertok

Tel Aviv, 5th Iyar, 5708, 14th May, 1948.

Contents

"If I forget Thee, O Jerusalem..." Panoramic View

Chapter 3 — THEY KEPT FAITH THROUGHOUT THEIR DISPERSION — 50

Chapter 4 — THEY RETURNED TO THEIR LAND, THEY REVIVED THEIR LANGUAGE — 68

Chapter 5 — AGAINST THE FORCES OF NAZI WICKEDNESS — 86

Tel-Aviv, Panoramic View

Introduction

"What are we doing here?
Why did we come here?"
(Rami, an Israeli teenager,
in a youth colloquium, Tel Aviv)

What are we doing here?

The answer to this question was crystal clear to the 14 young people, members of the BILU group (an acrostic for the Hebrew phrase *Beit Ya'akov Lechu VeNelcha* – "House of Jacob come and let us go," *Isaiah* 2:5) when they descended, hearts pounding, on to the beach of Jaffa on the 19th of the Hebrew month of Tammuz 5642 (8th July 1882). The 13 young men and one young woman who had sailed from the Russian port of Odessa, were the trailblazers of an idealistic youth movement, dedicated to an almost impossible dream: to establish a Jewish state in the Land of Israel.

Their path was not easy. Critics and cynics called them "dreamers," "retarded" or even "insane," opining that there was no chance to realise their dreams in this forgotten land, in a dark and neglected corner of the Ottoman Empire. There was no chance for this delusion, the critics surmised, and they treated the young group with disdain and mockery.

No one could have believed that within 120 years, the Land of Israel would have become a Jewish state with nearly seven million citizens, six million of whom were Jews; that this state would have to its credit amazing achievements in science, culture, agriculture, sophisticated industry, and military strength; that it would have brought over exiles from the four corners of the earth and transformed them into one nation In the course of the 20th century, great empires rose and fell; political ideologies swept over the globe, wars demolished the world order. Communism rose and collapsed, Nazism burst forth and was overcome, the Third World of newly-liberated states brought great hopes which too often melted away in bitter disappointment. But the biggest achievement of all, the most astounding in the annals of the preceding hundred years, was the establishment of the sovereign State of Israel.

What are we doing here?
Only a few decades ago, Jewish blood was freely shed in both the west and the east. Our Jewish brethren were slaughtered in horrible massacres, choked by poison gas, burnt in the crematoria of Auschwitz and Treblinka. The establishment of the State of Israel sent a clear message: Never Again! Nobody would be able once again to raise his hand against the Jewish people; should they do so – they would be hit hard in return. This applied not only to the Jews who had immigrated to Israel or had been born there, but equally to the entire Jewish people. Israel had given a whole people stature and had planted within their hearts the realization that now they had both a protector and a home.

What are we doing here?
Over the years, the collective memory of the Israeli nation became indistinct; the heroic struggles, the unforgettable characters, the extraordinary achievements – faded away into the shadows of the past. Truths that were once self-evident melted away or were challenged. Pseudo-historians, sceptics and scoffers twisted or dwarfed the awesome achievements that mark the State of Israel. Mistakes that Israel made along the way, mistakes that characteristically are alien to our religious, social and ethical principles, dimmed the light of our lives. The dream of a perfect society that acts according to the traditional commands of Judaism, is yet to be fully realised.

What are we doing here?
Many of us are not always aware of the deep, historical significance of the Return to Zion and our existence as a free people in a democratic Jewish state. Some of us are consumed by bitter self-criticism, which, even if sometimes deserved,

denies the unique achievements of Israeli society. There are those who choose the Jewish solution of yesteryear, and again take up the staff of the wanderer and depart across the seas in search of an easier life. Many of us forget either the reason or the goal of the renewed independence of Israel.

What are we doing here?

We have chosen to respond to this question not through our own voice, but through the voices of the dreamers, the men and women of action, the pioneers and the fighters, the ideologists and the spiritual leaders, the witnesses to both its successes and its failures. We have sought to gather together the major canonical texts from the past and from the present, which reflect the uniqueness and totality of the experience of Zionism and the State of Israel.

Moshe Dayan once said to me: "If you wish to understand the soul of a people – go to the poet." We went to poets and writers of prose, to lyricists, to painters and to caricaturists. We assembled here the most representative texts we could find which refer to the deep bond attaching us to Israel, without taint or hint of political bias. Beside expressions of patriotism we did not hesitate to present words of harsh criticism aimed at some of the negative phenomena in our lives, against which individuals, organisations and legal institutions constantly struggle. This too is patriotism; this too is democracy, this too is Zionism. When President De Gaulle was once asked why he lavished such respect on his bitter foe, the philosopher Jean Paul Sartre, he replied: "Sartre is also France." Israel's critics are likewise part of us.

In this book we have put together speeches and articles, poems and lyrics of popular songs, letters and military orders, extracts from diaries and excerpts from books and Supreme Court legal decisions, oaths of soldiers, verses from the Bible and the Talmud; all of these together with photographs and postcards, documents, newspaper articles and proclamations, stamps, paintings, caricatures and drawings of historical significance.

The book is constructed according to the Declaration of Independence of May, 1948. From its ringing phrases, we selected 12 sentences, which express the essential Israeli identity. Each sentence opens one of 12 chapters, in which we have gathered together extracts related to that topic.

I would like to express my appreciation to the people whose help was invaluable in helping me choose the material: Dr. Mordechai Na'or, a leading expert on the history of the Land of Israel; Yoram Teharlev, a distinguished songwriter and poet of Eretz Israel; Yossi Perlovitz, Yishai Cordova, and Arik Ben Shalom, of the Hotza'a Laor publishing house; editorial coordinator Nilly Ovnat, who expertly managed the massive day to day organizational work of the team - Noga Cohen and Limor Vidas. Yehuda and Danit Salomon designed the book with great flair. I was also helped by many of the country's leading authors and poets, whose advice was very important to me. My longtime colleague Asher Weill took responsibility for editing and supervising this English edition of the original Hebrew book.

The final responsibility for the choice and character of material is of course mine and mine alone.

Ultimately, this book is my response to the question "What are we doing here?" This is the land where we, the Israelis, became a free people again after two thousand years of exile.

Michael Bar-Zohar

Chapter 1

Israel's annual Independence Day celebrations are traditionally marked by the kindling of 12 torches - symbolizing the 12 tribes of Israel - on Mount Herzl, the burial place of the founder of modern political Zionism, Theodor Herzl. The torches are lit by citizens from all walks of life and each chapter of this book begins with one of their declarations.

 ## The Independence Day Torch

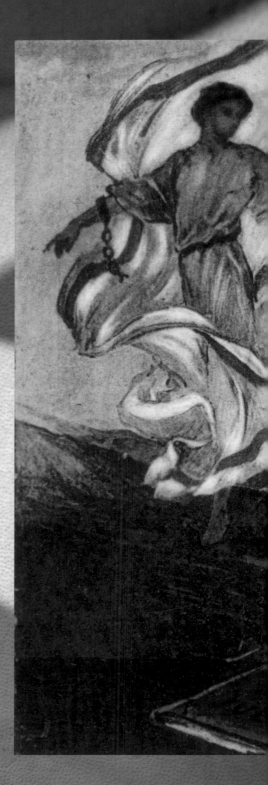

"I, Emanuel Cohen, son of Arthur and Naomi, born in Basel and a student at the Mount Zion Yeshiva; great-grandson of Rabbi Asher Michael Cohen, rabbi of Basel and a participant in the First Zionist Congress; grandson of Moshe Shapira, a leader of the religious Zionist movement and a signatory to the Scroll of Independence; have the honor to kindle this torch to mark the 49th anniversary of the State of Israel.

In homage to this place, Mount Herzl and the person buried thereon, Benjamin Ze'ev Herzl, who founded the Zionist Movement in his belief in the strength of the Jewish people to turn the legend into a state.

In honor of the uniting of different streams and factions, whether spiritual or practical, religious or socialist, liberal or revisionist, in the joint Zionist endeavor,

In honor of the promise to our father Jacob which has supported us through the generations and which is now revealed before our eyes: "For here am I, with you and I will preserve you whither you shall go and I will return you to this Land."

And to the glory of Israel.

Eve of Independence Day, 1997

בארץ־ישראל קם העם היהודי, בה עוצבה דמותו הרוחנית,
הדתית והמדינית, בה חי חיי קוממיות ממלכתית, בה יצר נכסי תרבות
לאומיים וכלל־אנושיים והוריש לעולם כולו את ספר הספרים הנצחי

THE BIRTHPLACE OF
THE JEWISH PEOPLE

לאחר שהוגלה העם מארצו בכוח הזרוע שמר לה אמונים בכל ארצות
פזוריו, ולא חדל מתפלה ומתקוה לשוב לארצו ולחדש בתוכה את חירותו

מתוך קשר היסטורי ומסורתי זה חתרו היהודים בכל דור לשוב ולהאחז

The Promise

The promise to Abraham.
Postage stamp based on a
drawing by E.M Lilien

The Promise to Abraham

The Lord said to Abram, after Lot had separated from him, "Lift up your eyes, and look from the place where you are, northward and southward and eastward and westward; for all the land which you see I will give to you and your descendants for ever. I will make your descendants as the dust of the earth; so that if one can count the dust of the earth, your descendants also can be counted. Arise, walk through the length and the breadth of the land, for I will give it to you."

Genesis 13: 14-17

The Promise to Jacob

And behold, the Lord stood above it and said, "I am the Lord, the God of Abraham your father and the God of Isaac; the land on which you lie I will give to you and to your descendants; and your descendants shall be like the dust of the earth, and you shall spread abroad to the west and to the east and to the north and to the south; and by you and your descendants shall all the families of the earth bless themselves. Behold I am with you and will keep you wherever you go, and will bring you back to this land; for I will not leave you until I have done that of which I have spoken to you."

Genesis 28: 13-15

The Chosen People

"For you are a people holy to the Lord your God; the Lord your God has chosen you to be a people for his own possession, out of all the peoples that are on the face of the earth."

Deuteronomy 7: 6

Shema Yisrael - Hear O Israel!

"Hear, O Israel: The Lord our God is one Lord; and you shall love the Lord your God with all your heart and with all your soul, and with all your might. And these words which I command you this day shall be upon your heart; and you shall teach them diligently to your children, and shall talk of them when you sit in your house, and when you walk by the way, and when you lie down, and when you rise. And you shall bind them as a sign upon your hand, and they shall be as frontlets between your eyes. And you shall write them on the doorposts of your house and on your gates."

Deuteronomy 6: 4 - 8

Hatikvah - "The Hope."
Right: an advertisement for a cigarette company, early 20th cent., USA.
Below: Postcard, Russia, 1902

Hatikvah ("The Hope")

Naftali Hertz Imber

"Hatikvah" is the symbol of the struggle to establish the State of Israel in our days. The song, which has become the national anthem of Israel, was composed by Naftali Hertz Imber (1856 - 1909). The melody was composed apparently under the influence of a traditional folk song. Some see it as derived from the Spanish folk tradition, or from cantorial music; and there are those who see a similarity to the "Moldava" symphony by the Czech composer Bedrich Smetana. Other authorities maintain it was based on a Romanian folk song. Imber offered "Hatikvah" along with "Mishmar HaYarden" ("The Jordan Guard") and other Zionist-inspired poems, to publishers in an original manner. In 1886, he published the following announcement in the *HaZvi* newspaper:

"To printers, lovers of Zion
I have a manuscript, which I have entitled "Barkai" whose contents are various poems which I wrote in the Holy Land, about Israel and the settling of Eretz Israel and about the settlements – all of which are in the national spirit. Whosoever among the printers wishes to purchase them, please contact me – Naftali Hertz Imber, Jerusalem."

In 1898, a publisher was found for "Barkai" and in it was the first version of "Hatikvah," called "Tikvatenu" –"Our Hope."

Tikvatenu

We have not yet lost our hope
the ancient hope
To return to the land of our ancestors
to the city where David lived.
All the while his heart beats
the Jewish soul yearns -
looking eastward
his eyes on Zion.
All the while, tears that fill our eyes
fall abundantly like rain
and thousands of our people
still visit their ancestors' graves.
All the while, the walls of our treasures

appear before our eyes
and over the ruins of our Temple
the eyes still weep.
All the while, the waters of the majestic Jordan
roll through its banks
and into the tumultuous Sea of Kinneret
they fall in a roaring voice.
All the while, there along the way
where a gate was destroyed in desolation,
amidst the ruins of Jerusalem
a daughter of Zion still weeps.
All the while the pure tears of my

people flow
to cry for Zion.
At the beginning of the watch
he will rise at midnight.
All the while the love of the nation
beating inside the Jewish heart –
we can still hope, even today
that the angry God will show mercy
to us.
Listen, my brethren in the lands of my wandering
the voice of one of our prophets,
"the last Jew
is also the last of our hopes."

The first two verses of the poem quickly became the anthem of Hovevei Zion (the movement "Lovers of Zion"), and it was sung at the Zionist Congresses from the sixth onward. With the establishment of the State of Israel, "Hatikvah" became the country's national anthem. The first verse of the song was changed according to a suggestion by Dr. Cohen-Matmon, the founder of Tel Aviv's Gymnasia Herzlia, the first Jewish high school in the land. Over time "the ancient hope" became "the 2000-year old hope" while "the city in which David lived" in the original version, became "The Land of Israel and Jerusalem."

As long as deep in the heart
The soul of a Jew yearns
And towards the East
An eye looks to Zion

Our hope is not yet lost
The hope of two thousand years
To be a free people in our land
The Land of Zion and Jerusalem

A Free People

Amnon Rubinstein

There are those who see in "Hatikvah" a worn-out declaration, whose time has passed. By contrast, Amnon Rubinstein penned a contemporary, more relevant, version of the national anthem. Prof. Rubinstein, a former minister of education and a Knesset member, is a professor of law, an author and journalist.

The weak-hearted among us stand powerless in the face of the difficulties that Israel is confronted with from within and without. We, who have attempted what no other nation has before us, know that the way is to become stronger and more steadfast. If the ground is burning, we have to run faster. If the situation is hard, we have to work harder. If political and social distress exists in Israel, then we have to do something to relieve it; the vitality and determination of Israeli society justify the hope that great disappointments will result in a return to the basic foundations of Zionism.

The essence of this return is freedom:

Freedom to be masters of our own fate.

Freedom from dependence on the goodwill of others.

Freedom from the spiritual burden that created this dependence inside us.

Freedom from dependence on the rich man's table.

Freedom to shape our own society.

Freedom of each of us to take part in the creative process.

Freedom to curb our individual freedoms in order to live together.

In order that this hope be not just a wish, but that it be transformed into reality, it is necessary to decide – that is, each of us has to decide – that there is no one else to look after us, that there is no one who can do the work instead of us, and that there is no one else to lead us if we don't lead ourselves. It is that simple.

The great decisions are always simple. Sometimes it seems that beyond the mask of endless words, the truth stands out, and that only simple words can express it. Simple words that define the central challenge of contemporary Israel, such as those which conclude "Hatikvah":

"To be a free people in our land

the Land of Zion and Jerusalem."

From *Lehiot Am Hofshi*, 1977

The Merit of "Hatikvah"

Yosef Lapid

Yosef (Tommy) Lapid was for many years a journalist for the "Ma'ariv" daily newspaper. In 1999, he was elected to the Knesset as head of a new political party, "Shinui" ("Change") He served as minister of justice from 2003 until leaving the government in 2004.

One of our ambassadors abroad suggested replacing the traditional version of Hatikvah with a more up-to-date text of his own creation:

"Peace and Justice are our goals

A Hebrew banner as a light unto the nations

our flag, blue and white, like a prayer shawl

Our capital Jerusalem."

The same ambassador also composed an anthem for Guatemala. Apparently he writes Spanish better than he does Hebrew. Otherwise the Guatemalan government would have good cause to sever diplomatic ties with Israel. Incredibly, the government secretary, Danny Naveh, placed on the daily agenda of the Ministerial

Committee for Symbols and Ceremonies, the suggestion to append this infantile text to the official version of Hatikvah. Fortunately, the Prime Minister, Benjamin Netanyahu, erased the absurd idea.

The new-old complaint is that Hatikvah no longer reflects today's reality. There had already been several suggestions: to replace it with Naomi Shemer's "Jerusalem of Gold" or Yaacov Rotblit and Yair Rosenblum's *Shir HaShalom* ("Song of Peace.") A member of Kibbutz Shomrat suggested adding to Hatikvah two verses from the "Song of Ascents" from the Book of Psalms.

Arabs complain that, with all due respect to the national anthem, the Zionist dream does not exactly express the yearning inside their hearts. Nevertheless, states are unlikely to change their national anthem, unless the regime changes radically, as happened in Russia.

Even after the fall of Hitler, the Germans retained their anthem, only ceasing to sing the verse *Deutschland über alles* ("Germany above all.") The British merely substitute the word "King" for "Queen" according to circumstances. The international anthem of the workers, the Internationale virtually disappeared from our stages with the demise of Marxism.

But Zionism is not dead. It only succeeded. There is no reason to abolish the anthem that accompanied the realisation of the dream. The whole beauty of Hatikvah lies in its innocence. The time that has elapsed has covered this innocence with a patina, which should not be erased. Whoever suggested changing Hatikvah because it is no longer relevant, should also call to change, too, the Menorah (candelabrum) as a symbol of the state, since who lights today with candles?

Would it occur to anyone to change the clothing worn by Venus de Milo because of changing fashions? Should one erase some of the prophets because their prophecies were fulfilled? Or because their prophecies were not fulfilled? Could you find a sane Frenchman willing to change the text of the *Marseillaise* because there is no equality in the world?

Naftali Hertz Imber wrote a song. Is everyone permitted to tinker with someone else's creation as if it were his own? Should we add verses to "Bialik's "City of Slaughter" because of what happened in the Holocaust? Apart from all that, who says that our period is so worthy of being remembered? In my opinion, it is not Hatikvah that should be adapted to reality, but that reality should strive to approach the spirit of Hatikvah.

From "I'm Still Talking," 1998

The Zionist flag
Above: A card for the New Year, New York, 1910
Right: The flag printed on cloth, early 20th cent.

Settling in Eretz Israel is Equal to all the Other Commandments

The Tana'im ("Teachers")

Back cover of a pamphlet, "Jugend," Germany, 1904

The fundamental essence of Zionism lies in the return of the Jewish people to Zion. This is not news. One thousand eight hundred years ago, the Tana'im (sages of the period of the Mishnah) had already made the decision in a responsum, and thereafter in the Talmud and Midrashim.

A person should dwell in the Land of Israel, even in a city where the majority are non-Jews, rather than in the Diaspora, even when all the inhabitants therein are Jewish. This is to teach us that settling in the Land of Israel is equal to all the rest of the commandments of the Torah and those who are buried in Eretz Israel, it is as if they were buried beneath the [Temple] altar. A person should not go to the Diaspora, except if wheat is unavailable. Rabbi Shimon said: "To what is being referred here? [Only] in a time when food is not to be found. But when it can be found, even the tiniest quantity - he should not leave."

Thus, too, did Rabbi Shimon say: "Elimelech was among the leaders of the generation and sustained the population, but because he left Israel, he and his sons died from starvation, and all Israel was sustained by their lands."

Tosefta Avodah Zara 4:5

To Found a Jewish Kingdom

Moses Hess

After generations of yearning and unfulfilled longings for Eretz Israel, there arose heralds of political Zionism who for the first time set the goal: a Jewish state in the Land of Israel. Moses Hess (1812-1875), philosopher, socialist and Zionist, wrote in his book "Rome and Jerusalem".

The Jews, who are destined to fulfil an exalted and elevated role in the world, need to be fortified on a basis of a true national existence, and this is possible only in the Land of Israel - on their ancestral land. The political situation today makes it possible to establish Jewish sovereignty in Eretz Israel... The practical work must begin with settlement of the land; with [Jewish] farmers working the soil. The kernel of the future Jewish state will not come from the Jews of the west, but rather, from the Jews of the east...

"Rome and Jerusalem," 1862

To be as the Other Nations

Peretz Smolenskin

In 1868, Peretz Smolenskin (1842-1885), editor of the monthly *HaShahar* ("The Dawn") published in Vienna, wrote:

They say to us: "Let us be like the other nations! I, too, will say, we shall be like all the nations; to pursue and achieve knowledge, to forsake evil and folly, to be loyal citizens in the countries of our dispersion; but we shall also be like the other nations by not being ashamed of the origins from which we are hewn, we shall be like all the nations in valuing our language and the respect of our people! We shall not feel ashamed or disgraced by our faith, for the end of our exile will come; a day will come and sovereignty will return to the House of Israel, just as the nations are not ashamed, and expect to redeem their souls from foreigners.

"HaShahar," 1868

The One and Only Refuge!

Yehuda Leib Pinsker

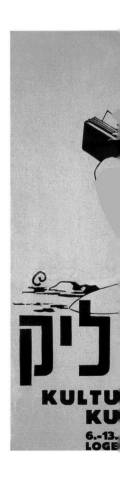

Score for the piano of the "Redemption March,"
London, 1922

Dr Yehuda Leib Pinsker (1821-1891) caused an intellectual revolution in the Jewish world when he published, anonymously, his pamphlet *Auto-Emancipation* ("Self-Emancipation") where he pursued the idea of the resurrection of the Jewish people. At the beginning of the pamphlet, Pinsker quoted the words of Hillel the Elder: "If I am not for myself, who will be for me? And if not now, when?" Pinsker drew the called-for conclusion and became one of the founders of the *Hovevei Zion* ("Lovers of Zion") movement in Russia.

What we desire to do is neither novel nor does it present a danger to anyone. Instead of the many shelters, which we are wont historically to request, we seek only one shelter, except that its establishment has to be politically secured as well.

The Jews are not a living nation; they are strangers in every place, and thus scorned.

Offering Jews equal civic and political rights is insufficient to give them standing in the eyes of the nations. The only correct and worthy solution is the creation of a Jewish nationalism, a people dwelling in its own land, the self-emancipation of the Jews, so as to bring about an equalisation of their status as a nation among other nations, through the acquisition of a homeland of their own.

Let us not delude ourselves by believing that humanism and intelligence will give rise at one time to a radical healing for the sickness of our people. A lack of national self-awareness and self-confidence, and the lack of political initiative and unity are the enemies of our national renaissance. Let us not be forced to wander from exile to exile; we require a wide, fertile land of refuge; a place of gathering that is our own... A congress of influential Jews must pave the way for a national Jewish revival...help youselves, and God will help you.

Y.L. Pinsker's "Auto-Emancipation," 1882

"The Last Generation of Slavery and the First of Redemption!"

Haim Nachman Bialik

In the above words from Bialik's (1873-1934) long epic poem "The Dead of the Desert" there is a strong and resounding echo of Pinsker's clarion call.

Yet sometimes the wilderness awakens and
grows weary of the eternal stillness
and awakens to be avenged with great
vengeance for its desolation by its Creator.
It lifts itself up against Him with a tempest and
with pillars of sand rebels against Him.
Suddenly it arises and kicks the Creator and
shakes Him on the Throne of Glory,
daring to heap abuse on His face and hurl it in
angry wrath to His feet
to confound Him because of all of His world
and restore chaos unto its former status.
Then the Creator shakes and grows angry and
the face of Heaven changes...
At that moment seized by violent strength

awakening the menacing might.
Suddenly arises a generation powerful and
strong, a generation strong for battle
Their eyes flashing and their faces burning,
and their hands to the swords!
The mighty thunder with their voices, sixty
myriads,
a voice splitting the tempest and contesting the
roaring of the angry wilderness,
round about them storming: round about them
raging.
They call out:
"We are warriors!
The last generation of slavery and the first of
redemption are we!

A Jewish State

Theodor (Benjamin Ze'ev) Herzl

Herzl: a commemorative stamp, Warsaw, 1917

"Death to the Jews" roared the inflamed French crowd who had gathered around the hall of the military law courts in Paris in which the Jewish army captain, Alfred Dreyfus, had been accused of espionage and treason. One of the journalists covering the trial stood amazed and horrified at the wave of hatred that consumed the crowd. He was convinced that Dreyfus was an innocent man, and he believed that the main motivation for his sentence was the profound degree of anti-Semitism that was rooted in the people of Europe. The journalist was a tall, young Jew with a full black beard and blazing eyes: Theodor Herzl (1860- 1904), a writer for the Viennese newspaper *Neue Freie Presse*. The expressions of hatred emanating from every side did not only shock him as a Jew; they also shattered one of his dreams: that the Jews could achieve equal rights in Europe.

Following the Dreyfus trial, a new idea took root in Herzl's mind that gave him no rest. He spent days and nights writing a short brochure in which he detailed his ideas. While he was writing, his soul was on fire, and he wrote that he "felt the fluttering of the wings of history" above his head. The book, *Der Judenstaat* - "The Jewish State" was published in German in Vienna in 1896. The following are some extracts from Herzl's brochure.

Petit-point wall hanging: early 20th cent.

Poster advertising a cultural week, Berlin, 1936

The idea I have developed in this essay is an ancient one: It is the restoration of the Jewish State. . . The decisive factor is our propelling force. And what is that force? The plight of the Jews. . . I am profoundly convinced that I am right, though I doubt whether I shall live to see myself so proved.

Those who today inaugurate this movement are unlikely to live to see its glorious culmination. But the very inauguration is enough to inspire in them a high pride and the joy of an inner liberation of their existence...

The plan would seem mad enough if a single individual were to undertake it; but if many Jews simultaneously agree on it, it is entirely reasonable, and its achievement presents no difficulties worth mentioning. The idea depends only on the number of its adherents. Perhaps our ambitious young men, to whom every road of advancement is now closed, and for whom the Jewish state throws open a bright prospect of freedom, happiness, and honor- perhaps they will see to it that the idea is spread....

It depends on the Jews themselves whether this political document remains for the present a political romance. If this generation is too dull to understand it rightly, a future, finer, more advanced generation will arise to comprehend it. I consider the Jewish question neither a social nor a religious one, even though it sometimes takes these and other forms. It is a national question, and to solve it we must first of all establish it as an international political problem to be discussed and settled by the civilized nations of the world in council. We are a people — one people...

We have no flag, and we need one. If we desire to lead many men, we must raise a symbol above their heads. I would suggest a white flag, with seven golden stars. The white field symbolizes our pure new life; the stars are the seven golden hours of our working-day. For we shall march into the Promised Land carrying the badge of honor.

We have sincerely tried everywhere to merge with the national communities in which we live, seeking only to preserve the faith of our fathers. It has not been vouchsafed us. In vain

Flag for the Jewish state
A suggested design drawn by Herzl, 1896

21

"In Basel I founded the Jewish State"
Postcard, early 20th cent.

are we loyal patriots, sometimes super-loyal; in vain do we make the same sacrifices of life and property as our fellow citizens; in vain do we strive to enhance the fame of our native lands in the arts and sciences, or her wealth by trade and commerce. In our native lands where we have lived for centuries we are still decried as aliens, often by men whose ancestors had not yet come at a time when Jewish sighs had long been heard in the country…

Oppression and persecution cannot exterminate us. No nation on earth has endured the struggles and sufferings as we have. Jew-baiting has merely winnowed out our weaklings; the strong among us defiantly return to their own whenever persecution breaks out… Wherever we remain politically secure for any length of time, we assimilate. I think this is not praiseworthy… The Jewish people are at present prevented by the Diaspora from conducting their political affairs themselves. Besides, they are in a condition of more or less severe distress in many parts of the world. They need, above all things a gestor. [ed. facilitator]. This gestor cannot, of course, be a single individual. Such a one would either make himself ridiculous, or — seeing that he would appear to be working for his own interests — contemptible. The gestor of the Jews must therefore be a body corporate.

And that is the Society of Jews. This organ of the national movement, the nature and functions of which we are now dealing, will in fact, be created before everything else. Its formation is perfectly simple. The Society will have scientific and political tasks, for the founding of a Jewish State, as I conceive it, presupposes the application of scientific methods. We cannot journey out of Egypt today in the primitive fashion of ancient times. We shall previously obtain an accurate account of our number and strength. The undertaking of that great and ancient gestor of the Jews in primitive days bears much the same relation to ours that some wonderful melody bears to a modern opera. We are playing the same melody with many more violins, flutes, harps, violinecellos, and bass viols; with electric light, decorations, choirs, beautiful costumes, and with the finest singers of the day.

The Society of Jews will gather all available declarations of statesmen, parliaments, Jewish communities, societies, whether expressed in speeches or in writing, in meetings, newspapers or books. Thus the Society will find out for the first time whether the Jews really wish to go to the Promised Land, and whether they must go there.

Palestine is our unforgettable historic homeland. . . Let me repeat once more my opening words: the Jews who will it shall achieve their State. We shall live at last as free men on our own soil, and in our own homes peacefully die. The world will be liberated by our freedom, enriched by our wealth, magnified by our greatness. And whatever we attempt there for our own benefit will redound mightily and beneficially to the good of all mankind.

From "The Jewish State," 1896

Herzl addressing the Second Zionist Congress, 1898

Wenn Ihr wollt, ist es Kein Märchen.

"If you wish it, it is no dream" the motto in Herzl's handwriting in his prophetic book *Altneuland* ("Old-New Land,") published in 1902

"A Tool for the People of Israel that they have not Previously Possessed"

Theodor Herzl

From Herzl's opening address at the First Zionist Congress, Basel, 29 August, 1897.

Since time immemorial the world has been misinformed about us. The sentiment of solidarity with which we have been reproached so frequently and so acrimoniously was in process of disintegration at the very time we were being attacked by anti-Semitism. And anti-Semitism served to strengthen it anew. We returned home, as it were. For Zionism is a return to the Jewish fold even before it becomes a return to the Jewish land. We, the children who have returned, find much to redress under the ancestral roof, for some of our brothers have sunk into deep misery. We are made welcome in the ancient house, for it is universally known that we are not actuated by an arrogant desire to undermine that which should be revered. This will be clearly demonstrated by the Zionist platform.

Zionism has already brought about something remarkable, heretofore regarded as impossible: a close union between the ultramodern and the ultraconservative elements of Jewry. The fact that this has come to pass without undignified concessions on the part of either side and without intellectual sacrifice, is further proof, if such proof is necessary, of the national unity of the Jews. A union of this kind is possible only on a national basis.

Consequently the only reasonable course of action which our movement can pursue is to work for publicly legalized guarantees. The results of colonization as it has been carried on hitherto were quite satisfactory within its limitations. It confirmed the much disputed fitness of the Jews for agricultural work. It established this proof for all time, as the legal phrase has it. But colonization in its present form is not, and cannot be, the solution of the Jewish question. And we must admit unreservedly that it has failed to evoke much sympathy. Why? Because the Jews know how to calculate; in fact, it has been asserted that they calculate too well. Thus, if we assume that there are nine million Jews in the world, and that it would be possible to colonize ten thousand Jews in Palestine every year, the Jewish question would require nine hundred years for its solution. This would seem impracticable…

At this Congress, we are creating a tool for the Jewish People that they have not previously possessed, although it is a need frequently required – a requirement for life itself… Our cause is too great to be left to the ambition or the whim of individuals. It must be elevated to the realm of the impersonal if it is to succeed.

And our Congress shall live forever, not only until the redemption from age-long suffering is effected, but afterward as well. Today we are here in the hospitable limits of this free city — where shall we be next year?

But wherever we shall be, and however distant the accomplishment of our task, let our Congress be earnest and high-minded, a source of welfare to the unhappy, of defiance to none, of honor to all Jewry. Let it be worthy of our past, the renown of which, though remote, is eternal!

First Zionist Congress
Above: Invitation to Congress delegates, 1897
Below: Postcard commemorating 50 years since the First Zionist Congress, 1947

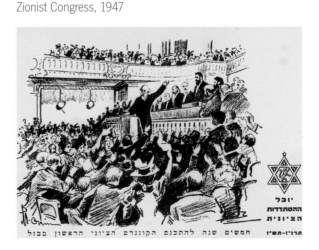

A National Home in Eretz Israel

The Basel Program

"The major contribution of Herzl," wrote Ben-Gurion, "was that he transformed the Jewish people into a political people." In founding the Zionist Movement, and organising the First Zionist Congress in Basel in 1897, he provided the Jewish people with the tools for the political struggle, for the right to return to its land, and to renew there its sovereignty.

Zionism aspires to create for the Jewish people a homeland in Eretz Israel, guaranteed by universal justice. To achieve this aim, the Congress intends to carry out the following acts:

1. The development of Eretz Israel by the return of Jews who will till the soil, and craftsmen and artisans possessed of manifold skills.
2. The organization and unification of world Jewry so as to create effective local and general mechanisms in accordance with each country's laws.
3. To elevate national Jewish feelings and the appreciation of Jewish nationalism.
4. To undertake exploratory actions so as to receive the agreement of governments, the cooperation of whom will be necessary in order to achieve the purposes of Zionism.

Basel Program, 1897

Stamp commemorating the centennial of the First Zionist Congress, 1997

"In Basel I created the Jewish State"

Theodor Herzl

Were I to sum up the achievements of the Basel Congress in one sentence – which through caution I would not state publicly – it would be this: "In Basel I created the Jewish State." Had I said this today in public, it would have been greeted by laughter from all sides. Maybe in five years time, but certainly in another 50 years, everyone will recognize this.

From Herzl's diary, 1897

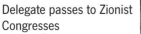

Delegate passes to Zionist Congresses
From above: First, Third, Fourth, Second, Sixth

A Clarion Call to the Whole World

Ahad Ha'Am

Ahad Ha'Am (1856-1927), was the pen-name of Asher Ginsberg, one of the most distinguished Jewish writers and philosophers of the19th and 20th centuries. He described the first Zionist Congress in an article in the magazine *HaShelach.* In this article, he poured scorn on the "professional" Jewish leaders who had attended the Congress. Even so, he described the Basel meeting with great enthusiasm.

Ahad Ha'am

"The Congress of the Zionists" – the battle over which filled the emptiness of our small world during the past few months - is now already an established fact.

Some 200 people from the House of Israel, from every country and party, gathered in Basel, and for days, from morning to evening, deliberated in public, in front of the entire world, about the establishment of a secure home for Israel in the land of its ancestors.

The national response to the question of the Jews thus burst through the barriers of "modesty" and entered the public domain; it spread over the whole world in a loud voice, in clear language, and with an upright posture – something that we have not known since the day Israel was exiled from its homeland.

And that is all. This Congress was unable to do more, and it had no need to do more. Because – why fool ourselves? – of all the great aims that Hibat Zion (or as they now say "The Zionists") strive for; only one up to now was truly in our power to achieve in the right way, and that was the moral goal – to free ourselves from internal slavery, from defeatism that led us to assimilation, and to strengthen our national unity through joint endeavors in every branch of our national life, until we are proved capable and competent for a future life of respect and liberty...

After thousands of years of evil and endless hardships, it is impossible for the people of Israel to be content with its lot. Eventually they would have reached the level of a small and lowly people... It is impossible for an ancient people, that was to be a "light unto the nations," to be satisfied, as a reward for all its sufferings, with this smallness, which many other nations, people without a name or a culture, achieved in a short time, without enduring even a minute portion of the suffering that the Jewish people suffered.

Not for nothing did prophets arise in Israel, who saw in their visions that justice would prevail over the earth at the end of days. Their nationalism, love for their people and their land, was the reason. But even then, the Jewish state was located between two lions; Assyria and Babylon on one side, and Egypt on the other. It had no hope of living at ease or developing in a way that it so yearned for. Thus the spread of Zionism in the heart of the prophets and the realisation of the great vision at the end of days – when the wolf will lie down with the lamb, and nation will no longer lift up sword against nation – then Israel, too, will dwell securely in its land. This human ideal was and will be of necessity, forever part of the national ideal of the Jewish people, and only "a Jewish State" will then be able to offer it respite, when universal justice will prevail over all the nations...

And thus we have come to Basel, not in order to found the Jewish state today or tomorrow, but to issue a clarion call to the whole world: the people of Israel is still living and wants to live! With this call we have to cry again and again. Not in order that the nations will hear and grant us our request, but rather, first and foremost, that we will hear the echo of our own voices in the valley of our souls, perhaps it will arouse and awaken us from our lowliness...

From "The First Zionist Congress;" HaShelach, Volume 2, 1897

The Land of our Fathers' Yearnings

Israel Doshman

Here in the Land of our Fathers'
yearnings
All our hopes will be fulfilled.
Here we will live and create
A life of freedom and liberty.
Here the Divine Spirit will rest
And the biblical tongue will flourish.
Plough the fallow land,

Sing a joyful song,
Come rejoice, come rejoice!
The blossoming has begun.
Plough the fallow land,
Sing a joyful song.
Come rejoice, come rejoice!
The seeds will yet be sown.

Redemption of the Land

Menachem Ussishkin

At the Fifth Zionist Congress in 1901, the Jewish National Fund was established. From 1923 the Director of the Fund was Menachem Ussishkin (1863–1941).

"When the people of Israel redeem Eretz Israel, then Eretz Israel will redeem the people of Israel."

Zionah Tagger; Ascent to Mount Zion, 1925

There is but one Truth and not Two

Uri Zvi Greenberg

The poet Uri Zvi Greenberg (1896-1981), a prominent leader of the Revisionist movement, outlined in this poem his concept of national Zionism.

Your leaders taught: Land is bought for money,
One buys a plot and plunges in the spade.
But I say: No land is ever bought for money
And with a spade one digs and there the dead are laid.
I say: A land is conquered with blood.
Only that won with blood is hallowed to the folk
With the holiness of blood.
Only he who follows the cannon in the field
Deserves to follow his good plough
Upon this conquered field.
Your rabbis taught: The Messiah will come in future ages
And Judea will arise without fire and without blood. She will rise with every tree, with every added house.
And I say: If your generation is idle
And does not haste on the end with its hands

and with its strokes
And enters not the fire with a buckler of David
And the hocks of its horses enter not into blood –
The Messiah will not come even in a distant age.
Judea will not arise.
And you will become forced labor for any alien ruler. Your home will become stubble for the spark of any insolent one.
Your trees will be cut down with their ripe fruit.
Your belly will be cleft to its bowels by the hand of the foe.
Your young men shall share the infant's fate
At the enemy's sword –
Only your chattering will be left – for yourselves…
And the testimony of your dishonor in the bookbindery.
And an eternal curse in your slashed visage.

Your rabbis taught: There is one truth for the gentile: Blood for blood – but it is not the truth of the Jew.
And I say: There is but one truth and not two
As there is but one sun and not two Jerusalem.
It is written in the law of conquest of Moses and of Joshua. And till the last of my wounded kings and lions, A truth that the teeth of exiles and betrayers burnt away.
And this will be a day when from the river of Egypt to the Euphrates
And from the sea to beyond Moab my young men will ascend
To summon my enemies and haters to the last battle.
And blood will decide who shall be the sole ruler here.

Translated by L.V. Snowman

The Hebrew People was Created on the Soil of Eretz Israel

Ze'ev Jabotinsky

Writer, journalist, and romantic dreamer about the Return to Zion – Ze'ev Jabotinsky (1880-1940) was all of these. He was later to become the leader of the Revisionist movement, and was considered the main ideologist of the Herut political movement, even years after his death. He conceived his Zionist philosophy, which won many adherents, at the beginning of the 20th century.

Poster welcoming Ze'ev Jabotinsky, founder of the Jewish Legion, to the USA, 1922

Before we came to Eretz Israel we were not a nation and neither did we exist. It was on the soil of Eretz Israel that the Hebrew nation was created out of fragments of various other nations. On the soil of Eretz Israel we grew, we became citizens; we consolidated our belief in one God, we breathed in the spirit of the land, and in our struggle for independence and for sovereignty its atmosphere inspired us and its grain nurtured our bodies. In Eretz Israel our prophets expounded their ideas and the Song of Songs was first heard. All that is Hebrew in our midst was bestowed on us by Eretz Israel; all else that exists within us – is not Hebrew. Israel and Eretz Israel are one and the same. There we were born as a nation and there we matured. And when the storm came and cast us outside the borders of the land, we could no longer grow, just as an uprooted tree can no longer grow. And our lives were devoted to preserving the unique qualities which were fostered in Eretz Israel. And here, in this way, we finally evolved the perfect form of that fundamental motive in the annals of our exile, the desire to formulate the true nature of the people's will: to preserve and to struggle for our national singularity, our pure Eretz Israeli singularity; that and nothing more. And hence, the inevitable conclusion is that the only truly popular movement in Eretz Israel will be that which sets itself the aim of guaranteeing the uninterrupted development of our Eretz Israeli national singularity…

Our belief in Eretz Israel is not a blind, semi-mystic emotion, it is the logical conclusion deriving from an objective examination of the essence of our history and our movement. Having said all this, I admit freely that, despite everything, I am a true believer.

From "Zionism and Eretz Israel," 1905

"The Answer for Hebrew Youth!"
A poster for the Bitzaron youth movement, Prague, 1930

We will Build our Land

Avraham Levinson

We'll build our land, our own homeland,
Because this land is ours.
We'll build our land, our own homeland,
Our blood commands it, our history commands it.
We'll build our land despite our foes,
We'll build our land by the force of our will.
The end of malignant servitude,
The burning flame of liberty,
And glorious shining hope
All these will fire our blood.
Thirsty for freedom,
For sovereignty,

We march as one to liberate the people.
We will march forward together
With added strength and greater power.
We will march forward together,
The nation's hope will light our way.
We are one, our standards on the march
We are one, as freedom's song sounds out.
The song of a wounded heart,
An unknown joy,
A path as yet unblazed,
All these will fire our blood.
With firm step
With heads held high
We march as one to liberate the people

The Greatest Political Zionist Since Herzl

Chaim Weizmann

Dr. Chaim Weizmann, a young scientist, impassioned orator and ardent Zionist (1874-1952) came to prominence during the First World War. In one of his first speeches he lauded the pioneers who were building up the country and those dying in its defense.

Have we any other path, one without dangers, are we indeed to wait till we are brought to Eretz Israel with cymbals and dance as the whole world rejoices? Were this so and were it only possible, then not only you sitting here before me would be Zionists but also the assimilated Jews of Paris. It gratifies us that we Zionists are considered "crazy;" if we were "normal" we would not have gone to Eretz Israel and we would have stayed where we were, like all "normal" people among us. Those who do not believe in the arduous path and think that we should not follow the hazardous road should stay at home. The fearful and the cowardly cannot build a lasting structure for a homeland. Without danger and perilous undertakings, no nation in the world can liberate itself from others. No nation was ever liberated by capital profit and interest, but only by investing energy and making sacrifices. And so far, we Jews have made few sacrifices and so only two per cent of the land in Eretz Israel is ours. Look at the value of great sacrifices: somewhere near Kiev there is a Jew named Barsky, whose son, a worker, was killed on the soil of Eretz Israel in Degania, and the bereaved father wrote a letter of consolation to the workers of Eretz Israel and sent them his second son to replace the dead one and confront the dangers in his stead. This is the continuation – wrote the bereaved father. That Jew is the greatest political Zionist since Herzl!

Speech in Paris, 1914

Foreign Office,
November 2nd, 1917.

Dear Lord Rothschild,

I have much pleasure in conveying to you, on behalf of His Majesty's Government, the following declaration of sympathy with Jewish Zionist aspirations which has been submitted to, and approved by, the Cabinet

His Majesty's Government view with favour the establishment in Palestine of a national home for the Jewish people, and will use their best endeavours to facilitate the achievement of this object, it being clearly understood that nothing shall be done which may prejudice the civil and religious rights of existing non-Jewish communities in Palestine, or the rights and political status enjoyed by Jews in any other country"

I should oe grateful if you would bring this declaration to the knowledge of the Zionist Federation.

A National Home for the Jewish People

The Balfour Declaration

Weizmann succeeded, together with other Jewish leaders and the House of Rothschild, to persuade the leaders of Great Britain to extend their support to Zionism, both because of the noble act of returning a persecuted people to its homeland, and also because of the political interests of Britain during the First World War. On 2nd November 1917, the British minister for foreign affairs, Arthur James Balfour, sent a brief letter to Lord Rothschild, for the attention of the Zionist Federation. This letter, which has become known as "The Balfour Declaration" was instrumental in paving the long way for the Zionist Movement to achieve political independence in the Land of Israel.

The original letter which become known as "The Balfour Declaration," sent from Arthur James Balfour (later Lord Balfour) to Lord Rothschild, London, November 2nd, 1917

The Granting of a Land

David Ben-Gurion

The Balfour Declaration brought joy to the Jews in the Diaspora. Eretz Israel had been granted to them! Only a few understood that a land is not given to a people. One of these was a young pioneer, David Ben-Gurion (1886-1973) who had been exiled from Palestine by the Turkish authorities and had reached the United States. In September 1915, two years before the publication of the Balfour Declaration, Ben-Gurion presented a forthright opinion in an article, "The Granting of a Land."

The ways of conquering a country are many. It is possible to capture a country by force of arms, it is possible to acquire a country by political strategems and diplomatic treaties; it is also possible to buy a country with money.

We – we do not ask for Eretz Israel for the sake of subjugating the Arab people. Neither do we seek there a market for selling the goods produced by the Jews in the Diaspora.

We ask for Eretz Israel as a homeland, to repair the curse of the exile. To connect with the Land - the source of vitality, creativity and humanity – and to renew our national existence. A homeland cannot be given neither be taken as a gift; it is not obtained through political manipulations or agreements, it cannot be bought with gold, and cannot be conquered with the fist. It can only be built by the sweat of the brow. A homeland – this is a historic creation and the collective production of a people – the result of its physical, spiritual and moral endeavors over generations. Eretz Israel will be ours, not when the Turks, the English or the next Peace Congress agree to it, and sign a diplomatic treaty – but when we, the Jews, build it...

We will receive our country not through a Peace Congress or this or another ruling regime – but through the Hebrew worker who will come to strike roots in the land, to revive it and to live in it. Eretz Israel will be ours when the majority of its workers and guardians will be ours. The real conquest of Eretz Israel – conquest through labor – this is the historical task that has fallen on the Jewish pioneers, the builders and guardians of the land.

New York, Kampfer Shtimme, 27 September, 1915

David Roberts: Tower of David, Jerusalem, 1839

Card designed by students of the Bezalel Academy of Arts, Jerusalem to mark the Balfour Declaration

David Ben-Gurion, 1915

It is Possible that God Knows the Secret of the Landscape

S. Yizhar

The writer, S. Yizhar (Yizhar Smilansky) stands on the edge of the Negev against a strengthening wind, on land on which "the footsteps of the first fathers have not yet been erased."

You are standing here, and the fields around you recede towards the horizon, you take two steps and the fields rise about you to the curve of the horizon, and at the same time the wind grows stronger with a nonchalant whistling, that is satiated within itself, and feeds off itself, a tranquillity emanating from the earth of the field, a tranquillity of the depths of the firmament, a tranquillity of open vistas, and behind it like a thief, dark and evil-hearted, the fear peeps through. And if you wish to, you will immediately discover on the land in front of you the footsteps of the first fathers that have not yet been erased; they are hidden in the holy scrolls from ancient times, and they are wandering around. At any moment they will reveal themselves to you -- respectable and old – walking in their own landscape …and what is it after all? Beetles, ants, and dust – and lots of earth and lots of sky, and something else that is there, and it is very possible that God knows what it is.

From "At the Edge of the Desert," 1945

This Land

Dan Almagor

If you ask people here: What's this land to you?
They won't find it easy to say.
Because each man and woman whose homeland it is
Sees this land in their own special way.

But if one of my children should happen to ask
That very same question of me,
Then I'd say, Let me tell you about it, my child,
And you'll tell your own children some day.

For this country of mine, this country of mine
Is a place of great pain and of greater delight,
It's a prayer without words, it's a dream from the past
It's the roots again sprouting green leaves in the light
It's a field of ripe wheat.
It's the laugh of a child, and an old man at prayer,
It's my home and my shrine
This country of mine.

For this country of mine is hot winds and dry sand
It's the perfume of orchards and a young maiden's smile
It's old-fashioned, I know.
No one says it today,
But I mean what I say
It's my home and my shrine
This country of mine.

It's a grove full of dates in a land without dew,
It's a dream that seemed crazy but now has come true
Some countries are bigger,
But for them I don't pine,
Because this one is mine.

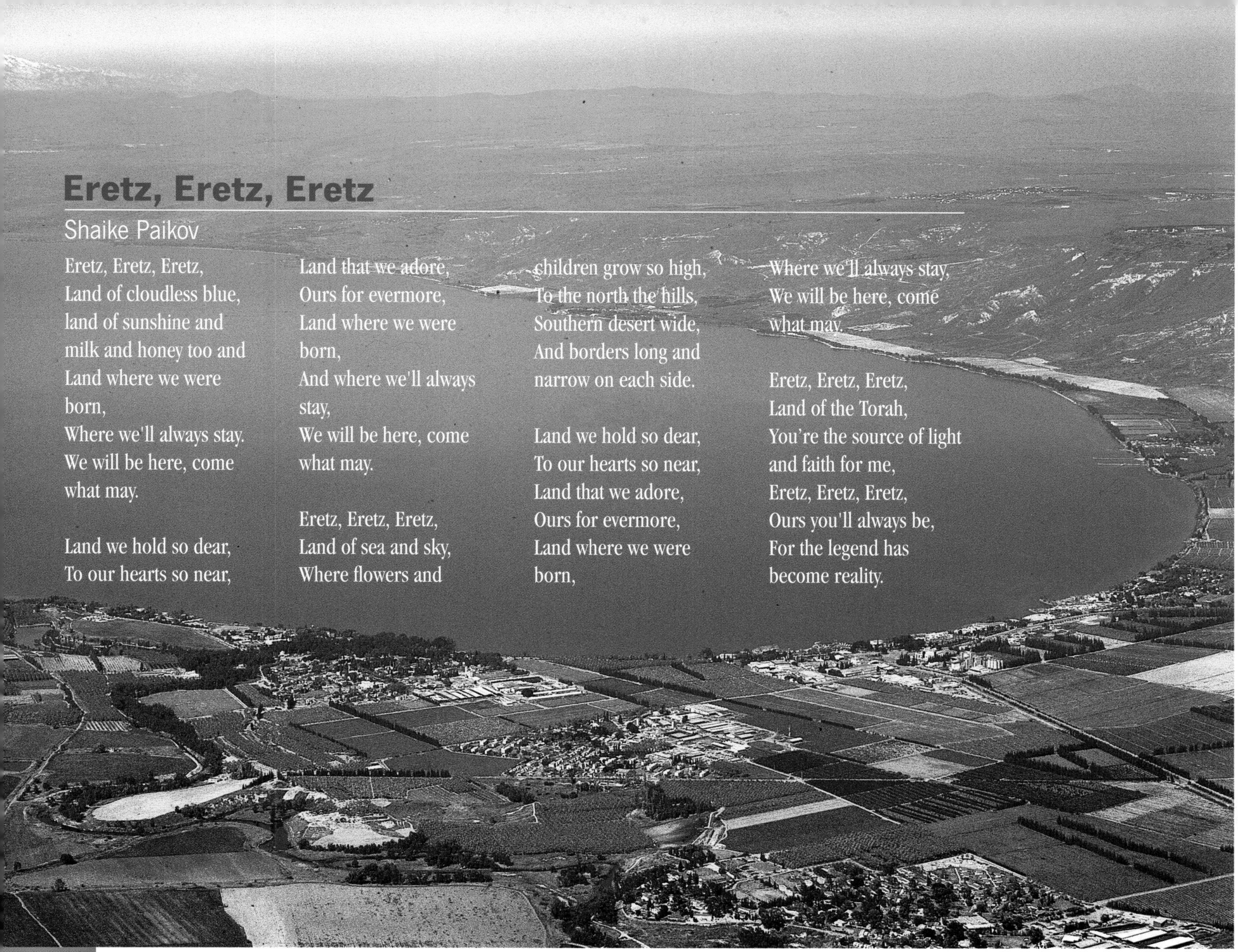

Eretz, Eretz, Eretz

Shaike Paikov

Eretz, Eretz, Eretz,
Land of cloudless blue,
land of sunshine and
milk and honey too and
Land where we were
born,
Where we'll always stay.
We will be here, come
what may.

Land we hold so dear,
To our hearts so near,
Land that we adore,
Ours for evermore,
Land where we were
born,
And where we'll always
stay,
We will be here, come
what may.

Eretz, Eretz, Eretz,
Land of sea and sky,
Where flowers and
children grow so high,
To the north the hills,
Southern desert wide,
And borders long and
narrow on each side.

Land we hold so dear,
To our hearts so near,
Land that we adore,
Ours for evermore,
Land where we were
born,
Where we'll always stay,
We will be here, come
what may.

Eretz, Eretz, Eretz,
Land of the Torah,
You're the source of light
and faith for me,
Eretz, Eretz, Eretz,
Ours you'll always be,
For the legend has
become reality.

"To the North, Kinneret; to the South – Sand"
Above: The Kinneret – Sea of Galilee
Below left: The Wilderness of Zin in the Negev

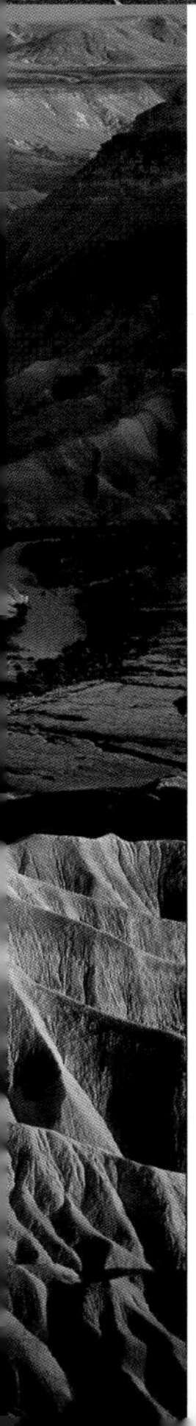

The Place and the Time

Aharon Megged

The writer and publicist Aharon Megged interweaves expressions of his love for the land with memories from his youth.

Winter 2003. I am standing on a hill, not far from the River Yarkon. On this pleasant sunny day the slopes of the Mountains of Ephraim can be seen in the east, bright in their blueness; in the west, the waves of the Mediterranean sparkle, coming and going, from here to Cyprus, to Greece, to Spain, and from there to here, again and again. A distinguished Jew who wanders between Geneva and Cambridge, once said "a Jew's birthplace is his suitcase." I don't sit on suitcases, in anticipation of the coming train, or the ship, or the aeroplane, that will take me to another country so that I might find there a new place of sojourn. Here "the land of the yearnings of my fathers" is my place. It is to that land that the soul of the poet Yehuda Halevi yearned from the edge of the west, and when he dreamt of his return to it, he was the harp to its songs. On it Haim Nahman Bialik hung his hopes, and from the Diaspora inquired after the well-being of the Jordan and its clear waters and of all the mountains and the hills, and he bade that he be given wings to fly to a land "in which the almond and date tree blossom."; This is my place, from my childhood it will recognise me. Behind the shack in the small settlement, there was a chicken run and a cowshed for one cow, lemon, orange, and plum trees, and in the summer vacation, my classmates came and together we weeded with hoes the weeds around the trees. We played in the Eucalyptus grove with the kids from the Arab village of Hirbat

Azun, Yitzhak and Ishmael, and my mother didn't say to my father: "Get rid of the son of that slave woman." In the summer of 1929, my father received a large club from the Hagana to defend us from the rioters that were expected to come from Kalkiliya, and we, the children, were evacuated to Ein Hai, known as Kfar Malal, which contained fortified concrete cowsheds... Five years later, we set out to cross the country by foot, a Bible in our backpacks. We headed eastwards, to Kalkiliya, Tul Karem, Kafr Kara, Um el-Fahm. In Jenin, some wild youngsters threw stones at us, but in the water canteen of the leader of our group a parabellum revolver was hidden. Thus we reached Ma'ayan Harod in the Valley of Jezreel. I have kept a map of Eretz Israel from 1936, the year of the beginning of the Arab revolt that lasted three years, and in which no day passed without murder or injury, without fields and orchards going up in flames... Today, too, I like to spread it on the table and spend hours looking at it. I glance at the names of hundreds of villages in the green coastal plain and in the orange mountains; Arab names alongside the biblical ones - Jeba –Geva; Far'ata – Faraton, Jiljulia – Gilgal, Shvekha – Shakha, Fandekumia – Pundaka, Hirbat Belama –Yeval'am, Jenin –Ein Ganim, and so on.

And I marvel how the biblical names survived during the hundreds of years in which the Jews were exiled from the land. Their retention surely contradicts the ridiculous assertion of a number of "new" historians, according to whom "The biblical period never existed."

In the early 1940s, I worked with Arabs and Houranis in the granaries of ships in the Haifa port, ten to 12 hours a day, under the supervision of their leader, Mahmoud Fayat, a broad-boned giant, with a huge voice; and we said to ourselves – together, yes, together we will live here, not one above the other but side by side. I am reminded of this every day, and I return, as though through a time tunnel, to the years of my childhood and youth, to the years of the renewed youth of this biblical land. When I think of my ancestors in Poland, I know that even though they lived there where their livelihood was even in poverty, even my grandfathers, Yaakov-Yehoshua and Avraham Meir, their heads buried in the Talmud from morning to night, and this was all their world; nevertheless, with their very being they knew that that was not their place, and that they were merely passers-by in that city, in that country. Today they are here, tomorrow who knows; today they are alive, tomorrow under the knife of the slaughterer. Eretz Israel, this is the place, a slither of a land between the sea and the Jordan, tortured by nature and by men for generations, that I am allowed to call "My Homeland." This is the land to which Nathan Alterman was not ashamed to sing: "We love you, Homeland, in joy, in song and toil." If that is so, then I am an Israeli.

When I look at the map, I remember all those names from the Book of Joshua, the conqueror who divided the territories of Canaan among the 12 tribes, each tribe according to its lot; names from the Books of Judges and Kings, from the time of the First and Second Temples, and from the days of the Tana'im and the Amoraim [the teachers of Mishna and Gemara] – I see how they disappeared - as if they had never been. 1,500 years of my history, these are the years of wandering in foreign lands, years of degradation and decrees from the destruction of the Second Temple to the expulsion from Spain, related in *Shevet Yehudah* ("The Rod of Judah") by Rabbi Shlomo Ibn-Verga, and the years of expulsion and pogroms throughout Europe, from Britain and France to the Ukraine and Poland, up to and including the Holocaust. And I am amazed to see that, despite the huge revolution which Zionism wrought upon the Jewish people, which radically changed its life in a manner never witnessed before in history; returning it to the land of its ancestors, the birthplace of its religion and the origin of its culture, so that today, in 2003 in Israel, I return to the cycle of Jewish time

Cover of a pamphlet published by the Jewish National Fund, New York, 1944

from pre-history till now, and the prophecy of Balaam 3,000 years ago. Just as then, so still today, we are "a people that dwells alone, not reckoned among the nations."

"A people that dwells alone" – our state is unique in the world in that hundreds of millions of people in other countries do not recognise its right to exist and threaten to obliterate it. And "not reckoned among the nations," because, again, our being here is a target for hatred, disdain and incitement that is spreading across the globe, in states where Jews have been among the builders of the culture, such as Germany, Austria, the Czech Republic, and in states where Jews enriched and developed their commerce, like Poland, Ukraine, France; and in states that did not even know Jews, like Japan or Indonesia. I, an Israeli, am attacked in that I live on this land, which is my homeland; I, a Jew, not just as an inheritor of the ancient Jewish culture, but also because my fate is the Jewish fate. When I look down the long, dark tunnel of hundreds of years of exile, toward the small circle of light of our existence here in our land, and I think of the ring of animosity that surrounds us; of all the Moslem countries, and their scheming to destroy us, animosity which breaks out in violence, and which is proclaimed from every prayer lectern and every school book – I say to myself that the chapter in which I am standing now, is only a mutation, improved in a certain way, of a phenomenon that has been extant since the time of the patriarchs, the crossing of the Sinai Desert, the conquest of the Land of Canaan; the destructions and the exiles... Here, too, there is no escape from the curses of the angry prophecies of Jeremiah. I know that the battle in which we are presently engaged to defend our lives is "the last battle" in the War of the Jews. If we lose, there will be no more survivors or remnants from the Jewish people, not here nor in another place.

Tel Aviv, 30 January, 2003

The Land which God Promised our Forefathers

Shmuel Yosef Agnon

An extract from Shmuel Yosef Agnon's speech on accepting the Nobel Prize for Literature, Stockholm, December 10, 1966.

As a result of the historic catastrophe in which Titus of Rome destroyed Jerusalem and Israel was exiled from its land, I was born in one of the cities of the Exile. But always I regarded myself as one who was born in Jerusalem. In a dream, in a vision of the night, I saw myself standing with my brother Levites in the Holy Temple, singing with them the songs of David, King of Israel, melodies such as no ear has heard since the day our city was destroyed and its people went into exile. I suspect that the angels in charge of the Shrine of Music, fearful lest I sing in wakefulness what I had sung in dream, made me forget by day what I had sung at night; for if my brethren, the sons of my people, were to hear, they would be unable to bear their grief over the happiness they have lost. To console me for having prevented me from singing with my mouth, they enable me to compose songs in writing.

The King of Sweden applauds S.Y. Agnon on his receipt of the Nobel Prize for Literature, Stockholm, 1966

I belong to the tribe of Levi, my forebears and I are of the minstrels in the Temple, and there is a tradition in my fathers's family that we are of the lineage of the Prophet Samuel, whose name I bear.

Never in all my life have I forgotten the Psalm [131:1] in which David said: "Lord, my heart is not haughty, nor mine eyes lofty; neither do I exercise myself in great matters, or in things too high for me." If I am proud of anything, it is that I have been granted the privilege of living in the land which God promised our forefathers to give us. Before concluding, I would like to say a brief prayer: He who giveth wisdom unto the wise and dominion unto princes, may He increase your wisdom beyond measure and exalt your sovereignty. In his days and in ours may Judah be redeemed and Israel dwell in safety. May the redeemer come unto Zion, may the earth be filled with knowledge and eternal joy for all who dwell therein, and may they enjoy much peace. May all this be God's will. Amen.

Chapter 2

The Independence Day Torch

I, Arieh Arazi, born in Ramat Gan, whose mother is a Holocaust survivor; a resident of Elkana in Samaria; a teacher of Israel studies at Bar Ilan University and a travel guide, have the honor to light this torch to mark the 47th anniversary of the State of Israel.

In honor of those who love the Land of Israel, its stones and its paths, its valleys and its hills, its fields and its deserts, its antiquities and its settlements, its heritage and its future.

In honor of those who hope and believe that "Old men and old women shall again sit in the streets of Jerusalem, each with staff in hand... And the streets of the city shall be full of boys and girls playing in its streets," because that is the true face of peace.

And to the glory of Israel.

Eve of Independence Day, 1995

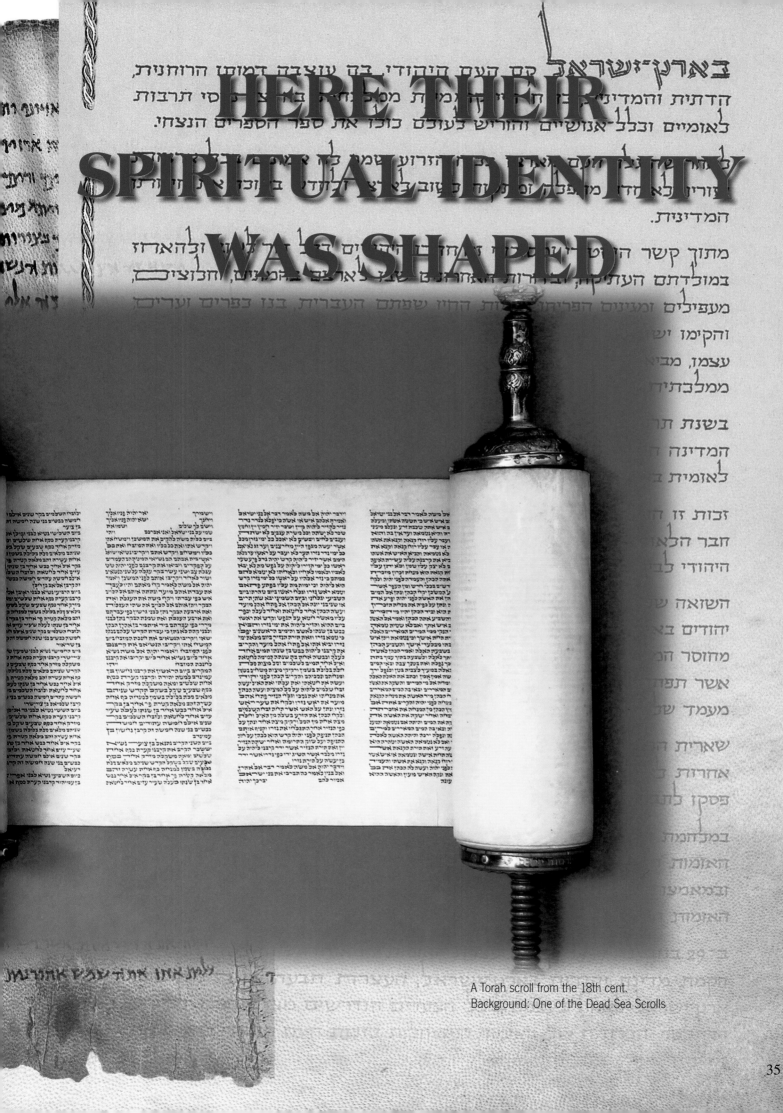

HERE THEIR SPIRITUAL IDENTITY WAS SHAPED

A Torah scroll from the 18th cent.
Background: One of the Dead Sea Scrolls

The Ten Commandments

And God spoke all these words saying,

"I am the Lord your God, who has brought you out of the Land of Egypt, out of the house of bondage.

"You shall have no other gods before me.

"You shall not make for yourself a graven image, or any likeness of anything that is in heaven above, or that is in the earth beneath, or that is in the water under the earth; you shall not bow down to them or serve them; for I the Lord your God am a jealous God, visiting the iniquity of the fathers upon the children to the third and the fourth generation of those who hate me, but showing steadfast love to thousands of those who love me and keep my commandments.

"You shall not take the name of the Lord your God in vain; for the Lord will not hold him guiltless who takes his name in vain.

"Remember the sabbath day to keep it holy. Six days you shall labor, and do all your work; but the seventh day is a sabbath to the Lord your God; in it you shall not do any work, you, or your son, or your daughter, your manservant, or your maidservant, or your cattle, or the sojourner who is within your gates; for in six days the Lord made heaven and earth, the sea, and all that is in them, and rested on the seventh day; therefore the Lord blessed the sabbath day and hallowed it.

"Honor your father and your mother; that your days may be long in the land which the Lord your God gives you.

"You shall not kill.

"You shall not commit adultery.

"You shall not steal.

"You shall not bear false witness against your neighbor.

"You shall not covet your neighbor's house; you shall not covet your neighbor's wife, or his manservant, or his maidservant, or his ox, or his ass, or anything that is your neighbor's."

Exodus 20: 1-17

The Giving of the Law

Uri Gnessin

Uri Nissan Gnessin (1881-1913), Ukrainian-born, was a writer, poet and translator.

'Twas not in the dark, in secret oblivion,
'Twas not in the gloom of the night, the depths of quiet
That the hand of God bestowed the sacred Torah,
The pledge of eternal peace.
In a great wide expanse
In the desert, open to the winds of heaven,
Open to all, no border to check us
There the Lord who dwells above was revealed to us:
"They who choose my Torah, let them
Approach Sinai" cried the thundering voice.

And as lightning flashed and thunder roared,
The voice of God sounded mightily
And echoed near and far
And all creatures on earth hearkened
To the voice of the Lord, coming down
In splendor and might to his people, Israel
Inspiring awe in both old and young
And the cedars of the forest trembled at his tread.

...And the people listened in awe and trembling
To the spirit of God in the silence
And they heard the word of the living God
"You are my chosen people and I am the Lord."

Rembrandt: Moses and the Tablets of the Law

36

Shrine of the Book,
Israel Museum, Jerusalem.
The Dead Sea Scrolls

Something Primal and Very Deep

Berl Katznelson

Berl Katznelson (1887-1944) one of the Zionist movement's most important leaders, was the first editor of the newspaper *Davar* and founder of the Am Oved Publishing House. Many regarded him as the chief ideologist of the Labor Zionist Movement. Together with his close friend, David Ben-Gurion, he unified the labor parties in the pre-State period. Berl Katznelson had profound Jewish roots.

A generation which renews and creates
Does not cast its ancient heritage
On to the rubbish heap.
It scans it and studies it,
From afar and from near.
And sometimes it clings to existing tradition and augments it.
And sometimes it gropes through that heap,
And uncovers a forgotten object,
Scrapes off the rust,
And revives an ancient tradition,
To nourish the soul of the renewing generation.
If in the life of a nation there is something primal and very deep,
Which can edify man and give him strength to face his future,
Is it in the true revolutionary spirit to ignore it?

From "Sources that do not Dry Up," 1934

The People Shall Rise up Again

Nathan Alterman

Nathan Alterman (1910-1970) was one of Israel's most admired poets. Just as Bialik was the poet of the renaissance, Alterman was the poet of the renewed independence, who identified totally with the struggle for statehood. He was also regarded as Israel's conscience and a zealous guardian of its moral values, drawing inspiration from Jewish sources. This poem describes a bitter moment in Jewish history; King Saul's suicide after his defeat by the Philistines. Alterman perceived a profound symbolic significance in the death of Saul.

The day and night of battle are over,
Filled with the tumult of retreat
When the king fell on his sword
And Mount Gilboa was shrouded in defeat.
And in the land, until the break of dawn
The messenger rode without cease
And his steed's blood-flecked nostrils
Brought the news that the battle was lost.
Day and night of battle have ended
And the king has fallen on his sword.

And daylight glimmered on the hills
As the messenger came to his mother's house
And as he fell at her feet in silence
His red blood covered her feet
Yes, his blood covered her feet
And the dust became a battlefield
And when she said: Arise, my son –
His eyes were dark with tears
As he told her of the day and night of battle
How the king fell on his sword.
And she said to her son – Yes, blood
Will cover the feet of mothers
But the nation will rise up seven-fold
From defeat upon their own soil.
The king has met his destiny
But some day his heir will arise.
For on his land he rested
The sword upon which he fell.
Thus she spoke and her voice trembled
And it came to pass, for David heard.

Right: Gustave Doré:
Saul falls on his sword
Below: David Roberts:
Jaffa Gate, Jerusalem

A Song of Ascents. Of David

I was glad when they said to me.
"Let us go to the house of the Lord!"
Our feet have been standing within your gates, O Jerusalem!
Jerusalem, built as a city which is bound firmly together,
to which the tribes go up, the tribes of the Lord, as was decreed for Israel,
to give thanks to the name of the Lord.
There thrones for judgment were set, the thrones of the house of David.
Pray for the peace of Jerusalem!
"May they prosper who love you!
Peace be within your walls, and security within your towers!"
For my brethren and companions' sake I will say, "Peace be within you!"
For the sake of the house of the Lord our God, I will seek your good.

Psalm 122

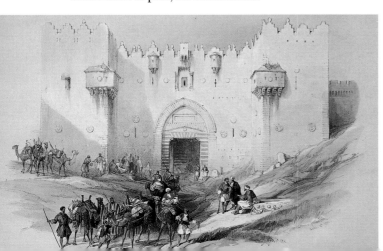

Let us Fight for Our People!

The Maccabees

In 167 BCE, the Hasmonean Revolt broke out in Modi'in against the Greek-Syrian king Antiochus, who had transformed Jerusalem into a Hellenistic city and looted the Temple. After the death of Mattathias, the leader of the revolt against the Greeks, his third son, Judah, and his Maccabee brothers took control, eventually conquering the Greek army in 164 BCE and liberating Jerusalem and the Temple. With the power of their spirit and their fighting skills, the Maccabees have become a symbol of heroism for generations.

When Judah and his brothers saw how misfortune had increased and that the enemies' troops were encamped within their territory, and they realised that the king had ordered the destruction of the people, they said to each other: "Let us rebuild the destruction of our people, and fight for our people and for the Temple".

First Book of Maccabees 3: 42-43

Who Can Tell Us?

Menashe Rabina

Who can tell us of Israel's great feats, who can count them?
In every generation a hero arises, the people's savior.
Hear!
In those days at this time
The Maccabees saved us and set us free,
And in our day the nation of Israel
Will unite, arise and be redeemed.

Judah the Maccabee depicted on a stamp for the Hanukka festival, issued by the Jewish National Fund, Chicago, 1938

"We Chose Death Rather than Slavery"

Elazar Ben Yair

The tragic story of the defenders of Massada has become the ultimate symbol of the struggle for freedom by the people of Israel. At the end of the Great Revolt against the Romans (70 CE) the stronghold of Massada became the last scene of the revolt of the Zealots. 960 men, women and children, under the leadership of Elazar Ben Yair held out with enormous courage against the massed legions of Rome. Finally, when it became clear that defeat was inevitable, Ben Yair gathered his people together and delivered a heartrending speech. The following is an extract from the speech as recounted by the Roman-Jewish historian Josephus Flavius:

"My loyal followers, long ago we resolved to serve neither the Romans nor anyone else but only God, who alone is the true and righteous Lord of men: now the time has come that bids us to prove our determination by our deeds. At such a time we must not disgrace ourselves: hitherto we have never submitted to slavery, even when it brought no danger with it: we must not choose slavery now, and with it penalties that will mean the end of everything if we fall alive into the hands of the Romans. For we were the first to revolt, and shall be the last to break off the struggle. And I think it is God who has given us this privilege, that we can die nobly and as free men, unlike others who were unexpectedly defeated. In our case it is evident that daybreak will end our resistance, but we are free to choose an honorable death with our loved ones.

This our enemies cannot prevent, however earnestly they may pray to take us alive; nor can we defeat them in battle.

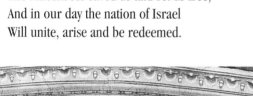

Michaelangelo: David and Goliath

From the very first, when we were bent on claiming our freedom but suffered such constant misery at each other's hands and worse at the enemy's, we ought perhaps to have read the mind of God and realized that His once beloved Jewish race had been sentenced to extinction. For if he had remained gracious or only slightly indignant with us, He would not have shut His eyes to the destruction of so many thousands or allowed His most holy city to be burnt to the ground by our enemies. We hoped, or so it would seem, that of all the Jewish race, we alone would come through safe, still in possession of our freedom, as if we had committed no sin against God and taken part in no crime – we who had taught the others! Now see how He shows the folly of our hopes, plunging us into miseries more terrible than any we had dreamt of. Not even the impregnability of our fortress has sufficed to save us, but though we have food in abundance, ample supplies of arms, and more than enough of every other requisite, God Himself without a doubt has taken away all hope of survival. The fire that was being carried into the enemy lines did not turn back of its own accord towards the wall we had built: these things are God's vengeance for the many wrongs that in our madness we dared to do to our countrymen.

"For these wrongs let us pay the penalty, not to our bitterest enemies, the Romans, but to God – by our own hands. It will be easier to bear. Let our wives die unabused, our children without knowledge of slavery: after that, let us do each other an ungrudging kindness, preserving our freedom as a glorious winding-sheet. But first let our possessions and the whole fortress go up in flames: it will be a bitter blow to the Romans, that I know, to find our persons beyond their reach and nothing left for them to loot. One thing only let us spare – our store of food: it will bear witness when we are dead to the fact that we perished, not through want but because, as we resolved at the beginning, we chose death rather than slavery.

From Josephus Flavius: "The Wars of the Jews"

Massada Shall not Fall Again

Yigael Yadin

Swearing-in ceremony for new recruits on top of Massada, 1962

Soldier, archeologist and statesman, Yigael Yadin (1917-1984) stamped his personal imprint on research into the history of the Jewish people. In effect he led the Israel Defense Forces in the War of Independence (since the chief of general staff, Ya'akov Dori, was ill), and afterwards became the second chief of general staff. But for the world at large, Yadin is known as the excavator of Massada, Hazor and Megiddo, and as the primary discoverer and interpreter of the Dead Sea Scrolls. In 1977, he was among the founders of a new political party, the Democratic Movement for Change, and served as deputy prime minister in the first government of Menachem Begin. He delivered the following address at a military swearing-in ceremony on the top of Massada.

We are standing today in this place, which is wrapped in ancient glory. First constructed by Jonathan the Maccabee; fortified by King Herod, it is the place from which Shimon Bar Giora and his companions set out to fight. Here, one of the most tragic events that our people has ever experienced ocurred. Here the last battle of Judea – Judea from the Second Temple – took place. Here 967 men, women and children, fighters and those survivors of the conflict, whose world and whose Temple had been destroyed, gathered together for the one last battle against the might of the Roman Empire.

When the Romans surrounded them on all sides in their siege camps, which have survived to this day, and when it became clear that they could no longer hold out; there took place – on this very spot – one of the most moving declamations known to history –

the speech of Elazar Ben Yair in which he convinced his brethren to chose death over slavery.

Massada has become a symbol, and the declaration, "Massada will not fall again" has become a clarion call and a symbol for the young and for all the Israeli nation. We do not exaggerate if we say that it is because of the heroic fighters of Massada – like many other links in the chain of heroes of the people of Israel – that we are standing here today, soldiers in an army of a young yet ancient people, surrounded by the vestiges of the siege-camps of our destroyers. We stand here no longer powerless against the might of our enemies; we no longer fight a hopeless battle. Rather, we are strong and confident, proud and calm, knowing that our fate lies in our own hands, in the power of our spirit, the ancient spirit of Israel which has been kindled anew...

Yigael Yadin at the swearing-in ceremony of soldiers of the IDF armoured corps, on the top of Massada, 1962

Aerial view of Massada

Not Monuments of Victory

David Elazar (known as "Dado")

Lieut. Gen. David Elazar (1925-1976) commanded the forces that captured the Golan Heights in the Six-Day War of 1967, and was chief of general staff of the IDF in the Yom Kippur War of 1973.

Lieut. Gen. David Elazar

We are a people whose monuments have never been those of victory. On our monuments are inscribed the names of the fallen. In other nations you will find triumphal arches celebrating victory, but our symbols of heroism are Massada, Tel Hai, the Warsaw Ghetto – places where, although defeated in battle, we were victorious in the struggle to ensure the nation's survival. A continuous historical chain of the Jewish struggle for life leads from the speech by Elazar Ben Yair on Massada, by way of the dying words of Trumpeldor [at Tel Hai] and to the last command of Mordecai Anielewicz [in the Warsaw Ghetto.] Just as the last warriors of Massada stood in a wall of defiance, so did the rebels of the ghettoes stand on the ruined walls of the Jews of Europe...

David Elazar, speaking at the commemoration of 30 years of the Warsaw Ghetto revolt, at Kibbutz Lohamei HaGeta'ot, April 1973

The Bar-Kokhba Scrolls

Yigael Yadin

"…Impatiently, I opened the box in which I kept the bundle of papyri and began to examine it closely for the first time since its discovery. I did not dare touch the papyri themselves, but I managed carefully to pull out of the bundle two of the four wooden slats which I had observed already in the cave. The other two were still folded inside the bundle. The two I took out had clear letters in ink, in cursive writing of the type discovered at Murabb'at. I copied the letters on to a piece of paper, one by one. My hand copied automatically without my mind registering the words. When I finally looked at what I had scribbled, I could not believe my eyes.

Yigael Yadin studying one of the Dead Sea Scrolls, 1960

A few weeks later, after the unfolding of the documents and their decipherment, I spoke about them before a crowd of guests in the house of the late President of the State, Yitzhak Ben-Zvi, and as I projected slides of the same four tablets, on the screen, I read out with great excitement the first line: "Shimon Bar Cosiba, President of Israel." Then I added: "Dear President, I have the honor of announcing that we have discovered 15 letters which the last President of Israel wrote, or dictated, 1,800 years ago." For a moment it seemed to me that my listeners were dumbfounded, but quickly their surprise found expression in sounds of joys, and unbounded amazement.

It is difficult to describe the reaction of the people gathered on that occasion, and indeed the emotion of the whole country, when the news was released. Newspapers came out with gigantic banners and leading articles, and everyone was elated. Obviously this was not received as just another archeological discovery. It was the retrieval of part of the nation's lost heritage.

From Yigael Yadin, "Bar-Kokhba," 1971

Rabbi Shlomo Goren, the chief military rabbi, opposite Mount Sinai

This is the Entire Torah

Hillel the Elder and Rabbi Akiva

Hillel, who lived in the first century CE, bequeathed to us sayings that point to the love of humanity, the pursuit of peace and forgivingness.

"Whatever is hateful to yourself do not do to your fellow – this is the entire Torah. As for the rest... go and study."

Talmud: tractate Shabbat 31a

Similarly, Rabbi Akiva, one of the great teachers of the Mishna and among the followers of Bar Kokhba, summed up the entire Torah in one verse:

Thus said Rabbi Akiva:
"And you shall love your neighbor as yourself,"
that is the great rule
the great rule of the Torah"

Torat Cohanim Kedoshim 45

A Covenant with Ourselves

Abba Kovner

Abba Kovner (1918-1987) poet, author, and a courageous freedom fighter with the partisans during the Second World War, brought with him to Israel painful memories of the loss of European Judaism. Together with the great hopes accompanying the rebirth of the state, he feared a loss of Jewish consciousness among Israeli youth.

It is no surprise that the Jews have become a universal people. In his wanderings, the Jewish wagoner reached the ends of the earth, old and new. The wonder is that our ancestors remained Jews when spread over their dispersion. But behold, one generation after Auschwitz, hundreds of thousands of Jewish families are being swallowed up by assimilation in the Diaspora. Just one generation after the establishment of the State of Israel the question is still being posed: "Does Judaism have any meaning for our youth?" And as much as the question hurts, it cannot be easily dismissed, and there is no way to silence the doubters with sermons and admonitions. This is a spiritual-national problem which calls for a serious and profound self-evaluation ...

While it is still not too late, one must make a decision to renew the covenant. Of all the covenants that obligate us in our return to Zion: a covenant with the land, a covenant with the neighboring peoples, and – as a sovereign people – a covenant with the nations of the world, it seems that the most difficult challenge is to renew the covenant with ourselves, a covenant of man with his source, a covenant of we Jews in Israel with the Jewish people that was wiped out and seemingly extinguished, but which is now alive and flourishing and encompasses the Jewish nation all over the globe...

A people that is only connected to its past is destined to die, but if the Jews draw on their past knowledge and love for their tradition, we will have the strength to open wide the gates to the future.

Speech at the opening of Beit Hatefutsot - The Museum of the Diaspora, Tel Aviv, 1978

"A Fossilized People" - The Challenge and the Duel

Michael Bar-Zohar

On 31 January 1961, a dramatic confrontation took place between the world-famous British historian, Arnold Toynbee and the Israeli ambassador to Canada, Dr Yaacov Herzog. A few days earlier, Toynbee, in a lecture at McGill University, had drawn a comparison between Nazi atrocities during the Second World War and those of the Israeli Army in the War of Independence. In the course of the speech Toynbee had also referred to the Jews as a "fossilized people." Horrified by the comparison and the use of the term "fossil" Herzog challenged the eminent historian to a public debate, despite the misgivings of Canadian Jewish groups that it was reminiscent of the medieval disputations in which Jews were forced to defend their faith in public.

Prof. Arnold Toynbee (right) in debate with Yaacov Herzog, Israel's ambassador to Canada; Montreal, 1961

That snowy morning in January 1961, hundreds of students thronged Hillel House at McGill University in Montreal. The auditorium was packed and loudspeakers were placed to transmit the event to those who failed to get into the hall. The audience was made up of students, local Jews, the press and diplomats, including someone from the consulate of the United Arab Republic. A public debate was about to begin between Israel's ambassador to Canada, Yaacov Herzog, and the British historian, Professor Arnold Toynbee. The debate caused unprecedented excitement among the Jews of Canada – as well as in Israel – even before the first word was spoken. Toynbee was a world-famous historian, an Oxford graduate who had served in the Foreign Office and been a member of the British delegation to the Paris Peace Conference in 1919, and had opposed the Balfour Declaration.

Part of a mosaic floor with the inscription "*Shalom al Yisrael*" - Peace be upon Israel - dating from 747 CE, found in the ancient synagogue of Jericho

Between 1934 and 1961 he devoted himself to research and writing, and had published many books, of which the best known was his 12- volume, "A Study of History." He claimed to have deciphered the underlying significance of the historical movements of nations and human communities and of all history. Historians, according to Toynbee, ought to concentrate not on nations, countries and states, but on cultures. He isolated 21 civilizations, among them "backward," "failed," and "fossilized" civilizations. The last category included the Zoroastrian Parsee community in India and the Jews.

Toynbee's theories were controversial, and not only his doctrine, but also his methodology and conclusions were widely criticized. But he was a gifted writer and charismatic speaker and after retiring from academia he continued to draw large audiences to his lectures all over the world. He opposed Zionism and the State of Israel, and argued that in 1948 the Jews had treated the Palestinians the same way the Nazis had treated them.

In January 1961, Toynbee came to McGill University to give a series of lectures known as the Beatty Lectures. These drew vast audiences – some 4,000 people at every lecture – as well as extensive press coverage. When he addressed the Jewish students at Hillel House he was asked if he continued to view the Jews as "historic fossils" and whether he still maintained that the Israelis treated the Arabs as the Nazis had treated the Jews. Toynbee confirmed that he did, and proceeded to explain why he thought so.

Herzog was appalled. "A foreign ambassador" he said to a friend, "cannot remain in a country in which such things have been said about his people … in which his nation's honor is violated not only from a political standpoint, but from the standpoint of its moral and historical character. If he keeps silent and stays on, it is as if he concurred with the shedding of his people's blood... I felt that the only way to try and puncture the bubble was to challenge him to an open debate."

Toynbee accepted Herzog's challenge… Hearing this, Rabbi Shmuel Kass, director of

Opening page of the "Eviyatar Scroll" recounting the story of the settlement of Israel, 11th cent. BCE

Hillel House on the McGill University campus, invited Toynbee and Herzog to hold their debate at his venue, where Toynbee had made his original statements. The two disputants accepted the offer.

On 31 January, at exactly 12 noon, Yaacov Herzog and his wife Pnina entered the crowded auditorium and made their way to the stage… A tense silence fell in the hall. Herzog and Toynbee shook hands and exchanged a little polite small talk. Their wives sat side by side in the front row.

The debate began with a long exchange of views on the comparison from a moral standpoint, of the attitude of Israel to the Arabs in 1947-8, with the Nazi slaughter of six million Jews. After a detailed discussion Herzog reverted to the question of the historical connection to the Land of Israel to which Toynbee had referred. "You are quoted as having said that the Jewish people have no historical right to Israel. May I say some facts in this respect? Number One, the continuity of Jewish residence in the Land of Israel never ceased at any time in history, and I can quote you records on that century after century. Secondly, the return to Israel has been central in our religious faith – In our prayers, in our festivals and in every aspect of our national aspirations. Thirdly, the international community has recognised the validity of that right: the Balfour Declaration, the League of Nations, the United Nations. Fourthly, even the Arabs in the beginning did. There is a message from Emir Feisal to Dr Weizmann. He headed the Arab delegation to the peace conference in Versailles, and there was an agreement between them in which Feisal wrote that he "welcomes the Jews home…"

Herzog went on to argue that the Jewish right to the land did not "become obsolescent in 132 CE [the final collapse of Judea under the Romans]. Some of our greatest religious thought and works have been produced there: the Mishna, the Jerusalem Talmud, the Midrash…right down to the Shulkhan Aruch, which is the basic code of Jewish law. We feel that the present revival of the Third Commonwealth of Israel is a vindication of immortal prophecy. That has been our course down the ages. We have traversed the valley of death, and now, under Providence, we have come to the uplands of fulfillment. That is how we see our history. You feel that we are a fossil that went off somewhere and fell into the skating rink, in Montreal terms. We didn't. We remained vital and alive and creative.

Toynbee responded: "The Ambassador [has] raised two questions. One was the question about the Jewish claim or title to Palestine, and the other was about the word "fossil" that I have used. Not only about the Jews but about quite a number of different people, for instance, the Parsees and various Christian sects and to some extent, the Greeks."

Herzog rejected these definitions: "You do differentiate between fossilism – I've been reading your books – and archaism. The Parsees and we are in the fossil category… In your study, you say the Jews live on, the same peculiar people long after the Phoenicians and the Philistines lost their identity like all the nations. The ancient Syriac neighbors had fallen into the melting-pot, while Israel has proved impervious to this alchemy performed by history in the crucible of universal states and universal churches and wanderings of the nations. An extremely eloquent description, if I may say so, of Jewish survival… we are the only people today in the Middle East speaking the same language, practicing the same religious faith, living in the same category of aspiration and spiritual continuity as our forefathers thousands of years ago and those who were exiled from there. There is nobody else from 132 CE in that category in terms of continuity…"

Then Herzog sought to draw the debate back to its main issue. "As you have said, Professor, the title "fossil" has almost entered the international vocabulary since you used it in the context you did and as I understand from reading your works in the past few days and nights I might add - there are fossils and also peoples in the archaic sense…we seem

Charles Wilson: Jews prostrating themselves on the tomb of Yohanan Hasandlar; in the background, the tomb of Rabbi Shimon Bar Yochai

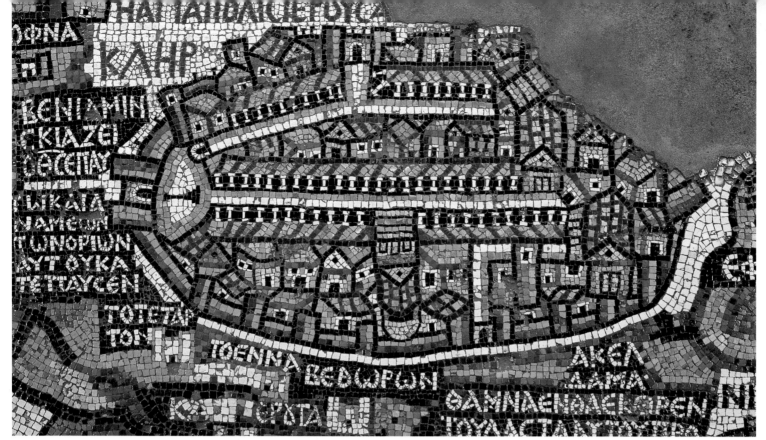

Part of the celebrated Byzantine mosaic Madeba map, depicting Jerusalem, 5th cent. CE

to be in both…I am not a historian but your thesis has been challenged by historians of great eminence and writers…"

Toynbee: "Don't I know it! Aubrey [Abba] Eban calls it the 'Toynbee Heresy.'"

Herzog replied by elaborating his religious spiritual view of the persistence of the Jewish people… "I could sum it up in a verse from the Psalms. It is 'I shall not die but I shall live!' A fossil does not die but he also does not live. Here we part ways. And as we live, and through our survival down the ages, we see the hand of Providence. …As a modern Israeli representing my country and one who has seen the country come to life and independence, is there no significance in the following facts which cannot be denied? Number One; of all the ancient peoples of the Middle East, we are the only one living in continuity, speaking the same language, practicing the same religious faith. Secondly…we have come to life in our time…. We have come to life without rancor despite all that has passed between us and our Arab neighbors…there is no rancor, there is no hatred. There is grief, but there is a hope for peace.

Thirdly, after these thousands of years we have assembled our people from 70 lands…has that link got no vitality? Is that a fossil? Is that how a fossil reacts…? Finally, the question of democracy… we are the only viable democracy in terms of the Israel-Arab complex in the area… We do have a message for the world and not, Sir, as you suggested, that our message ceased some 2,300 years ago… We believe in all humility that it has a relevance to the broad experience of mankind today. I would ask you, Sir, in all respect, whether you don't think all these elements have any basis on which you could possibly reconsider your concept of us as a fossil, non-creative, which… neither died nor lived [during] these past 2,000 years?

"…I have never used [the word fossil] of the Jewish people alone," Toynbee replied; "I have always used it of a whole class of peoples… I have tried to map out a picture of civilizations, and I found there were several civilizations or series of civilizations, some of which died out perhaps several thousand years ago; others are alive today... What I wanted to express in the word fossil was that these exceptional communities had survived from a previous age, just as fossils are a surviving record of forms of life that existed in a preceding age. Under the shock of the Roman wars I do think that the Jewish communities withdrew into a kind of shell; they gave up writing and speaking Greek and went back to Hebrew, or rather Aramaic, and for many centuries they remained encased partly by their

The Western ("Wailing") Wall; handpainted photograph by Felix Bonfils, late 19th cent.

own will, partly by the bad treatment they received from Christians, especially the western Christians. It is only since Napoleonic times you might say, except in some very early enlightened countries like Holland and Tuscany ...in the 16th and 17th centuries, that the doors were opened to the Jews and they were brought back into the full stream of life... The Jews in present times have, of course, become part of the general stream of life and have played an enormous part in it."

This was, in effect, a refutation of Toynbee's essential argument, and Herzog seized on it at once. "Defossilized, Sir?" Toynbee was disconcerted: "Israel can defossilize just as you can defrost a car... I have not found another word to express what I mean...Find me a better name and I will use it. That is all I can say really. It is not meant as an insult...."

Herzog relished his triumph: "...what I am very happy about, is that you have agreed today that the fossil has become defossilised, and the problem is not so much now finding an alternative term for the fossil...but to find a new term for the creature which has become defossilised."

Herzog concluded the debate: "On the morality issue you have agreed that we are like other peoples, and that again can be looked into when you visit Israel."

The audience applauded vigorously. Herzog was clearly the victor in the joust, and Pnina Herzog overheard Mrs Toynbee saying to her husband, "I told you not to take part in the debate!"

***

The passing years have not erased the memory of the debate between the young Israeli ambassador and the elderly British historian, who was scarcely able to conceal his animosity towards Jews and Israel. Decades after his death Yaacov Herzog's name remains associated with the debate, which grows in significance over time. But he could not have known that, ironically, that day in the depths of the Canadian winter, in a crowded auditorium in snowy Montreal, before a captivated young audience, this was his finest hour.

From "Yaacov Herzog: A Biography" by Michael Bar-Zohar

Bar-Kokhba's Grandson

Amos Kenan

Painter, sculptor, novelist, journalist and poet, Amos Kenan is politically a left winger but formerly a fighter in Lehi (the pre-State underground militant group, "Freedom Fighters of Israel" – known to the British as the "Stern Gang.") His love for the Land of Israel is given expression in his article "Why the Judean Desert?" in which he responds to a suggestion to establish a hotel and holiday center in the area.

Anyone who has gone thirsty in Wadi Tze'elim. Anyone who has drunk water from the spring of Anava. Anyone who has walked with a backpack and drunk water from a brook. Anyone who has seen the awesome rocks of Wadi Hever. Anyone who has done all these things is a son of this land and a son of the traditions of this land...

Anyone who has gone with a knapsack on his back, has seen where the embittered people fled with King David ... has seen where the zealots, the sicarii and the ascetics, fought in the last war for freedom, that last war without which we would have not been redeemed 1,800 years later, and would not have gone into the desert in order to take an oath on Massada, that Massada would not fall again, and we would have not fought the War of Liberation...

These caves hanging like eagles' nests above the chasm. The wadis with awesome rocks suspended above them. The white desert where the sicarii and the freedom fighters, prophets and visionaries found a final refuge. History makes our spines shiver, but it also elevates our spirit. The place to which you come in awe and to take an oath, is a place which entails a memory of destruction, yet it is from there that you draw the strength to fight for your lives and your freedom. If a place like this is not a protected national value, then what is a protected national value?

Will the television bill be the reservoir from which our grandchildren will draw strength and the power of the soul? Where will the visionary hermit flee to, and the poet and the dreamer and the prophet? And from where will it be possible to view the heavens? Are the heavens a protected national value? Are the spirit of freedom and the desire for liberty, national values which are not to be protected?

And where will the gazelle dwell or the ibex? And where will the leopard dwell and where the viper and the eagle, and the vulture? And where will a mountain remain, and on what mountain will the poet sing "Hawk, hawk, upon your mountain?"

Where will the Hebrew child be able to stroll along the paths of his homeland? Where will the child of a hotel room cleaner know that he is also the descendant of Bar Kokhba? And behold there, in Wadi Hever, we found the scrolls of Shimon Bar-Kokhba, President of Israel. Isn't Wadi Hever a protected national value?

Yediot Aharonot, May 1981

The Shulamit Waterfall at the Ein Gedi Nature Reserve

My Bible is Open

Rachel

The poetess Rachel Bluwstein (1890-1931) who was known simply as "Rachel," a romantic and loving but tragic figure, lived in Kinneret, Degania, Rehovot, Jerusalem and Tel Aviv, although her heart always remained in Kinneret. She was buried on the shores of the Sea of Galilee after her death from tuberculosis, bowed under by sorrow and pain.

My Bible is open at the Book of Job,
Wondrous man! Teach us too
To accept the bad as we accept the good
Blessing the God who smote us.

Let us learn like you with words and tears
To pour out our hearts to him.
Nestle like you in his fatherly bosom
And rest our weary heads.

November, 1935

The poetess Rachel seated on left with a group of friends from the second aliya (wave of immigration), early 20th. cent.

My Family

Moshe Dayan

Moshe Dayan (1915-1981) was born on Kibbutz Degania and was named after 19 year-old Moshe Barsky, who was killed in the fields of the kibbutz by Arab marauders. In the eyes of many, Dayan was the prototypical Israeli. A soldier and man of the soil; a lover of poetry and rooted in the landscape of the country, a fearless fighter and yet a friend to the Arabs. As a member of the Haganah, he was seconded to the British army and lost an eye in a fight against pro-Nazi Vichy French forces in Lebanon in 1941. He was commander in chief of the IDF in the Sinai Campaign of 1956, and minister of defense in the Six-Day War of 1967 and the Yom Kippur War of 1973. As foreign minister in Menachem Begin's government, he led the secret talks leading to the peace treaty with Egypt. The following passages which conclude his autobiography "Story of My Life" were written after his resignation from the government.

After seven years in the Defense Ministry, I returned to civilian life. The nights were undisturbed by the telephone, and there was no dashing to the office in the morning. I spent my first free day out of the government at Nahal Beersheba, a wadi in the Negev desert. That year we had enjoyed a very wet winter. I remembered the rains pouring down

the slopes of the Hebron hills, streaming southward and producing flash floods in the desert wadis. The waters rushing through these normally dry river beds and overflowing their banks soften the sides of the gullies and cause great chunks of earth to crumble. So I went south.

It was now early summer. The water had vanished, but not its impact. I drove along the edge of the winding Beersheba wadi, and at one of its bends I saw what I had hoped to find. Glinting in the sunlight were several white stones embedded in the middle of the north wall of the gully. They were oddly out of place.

Six thousand years ago, this area was inhabited by people who existed by hunting and pasture. They lived in caves burrowed in the hillside, with narrow openings to make them easier to defend. The interior of the cave would be broad and comparatively high. A strip of floor skirting the walls would be paved with stones, usually smooth pebbles taken from the gully, to serve, probably with a covering of animal skins, as sleeping pallets.

I attached a rope to the bumper of my jeep and clambered over the side, letting myself down the steep cliff toward the white stones. At first I had difficulty finding a hold for my toes, but after swinging and scrambling around I detected a soft stratum, a mixture of earth and ashes. It proved to be part of the floor of a cave. I crawled inside and started exploring. In one corner I noticed a depression in the ground surrounded by small rocks. This was the hearth, its fires used for cooking, for warmth, and for lighting the dwelling. Scattered among the ashes which covered the floor were potsherds, part of a milk churn, a cup, and the bottom section of a soot-laden cooking pot. Beneath the ashes, on the surface of the floor itself, were flint objects, mostly broken blades. I also found an axe head with an oblique edge fashioned from a large pebble. The inhabitants must have taken the rest of their vessels and implements with them when they left the cave, driven out by drought or by enemies, and wandered to another territory.

As I tried to learn more about this ancient cave community and recapture their daily pattern of living, the quiet was occasionally shattered by the ultra-modern sounds of jet fighters roaring overhead. I examined the animal bones left over from their last meal, saw the fingerprints of the potters on the vessels they had molded. These cave dwellers had lived here some two thousand years before our Patriarch Abraham. They could neither read nor write, but they occasionally drew and painted on rock and stone and decorated

Moshe Dayan overlooking the Wilderness of Zin, 1971

their pottery with deep-red stripes. This was their home, the center of their lives. From here they would go out to hunt in the Negev and in the Sinai desert, and they were familiar with every wadi, every hill, every fold of the ground. This was their land, their birthplace, and they must have loved it. When they were attacked, they fought for it. And now here was I, at the end of a rope, having crawled through an opening in a cliff side across their threshold and inside their home. It was an extraordinary sensation. I crouched by the ancient hearth. It was as though the fire had only just died down, and I did not need to close my eyes to conjure up the woman of the house bending over to spark its embers into flame as she prepared the meal for her family. My family.

From "Moshe Dayan: Story of My Life," 1976

Cover of a postcard collection, Jerusalem, 1918

Chapter 3

The Independence Day Torch

I, Moshe Benziman, son of Zippora and Zalman, eighth generation of a family from the Old City of Jerusalem, a descendant of the Hillel Rivlin family from Shaklev, disciples of the Hagra of Vilna, who established the Hazon Zion Movement and who immigrated to Safed and Jerusalem in 1840; professor of biochemistry at the Hebrew University of Jerusalem; am honored to kindle this torch to mark the 49th anniversary of the State of Israel.

In honor of generations of simple and believing Jews, who continually yearned for the Land of Israel, and arrived there in a small but steady stream which never ceased and through steadfastness and despite dangers, created the link between the people and the land.

In honor of the far-sightedness of the first Zionists who combined educational vision with political activism and laid the foundations for the development of scholarship and science in the Land of Israel.

And to the glory of Israel.

Eve of Independence Day, 1997

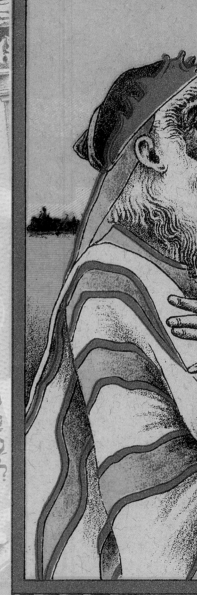

Mizrach ("East" - A synagogue wall-hanging facing in the direction of the
Temple and the Holy Land) based on a drawing by E.M.Lilien, Warsaw, 1920
Background: *Shir Zion* ("Song of Zion") Russia, 1888

If I Forget Thee...

In the whole history of the world, there has never been a nation for whom the yearning to return to their own land has been so passionate as that of the Jewish people. From the Babylonian exile to the immigration waves of our time, the Land of Israel has been the longed-for homeland, the inspiration for dreams and prayers, the subject of poetry, laments and hopes.

A Song of Ascents

When the Lord restored the fortunes of Zion,
we were like those who dream.
Then our mouth was filled with laughter,
and our tongue with shouts of joy;
then they said among the nations,
'The Lord has done great things for them"
The Lord had done great things for us;
we are glad.

Psalm 126: 1-3

By the Rivers of Babylon

By the rivers of Babylon,
there we sat down and wept, when we remembered Zion.
On the willows there we hung up our lyres.
For there our captors required of us songs, and our tormentors, mirth, saying,
"Sing us one of the songs of Zion!"
How shall we sing the Lord's song in a strange land?
If I forget thee, O Jerusalem,
Let my right hand wither
Let my tongue cleave to the roof of my mouth,
If I do not remember you,
If I do not set Jerusalem above my highest joy!

Psalm 137: 1-6.

By the Rivers of Babylon: Jerusalem, 1910

Comfort ye, my People

The Prophet Isaiah

Comfort, comfort ye, my people, says your God. Speak tenderly to Jerusalem, and cry to her, that her warfare is ended, that her iniquity is pardoned that she has received from the Lord's hand double for all her sins. A voice cries: "In the wilderness prepare the way of the Lord, make straight in the desert a highway for our God."

Every valley shall be lifted up, and every mountain and hill made low, the uneven ground shall become level, and the rough places a plain. And the glory of the Lord shall be revealed and all flesh shall see it together, for the mouth of the Lord has spoken.

The Vision of the Dry Bones

The Prophet Ezekiel

The hand of the Lord was upon me, and he brought me out by the Spirit of the Lord, and set me down in the midst of the valley; it was full of bones. And he led me round among them; and behold there were very many upon the valley; and lo, they were very dry. And he said to me, "Son of man, can these bones live?" And I answered, "O Lord God, thou knowest." Again he said to me. "Prophesy to these bones and say to them, O dry bones, hear the word of the Lord.

Thus says the Lord God to these bones: "behold I will cause breath to enter you and you shall live. And I will lay sinews upon you and will cause flesh to come upon you, and cover you with skin, and put breath in you, and you shall live; and you shall know that I am the Lord."

So I prophesied as I was commanded; and as I prophesied, there was a noise, and behold, a rattling: and the bones came together, bone to its bone. And as I looked, there were sinews on them, and flesh had come upon them and skin had covered them, but there was no breath in them. Then he said to me, "Prophesy to the breath, prophesy, son of man, and say to the breath, thus says the Lord God: come from the four winds, O breath and breathe upon these slain, that they may live." So I prophesied as he commanded me, and the breath came into them, and they lived and stood upon their feet, an exceedingly great host.

Then he said to me, "Son of man, these bones are the whole house of Israel. Behold, they say, 'Our bones are dried up and our hope is lost; we are clean cut off.' Therefore prophesy, and say to them: Thus says the Lord God; Behold I will open your graves and raise you from your graves, O my people; and I will bring you home into the land of Israel. And you shall know that I am the Lord, when I open your graves, and raise you from your graves, O my people. And I will put my Spirit within you, and you shall live, and I will place you in your own land; then you shall know that I, the Lord, have spoken, and I have done it, says the Lord."

Ezekiel 37: 1-14

Will Foxes Dance Upon It?

Sefer Ha'Agadah ("Book of Legends")

Master of the World! My soul is devastated, when I pass by your house and it is destroyed, and a silent voice inside it says: "A place where Abraham's seed brought sacrifices before you, and the priests stood on the podium, and the Levites praised with harps – will foxes dance upon it?

"Book of Legends"by H. N. Bialik and Y. H. Ravitsky:
An anthology of legends from the Talmud and Midrash, 1948

Ze'ev Raban: The destruction of the Temple and longings for its restoration

"My Heart is in the East and I am at the Edge of the West"

Yehuda Halevi

The songs of yearning of Yehuda Halevi (1075-1141), became a symbol of the longings of the Jewish people to return to the Land of Israel. Halevi, born in the Spanish city of Toledo, was by trade a merchant and physician, but a poet and philosopher in his soul. He was not able to fulfill his longings to see the Land of Israel and on his way there, he died in Cairo. (However, there is a legend that he did arrive in Jerusalem, only to meet his death trampled under the hooves of a Crusader horse).

Ode to Zion

Zion! Wilt thou not ask if peace be
with thy captives
That seek thy peace – that are the
remnants of thy flocks?
From west and east and north and
south – the greeting
"Peace" from far and near, take thou
from every side;
But greeting from the captive of
desire, giving his tears like dew
Of Hermon, and longing to let them
fall upon thine hills.
To wail for thine affliction I am like
the jackals; but when I dream
Of the return of thy captivity, I am a
harp for thy songs.

Translated by Nina Salaman, 1924

My Heart is in the East

My heart is in the East and I am at the
edge of the West. Then how can I taste
what I eat, how can I enjoy it? How
can I fulfil my vows and pledges
while Zion is in the domain of Edom,
and I am in the bonds of Arabia? It
would be easy for me to leave behind
all the good things of Spain; it would
be glorious to see the dust of the
ruined shrine

Translated by T. Carmi, 1981

Above: From "By the Rivers of Babylon, print, Jerusalem, 1910
Left: Calendar for the year 1903-4, St. Petersburg

First we will Take Eretz Israel

David Hare'uveni

Fascinating messianic leaders, veiled in a halo of mysticism, burst onto the Jewish world from the beginning of the 16th century onwards. One of them was Shlomo Molcho, descended from conversos, who reached the position of secretary of the Royal Council of the King of Portugal. He met the charismatic and hypnotic David Hare'uveni (16th century) who presented himself as a prince of an independent Jewish state, of the tribes of Reuben, Gad and the half tribe of Menasseh. Under his influence, Molcho returned to Judaism and studied kabbala with the expectation of redemption. Molcho and Hare'uveni believed as did many kabbalists, that redemption would come in the year 1540. The two caused great excitement across Europe but their fame was short-lived. Molcho was imprisoned and burnt at the stake in Italy by the Inquisition, while David Hare'uveni was exiled to Spain, where he disappeared. In his diary Hare'uveni wrote:

Page from the book by David Hare'uveni

"From our youth we have been at war, our war is with a sword and a spear and bow, and we wish to go — with God's help – to Jerusalem to take all of Eretz Israel from the hands of the Ishmaelites, for the end and salvation have arrived; I have come to ask for skilled people who know how to make weapons and firearms They should come into my land to make them and to teach our men-at-arms… Initially we shall take Eretz Israel and its surroundings, and thereafter officers of the army will go out westwards and eastwards to gather in the outcasts of Israel... I am neither a wise man nor a prophet, nor the son of a prophet. I am only an officer and a descendant of King Solomon from the seed of David son of Jesse, and my brother, King Joseph rules over three hundred thousand in the wilderness of Havor...

From "The Story of David Hare'uveni," 1948

Cover of the "Shulhan Aruch" by Rabbi Joseph Caro, Amsterdam, 1661

Hurry up and Ascend!

Rabbi Joseph Caro and Rabbi Shlomo Halevi Alkabetz

Rabbi Joseph Caro (1488-1575) who wrote the *Shulhan Aruch* [literally "The Prepared Table" – a classic compilation of religious laws] and a commentary on Maimonides' *Hayad hahazaka* ("The Strong Hand") was born in Portugal, and emigrated to Safed, the Upper Galilee town that was a magnet for some of the greatest scholars of Judaism in the Middle Ages. This was a time of fervor in the imminent expectation of the coming of the Messiah and the resulting redemption of Israel. His friend, Rabbi Shlomo Alkabetz, a liturgical poet and kabbalist, who wrote *Lekha Dodi* ("Come my Beloved" - a hymn in honor of the Sabbath) emigrated to Eretz Israel following words that he had purportedly heard from a mystical being known as "The Preacher" whose voice – according to Alkabetz – came through the mouth of Rabbi Caro. These are the words he heard:

"Happy are you my children, return to your studies and do not pause for one second, and then ascend to the Land of Israel, since not all times are equal and there is no stopping redemption (either in a large or a small way), and let your eyes not have pity on your possessions If you want and listen well, you will eat from the choicest of the produce of this goodly land. Therefore hurry up and ascend ...

From a letter from Rabbi Shlomo Halevi Alkabetz, in "Two Tablets of the Covenant" by Yeshayahu Halevi Horowitz, Amsterdam, 1698

Felix Bonfils: hand-colored photograph of Jerusalem seen from Mount Scopus, late 19th cent.

You Could have Come to the Land of Israel

Rabbi Avraham ben Mordechai Azulai

A raging storm that occurred in the Mediterranean Sea in 1613 rocked the little boat on which one of the outstanding rabbis of Morocco, Rabbi Avraham ben Mordechai Azulai (1570-1643) was traveling. The waves drenched the deck of the boat, engulfing all the manuscripts that he was carrying with him to Eretz Israel. He nevertheless survived and settled in Hebron where he wrote many books, calling on his brethren to emigrate to Israel.

Know that there is a kabbalistic tradition, that on the very same day that the King Messiah will arrive with a gathering of exiles in Eretz Israel, he will find in the land seven thousand Children of Israel. Then shall the dead from Eretz Israel return with a newly revitalized soul... And the seven thousand that live there at that time will also be created anew in a completely spiritual body like that of Adam before he sinned... and all this will appear before the people of the ingathering of the exiles. And these people will see how their brethren have been transformed into new beings and fly in the air to dwell in the Garden of Eden, to study Torah with the Holy One Blessed be He. Then the ingathered exiles will be brought together and they will be worried and will complain to the King Messiah in anguish saying : Are we not Children of Israel just like these, and how did they merit to be spiritual in both body and soul, unlike us, why are we any less ?

And the Messiah will answer them: "Surely the ways of the Holy One Blessed Be He are well- known... Those who were outside Israel and strove mightily to reach the land in order to merit a pure soul and not to concern themselves with their bodily welfare or their wealth, and came by sea and land and did not fear being drowned at sea nor robbed on dry land or to be captured by cruel masters – all this they did in essence for their spirits and their souls. Thus they returned to spirituality by way of reciprocity. But you, who had it within yourselves to emigrate to Eretz Israel like them, failed to do so because of your lust for money or the fear of losing your bodies and your goods, while your spirits and souls where only secondary.

From "Chesed LeAvraham" Amsterdam, 1685

Jerusalem, Jerusalem

Avigdor Hameiri

From the height of Mount Scopus
Let me bow down to you;
From the height of Mount Scopus,
I greet you, Jerusalem.
For generations I dreamed of you,
Of seeing the light of your countenance.

Jerusalem, Jerusalem
Cast your light on your son.
Jerusalem, Jerusalem,
I shall build you up out of your ruins.

My holy city is open, without a wall,
All its locks are shattered;
But one gate remains closed,
The gate of the Messiah.
Your myriads of sons have sent me to you,
To entrust your keys to me.

Jerusalem, Jerusalem,
I shall not move from here,
Jerusalem, Jerusalem,
let the Messiah come at last!

David Roberts: Horses in the Land of Israel, 1839

Foreign leaders and monarchs responding to the yearnings of the Jewish people, frequently became enamored with the dream of returning them to their ancient homeland

Who of you will Ascend?

Cyrus

Cyrus the Second, who reigned from 559 to 530 BCE, created the Persian Empire and befriended the exiles from Judea in Babylon. He encouraged them to return to Eretz Israel and rebuild the destroyed Temple.

"Thus says Cyrus King of Persia: the Lord, the God of heaven, had given me all the kingdoms of the earth, and he has charged me to build him a house at Jerusalem, which is in Judah. Whosoever is among you of all his people, may his God be with him, and let him go up to Jerusalem, which is in Judah, and rebuild the house of the Lord, the God of Israel – he is the God who is in Jerusalem."

Ezra: 1:2-4

Gustav Doré: Building the Second Temple

All the Exiles will be Gathered-in Again

Antiochus III

Antiochus the Third, king of Syria, was the victor in the wars of the diodochs – the successors of Alexander the Great who conquered the country in 332 BCE. In a bill of rights that he conveyed to the Jews through the governor he had appointed (198 BCE), he permitted the Jews to return to their country and to rebuild Jerusalem.

King Antiochus to Ptolemy, greetings! Since the Jews have displayed their fervor for us from the moment we trod their soil, and when we came to the city they received us lavishly… We see fit to reward them for their deeds and to rebuild their city which has suffered sorely from tdhe events of the war and to settle it by permitting all the exiles to be gathered in again… And it is my wish…that the work in the Temple be completed, the porticos and all other parts which need to be restored. And trees will be brought from Judea itself and from other nations and from Lebanon without payment of customs dues…And the same shall be done with other materials, which are required in order to restore the Temple to its former glory.

Return to Judea as Soon as you Can

Voltaire

The French philosopher and writer, François Voltaire (1694-1778) was one of the leading fighters for human rights and the freedom of mankind. His witty tongue and courageous opinions endangered him with both the authorities and the church, and he was exiled from France on several occasions. Nevertheless, many of his letters had a distinct anti-Semitic tone and evidently his apparent support for the return to Zion was more influenced by a desire to get rid of the Jews than love of Israel.

Do not reproach me with not loving you. I love you so much that I wish you were in Hershalaïm [Jerusalem], instead of the Turks, who ravage your country; but who, nevertheless, have built a very fine mosque on the foundations of your temple, and on the platform constructed by your Herod.

You would cultivate that miserable desert, as you cultivated it formerly; you would carry earth to the bare tops of your arid mountains; you would not have much corn, but you would have very good vines, a few palms, olive trees, and pastures.

Though Palestine does not equal Provence, though Marseilles alone is superior to all Judea, which has not one sea-port; though the town of Aix is incomparably better situated than Jerusalem, you might nevertheless make of your territory almost as much as the Provençals have made of theirs…

It is true, that you would have no horses; for there are not, nor have there ever been, about Jerusalem, any but asses. You would often be in want of wheat, but you would obtain it from Egypt or Syria. You might convey merchandise to Damascus and to Saïd on your asses — or indeed on camels — which you never knew anything of in the time of your Melchim [kings] and which would be a great assistance to you. In short, assiduous toil, to which man is born, would fertilize this land, which the lords of Constantinople and Asia Minor neglect…

Go back to Judea as soon as you can.

Sixth Letter to the Jews – "Beauty of the Land of Promise," from Voltaire's "Philosophical Dictionary," Paris, 1876

Arise! Make Haste!

Napoleon Bonaparte

Napoleon Bonaparte (1769-1821), who was later to become Emperor of France, regarded the Jews as the legitimate heirs of the Land of Israel and as such urged them to return to their homeland. Had it not been for his defeat at Acre, Bonaparte might have created a State of Israel with this proclamation dated April 20, 1799. The proclamation was at least partially responsible for the rebirth of Zionism.

Jews, a unique nation that conquerors and tyrants have, for thousands of years, deprived of their ancestral homeland but not of their name or their national existence! Stand upright in joy, you exiles! This war, unprecedented throughout history, has been pursued for self-defense by a nation whose ancestral lands have long been considered by its enemies as a prey to be offered up and cut into pieces. Now this nation is revenging itself for two thousand years of humiliation. Although neither the time nor the circumstances appear propitious for you to affirm or even give expression to your demands, this war now offers you…
a Jewish homeland.

Legitimate heirs to Palestine!

Arise! Show that the strength of your aggressors failed to destroy the courage of the descendants of those heroes who would have brought honor to Sparta and Rome (Maccabees12:15). Show that two thousand years of enslavement did not wipe out your courage. Make haste! This moment may not return for thousands upon thousands of years, the chance to demand the restoration of your civil rights and to claim your place among the peoples of the world. You have the right to a political existence as a nation among other nations. You have the right to worship the Lord freely according to your own religion.

Jacques-Louis David: Napoleon Bonaparte

Quoted in F. Kobler, "Collection of Political Documents" New Judea 6, December, 1940

By Wagon, Carriage or Raft

Rabbi Jacob Ben Harav Zvi Emden

Rabbi Jacob Emden (1698 -1776), known as the Ya'abetz, was a zealous polemicist. In the town of Altona, Germany, he preached with fervor the call for emigration to Eretz Israel.

"Hear, my brothers and friends, who dwell in a country that is not ours, on impure soil. Remember this and revive. Remember God, and let Jerusalem arise before you... draw close, feel and do not think about living outside Israel, God forbid, so as not to make true the verse "And the land of your enemies shall consume you." (*Leviticus* 26: 38). This was the sin of our ancient ancestors, which led to tears for generations, since they rejected the pleasant land. .. We forgot the land of the hart; we did not remember to return to the land of our homeland, we did not seek out the city where our ancestors are buried.

We, the poor and destitute, who abide close to the North Pole, where the light of the divine presence has never dwelt, and are far from the holy land and the holy tongue, how much more so do we have to make the effort to go up to the pleasant land, by wagon, carriage or raft. The rain and snow will not stop us from going to the workplace, and there is no fear for danger, for in a time of peace there is not such a danger and the dangers of the desert and the sea certainly do not exempt us from this great religious commandment, that can save and defend us.

From "God's Palace," 1745

A True Desire to Go to Eretz Israel

Rabbi Nachman of Bratslav

On the way to Eretz Israel
Members of the Polish Hashomer Hatza'ir movement, at the Congress of Vienna, 1925

Great grandson of the founder of Hassidism, Rabbi Eliezer Ba'al Shem Tov (c1700-1760), Rabbi Nachman of Bratslav (1772-1810), was one of the first hassidic leaders to create a court of adherents around himself. After a short sojourn in the Land of Israel, he composed a prayer for those immigrating to the Land.

Keren Hayesod poster, Russia, 1921

Lord, Lord, God of mercy and kindness, slow to anger and full of loving kindness and truth. Grant me your bountiful mercy, so that there should be yearning, longing and a passion and a true desire to come to Eretz Israel, so that I will merit your bountiful mercy and your awesome love... For you know the strength of my desire, how much I wish to be in the holy land because of the pain of being so distant from you... And because of this I desire to be in Eretz Israel, for there is the essence of the source of the holy belief; there is the fundamental root of the holiness of Israel... The pleasant land, that you desired and deeded to our ancestors, is good and spacious, a land in which is situated the city of our God, his holy mountain, a beautiful vista, the delight of all the earth.

Please, O God, full of mercy, full of love, full of goodness, full of righteousness, savior; let your goodwill be with me, in mercy and love; and let me reach Eretz Israel soon...

The writings of Rabbi Nachman of Bratslav, 1951-62

The Land Gives Tidings

Students of the Ga'on of Vilna

The students of Elijah ben Solomon Zalman (1720-97) known as the Ga'on of Vilna, one of the greatest spiritual leaders of Jewry, left Lithuania in three groups, in order to fulfill the command of their rabbi to emigrate to Eretz Israel. The Ga'on of Vilna himself did not succeed in fulfilling the dream of reaching the Holy Land. In 1810, his students sent a letter to the Jews of Vilna.

The land gives tidings, the land awakens/ land – what can the tongue say?

I remember days when I was a strong nation/ famous and crowned with glory/ even now, I lack for nothing / within me the Torah is clear / within me the awe of God is strong/ within me the soul is free...

In truth how wonderful it is to dwell in the goodly land! / in truth how wonderful is the love of our land / in truth how pleasant is holiness, a glowing light whether sitting or walking/ calm and peaceful/ even in its destruction there is no comparison/ in her desolation there is nothing like her/ in her peace there is no second / her dust and stones are good/ her produce and her fruit and vegetation are good/ the clear air is good.

To grasp her Torah is good/ adhering to the multiplicity of her commandments is good/ the purity of her holiness is good/ walking the land is good...

Charles Wilson: Jewish quarter of Safed, 1880

Avraham Ya'ari "Letters from Eretz Israel," 1950

To Prepare the Kingdom of Israel

Benjamin Disraeli, First Earl of Beaconsfield

Neither his baptism at the age of 13, nor his deep involvement in the political life of Great Britain were able to detach Benjamin, Lord Disraeli (1804-1881) from his Jewish roots. The person who was to become prime minister of Great Britain and receive a peerage from Queen Victoria, remained a Jew and a convinced Zionist at heart. In his novels, "Alroy, "Tancred" and "Lothair," his deep feelings for the Land of Israel burst forth.

"T'is singular! But when I am thus alone at this still hour, I ever fancy I came upon the Land of Promise. And often, in my dreams, some sunny spot, the bright memorial of a roving hour, will rise upon my sight, and, when I wake, I feel as if I had been in Canaan. Why am I not? The caravan that bears my uncle's goods across the desert would bear me too. But I rest here, my miserable life running to seed in the dull misery of this wretched city, and do nothing. Why! The old captivity was empire to our inglorious bondage....

...we must establish the throne of Israel – that is my mission, and for the means no matter how – or where... You ask me what I wish: my answer is, the Land of Promise. You ask me what I wish: my answer is, Jerusalem. You ask me what I wish, my answer is, the Temple – all we have forfeited, all we have yearned after, all for which we have fought – our beauteous country, our holy creed, our simple manners, and our ancient customs"...

We must leave off dreaming – we must act. We must build and we must ascend...

From "Alroy"

Raising a toast to Benjamin Disraeli (seated center) after his success at the Congress of Berlin, 1878

To Serve as your Maidservant

Rachel Morpurgo

The first Hebrew poetess in modern times, Rachel Morpurgo (1790-1871), who lived in Italy, dreamed of going to Eretz Israel. She offered to serve as "Maidservant to the Minister" Sir Moses Montefiore on one of his journeys. She described her hopes and her disappointment in a poem.

Sir Moses Montefiore

The precious and noble man of piety, for whom waiteth praise, Sir Moses Montefiore and all those who accompany him, may the Lord preserve and bless them, passed through our city here on their way to Jerusalem the Holy City, and I, who am worthless, sought to serve his noble wife as one of her maidservants, in order to go up there and reside with them, but I did not succeed. And after they had left in peace, I received greetings and blessings from the great sage who accompanied them, our esteemed mentor and rabbi Eliezer Levi, may God protect and preserve him, and so I hope that when the righteous man returns safely from his journey, I may presume to come before him and beseech him to tell me if the dawn has risen and our land has brought forth its produce as it is written: But ye, O mountains of Israel, ye shall shoot forth your branches and yield your fruit to my people, Israel, for they are at hand to come.

And I said in my haste:

How I yearned to come to the Minister's
house. Impatient to stand on the holy soil.
My hopes were dashed as the month went by
I was too late to meet the great man...
Noble sir, how glad and joyous I am
To learn that there is hope,
When you return pray tell me if the land
bears crops

For it is a good sign that the calamity is
ended.
I rejoiced when I saw his noble countenance
For this man Moshe, a humble man
Has built the tabernacle with his Lord

Poem of praise, 1855

E.M. Lilien: Postcard commemorating the Fifth Zionist Congress, 1902

Our Future and our Fate

Mordecai Manuel Noah

The American philanthropist Mordecai Manuel Noah (1785-1851) was a man of many parts. He was an author and playwright, a judge, American consul in Tunis (eventually dismissed from the post because he was a Jew) and he had a vision of a Jewish state – to be called "Ararat," to be established in the state of New York. However, in his later years, he understood that there could be only one place in the world where the Jews could create a state of their own.

England must possess Egypt, as affording the only secure route to her possessions in India through the Red Sea; then Palestine, thus placed between the Russian possessions and Egypt, reverts to its legitimate proprietors, and for the safety of the surrounding nations, a powerful, wealthy, independent and enterprising people are placed there by and with the consent of the Christian powers, and with their aid and agency the Land of Israel passes once more into the possession of the descendants of Abraham. The ports of the Mediterranean will be again opened to the busy hum of commerce; the fields will again bear the fruitful harvest, and the Christian and Jew will together, on Mount Zion, raise their voices in praise of Him whose covenant with Abraham was to endure forever, and in whose seed all the nations of the earth are to be blessed. This is our destiny".

New York, 1905

Your Dwelling Place, Zion!

Abraham Mapu

The book "Love of Zion" composed in a mellifluous biblical Hebrew, excited and ignited Zionist dreams throughout the Jewish world; in Eastern and Western Europe, in the Balkans, and in North Africa. Its author, Abraham Mapu (1808-67) is considered the first novelist in modern Hebrew literature. He also wrote "The Shame of Shomron" and "Hypocritical Vulture" weaving in them a fervent Zionist message.

How friendly are your dwelling places, Zion! Your hills are girdled with joy, peace to your ramparts, happiness and salvation to your palaces, the thunder has nearly stunned you, wicked streams frightened you, but the fear has passed and silence came and like a delicate lily you will now be free from restraint, you will flourish; you will continue to exude scents. Your children lie quietly in their beds with praises to God in their throats; here a father shows his son the righteousness of God and his wonders; they will be happy in the strength of God and rejoice in His salvation; here a woman embraces her baby, she rises quietly and with confidence crowns him with kisses, and her tongue expresses a multitude of blessings to the God who causes a mother to be happy with her children; here a groom rejoices with a bride, for sadness and despair have fled from Zion and joy and happiness now cheer their hearts... the voice of God will call to the city, a pleasant cry will be heard to the ends of the earth, hush, all flesh!

From "Love of Zion" Warsaw, 1970

Cover page of the United Jewish Appeal for Palestine Yearbook, New York, 1937

Return And None
Him Afraid.. Jeremiah

TINE APPEAL

To a Bird

Haim Nachman Bialik

A part of Bialik's first poem

Greetings! Peace to you, returning
Lovely bird, unto my window
From a warmer clime!
How my soul for songs was yearning
When my dwelling you deserted
In the winter-time!

Chirping, singing, dearest birdling,
Tell the wonders of that distant
Land from which you came.
In that fairer, warmer climate
Are the troubles and trials
Multiplied the same?

Do you bring me friendly greetings
From my brothers there in Zion,
Brothers far yet near?
O the happy! O the blessed!
Do they guess what heavy sorrows
I must suffer here?

Does your singing bring me greeting
From the land, its glens and valleys,
Mountain height and cleft?
Has her God had pity on Zion?
Are her graves still deserted,
Only ruins left?

Tell me, are the Vale of Sharon
And the Hill of Incense flowing
Still with nard and myrrh?
Does the oldest of the forests
Wake from sleep? Is ancient, slumbering
Lebanon astir?

Falls the dew like pearls on Hermon,
From its snowy heights descending,
Tearlike does it fall?
How fare Jordan's shining waters,
How the hills and how the hillocks
And the mountains all?

And the laborers, my brothers –
Have not these who sowed with weeping
Reaped with song and psalm?
Oh, that I had wings to fly with,
Fly unto the land where flourish
Almond tree and palm!

Translated by Israel Efros

Mikveh Israel, 1917

Conquer in Peace

Charles (Karl) Netter

Charles Netter (1826-82) had multiple interests and was deeply involved in the Zionist undertaking. He was a founder of the Alliance Israelite Française, a fighter for the rights of the Jews of Morocco and the Balkans, an initiator in the setting up of an institution for encouraging immigration and the establishment of the agricultural school of Mikveh Yisrael.

…Mark it clearly, that the Jew is capable of being a toiler of the soil anywhere... can provide bread for sustenance for an important percentage of the Jewish people, and prepare a field of refuge for the many, who will need in the future to flee in large numbers because of the determination of the nations. Ultimately, conquer by peaceful means the holy land upon which our ancestors announced the unity of the Creator.

Yaakov Ya'ari-Polaskin: "Karl Netter and his Creation - Mikveh Israel," 1926

Yesterday, One Hundred Years Ago

Amos Carmel

Amos Carmel is a writer, journalist and editor.

One hundred years ago, on 23rd August 1903, the Sixth Zionist Congress began to debate the Uganda Program. Theodor Herzl, the charismatic founder and leader of the young World Zionist Organization which had been inaugurated only six years before "in order to establish a homeland for the Jewish people in Eretz Israel," suggested a shift in direction: to consider the distress of the Jews of Eastern Europe at that time, and the failure in his contacts with the Ottoman Sultan – and to establish a temporary homeland in East Africa. He did this on the basis of a suggestion by the British home secretary who sought to strengthen the control by the British Empire and the white race in that territory and was prepared to cede for that purpose, a valley of 8,000 square kilometers (in the present area of Kenya) for an autonomous Jewish region to be called "New Palestine."

After the initial excitement in support of Herzl, the Congress blew up in a storm. Many caucuses, in particular those who came from the center of Jewish distress, dismissed the idea out of hand, even after Herzl explained that what one was talking about was merely a "transitory location." Max Nordau described the initiative as a *Nachtasyl* - "refuge for the night" for the suffering and oppressed, and as a school for learning the art of national independence.

When the voting terminated with a victory for the leader – 295 caucuses voted to send a mission of experts to East Africa, 178 opposed and 99 abstained – the opponents left the Congress, locked themselves in an anteroom, and in the words of an eye-witness "sat on the floor, mourning in the traditional fashion as if it was over the destruction of Jerusalem." Lev Trotsky, an anti-Zionist Jew, aged 24, who sat at the edge of the press gallery and did not dream that within less than 20 years he would be one of the instigators of the October Revolution and a leader of the Red Army, was certain that Zionism was on the verge of collapse.

He was not the only one to be mistaken. Herzl, too, was mistaken – twice: first, by underestimating the strength of the connection of Eastern European Zionists to Eretz

Israel, and second, in giving such weight to the seriousness of the British proposal. In the political echelons of London and among the British settlers in East Africa, immediate opposition arose to the arrival of "Jewish peddlers in the finest areas of the colony." On 12th December, 1904, less than four months after the outbreak of the storm, Herzl was himself forced to announce that the program was "impractical." At the end of July 1905, a year after Herzl's death, the Seventh Zionist Congress decided to abandon the idea completely.

In the hundred years that have passed since then a number of major historical events have taken place – most importantly, two world wars – that created a new reality in the Middle East that allowed the Zionist Movement to root the project firmly in Eretz Israel. The "Zionist Zionists" of the summer of 1904 could not, of course, have visualized such revolutions even in their wildest imagination. Yet without the determination that they demonstrated then, without their burning faith regarding the living historical connection with Eretz Israel and the ability to give it real content connected to reality, there would not be today a sovereign Jewish state, with all its shortcomings, but mainly with all its virtues.

Yediot Aharonot, August 2003

Cover page of the pamphlet "Jugend," Hamburg, May, 1904

Against Uganda

Chaim Weizmann

There is one good outcome to the African proposal in that it has opened our eyes to see our path and our objective more clearly... Zionism is not just the answer to the present-day afflictions of the Jewish people; for us it is an overall outlook which encompasses all aspects of our lives. The Jewish people are seated on a volcano and this situation will endure until a terrible catastrophe occurs and drives us towards the solution of the Jewish question, the sole and unique solution which Zionism offers: the rebirth of Israel in the historic homeland. To exchange Zion for another country is an impossibility for us because Zion is interwoven with our history, and only there can that element exist within us which is described in the ancient legend of the giant whose strength was restored when he touched the soil.

What work should we Zionists do now? Let me answer: the settlement of Eretz Israel! We must dedicate all our efforts now to the settlement of Eretz Israel! First we must settle a certain number of Jews in Eretz Israel and then strive for political rights. In one word: we must deal with settlement. A Jewish state cannot be created in a country without Jews.

Collected speeches, 1937

And Nevertheless

David Shimoni

And nevertheless, and despite it all
The Land, the Land, the Land of Israel.
And as long as somewhere in the world there beats
A Jewish heart,
As long as somewhere there resounds
Shma Yisrael, Hear O Israel, Hear O Israel
You're Eretz, Eretz, Eretz Israel.

Poster of a Jewish school in Breslau, Germany, 1932

New Year Card,
New York, 1925

Have You Tasted the Taste of the Garden of Eden?

Rabbi Yitzhak Hacohen Kook

Rabbi Abraham Yitzhak Hacohen Kook

Among the proponents of religious Zionism, Rabbi Kook (1865 -1935), who is considered among the great rabbis of the generation of the rebirth of the state, holds a very special place. Rabbi Kook established the Mercaz HaRav yeshiva in Jerusalem, the most influential one in the country and in 1923, he was appointed chief rabbi of Eretz Israel.

Oh, blind ones, who will give you eyes to see with the inner heart! Oh, dwellers in the dark lands, are you able to guess and understand the splendor of the holiness, the joy of the world, the outpourings of the streams of pleasures that pour through the heart of a son of Israel who dwells in the holy land? Have you tasted the taste of the Garden of Eden?

From "The Vision of the Redemption," 1941

In the Name of our People and our Land

Yosef Vitkin

In 1905, "The Young Group from Eretz Israel" published a fiery, exciting manifesto that called upon young Jews to immigrate and work on the land. "Awake, awake, youth of Israel," the manifesto cried enthusiastically; "Arise to help the people!" Behind the name of the group hid an enthusiastic and eloquent young man, Yosef Vitkin (1876-1912). He had immigrated to Palestine in 1898, and become one of the ideologists of the second aliyah that promoted "Hebrew labor" and the "Conquest of the land." Vitkin died prematurely at the age of 36.

Brothers!

...Our long hard war, demands of its warriors not money, as we foolishly thought up to now, but rather boundless love for our people and our land, strength and tremendous patience. From among the precious talents, we shall choose the true soldiers of the people; from these precious talents we must select a number of people who, in light of their health, their age, and their family situation, impress us by their ability to join a meaningful organization, and become dedicated to working for the people. But what will they do, and how will they serve the people and fight its war?

These soldiers must be divided into small groups of 100 or even 50 each, to come to Eretz Israel to work its soil and ultimately to settle on the land with almost no help from elsewhere. We want to establish new settlements that will contradict the mistaken outlook of the people as a whole and of the present settlers of the land itself, and the possibility of settling the land within the existing conditions. We want these settlements to be founded not through a private individual or through the public, but only by the settlers themselves...

What did we do as a people in order to save ourselves; what did we do when we gathered around the Zionist flag? We spoke, particularly in the latter days, in 70 languages, we raised dust to the heavens... We had noisy meetings; we delivered our fiery speeches, we donated – in moments of excitement – a few coins as well, but can one redeem a people thus? ...How can thousands of youngsters who are battling in foreign camps reach us...?

They must... organize a strong movement with absolute discipline and come to Eretz Israel. At first they will have to toil as workers in the settlements and in the cities with Jews and foreigners, in any place in which they can find work; after they have become more used to the country and the climate, after they have learnt from the experience of their predecessors, they will have to take possession of specific tracts of land either by purchasing them or renting them for a reasonable number of years... and to establish on them settlements which will flourish, but thanks to their work that knows no bounds... Now pay heed to the voice that calls to you from the mountains of Israel: Awake, Awake, youth of Israel, Rise up to help the people! Our people are dying, our land will soon disappear for ever, hasten quickly to help us!... Help, forget all that was precious to you up to now, leave it for good without the slightest shadow of regret, and come to work for the people! You are not extraneous as you are used to thinking; you are needed by the people and the country like breathing needs air. Arm yourselves with boundless love for the land and the people, with love of freedom and work, endless patience and come...

Hasten and come, heroes of Israel, renew the days of the "Biluim" with even greater effort and strength, for if you do not, all might be lost!

Lionel Reiss: etching. The pogroms in Eastern Europe were among the main reasons for Jews setting out to the Land of Israel

Hasten, my Brothers

Yehiel Michel Pines

Hasten, brothers, hasten,
With light footsteps.
Rush, my brothers, rush
To our motherland.
No rest for us,
No ease for us
In the land made barren
By the violent forces.
Bear the standard to Zion,
To our glorious city.
On the wings of the dove
We shall ascend to the hills of Judea.

All Hope was Lost

Avraham Tabib

Avraham Tabib (1889-1950) emigrated to Palestine from Yemen in 1908, and became one of the leaders of Yemenite Jewry in Israel. He founded the Organization of Yemenites and was a member of the first Knesset.

During the last seven years, immigration from the Yemen has almost ceased... It is not right that your pure hands will not participate in the building of the land, alongside brothers that come from the east and the west and it is not right that you remain waiting in your beautiful houses and stand aside to see who was defeated, for concerning this remember that the prophet Haggai raised his powerful voice against the House of Israel saying: "Is it a time for you yourselves to dwell in your panelled houses, while this house lies in ruins? " *(Haggai 1: 4,8).*

Avraham Ya'ari "Letters from Eretz Israel," 1950

We have a Homeland

Yitzhak Shinhar

Our faces are turned toward the rising sun,
Our path leads us eastward again.
We await that auspicious hour
Our heads are high, our spirits have not fallen.
We carve our destiny with firm hands
We bear a burning hope in our hearts.
We remember that we have a nation,
We know that we have a homeland.
We march towards the end of exile,
Together we will realize the dream of liberty.
We raise the banner of tomorrow
And column by column we march forward.

"I now know whither I shall go." Painting on a gramophone record of a popular Yiddish song from the 1950s, Kinnor Publishers

Those Who Left the Land will Return

Chaim Arlosoroff

In the summer of 1933, Dr Chaim Arlosoroff (1899-1933) was assassinated while walking along the beach of Tel Aviv. An intellectual and brilliant polemicist, he served as the head of the political department of the Jewish Agency.

This land is magical. Anyone who breaths its air and gazes at its heavens, is forced to return to it. Maybe hidden power like this is part of the Orient in general, or, if this is so, then Eretz Israel adds to this power a special and wondrous touch of its own. All those who leave the land, or who are about to leave, return here, either directly or circuitously, one way or the other. One returns immediately, one returns after many days; one returns from bitter despair, and one returns and breathes deeply when he stands on the soil of the country... one returns after being a settler in Australia, and one returns after having sailed to America with the troops.

From "Writings," 1934

I Shall not Forget Thee

Menahem Mendel Dulitzki

Zion my bride, Zion my beloved,
My heart yearns for thee from afar.
May my right hand wither if I ever forget thee.
Until my grave closes over my head.
May my tongue ever cleave to the roof of my mouth
If I remember thee not, soul of Zion.
May my heart wither from hardship and sickness
If my tears at thy sorrow ever end.

Chapter 4

 ## The Independence Day Torch

"I, Shulamit Cohen Peretz, born on Kibbutz Degania; daughter of Shlomo Cohen, who immigrated from Russia to Israel in 1924, and of Betty Yirmias who immigrated from Germany in 1936; sister of Eran Cohen, a Phantom fighter plane navigator who was killed in the Yom Kippur War; mother of Eran Hai Peretz, who was killed in the helicopter crash at Sha'ar Yishuv; am honored to kindle this torch to mark the 49th anniversary of the State of Israel.

In honor of my parents and their friends, members of the various waves of Zionist immigration, founders of the agricultural pioneering movements of the kibbutzim and the moshavim.

In honor of all those who strive to strengthen the Jewish people on the land of its forefathers, those active on behalf of the National Funds – the Jewish National Fund and Keren Hayesod; the redeemers of the land, excavators of the wells, layers of the pipelines, builders of the agricultural foundations.

In honor of the ability and the strength to carry on living through belief and hope and despite the ever-present pain of bereavement.

And to the glory of Israel.

Eve of Independence Day, 1997

Jewish National Fund poster, New York, 1930s
Background: Hebrew language class

68

THEY RETURNED TO THEIR LAND; THEY REVIVED THEIR LANGUAGE

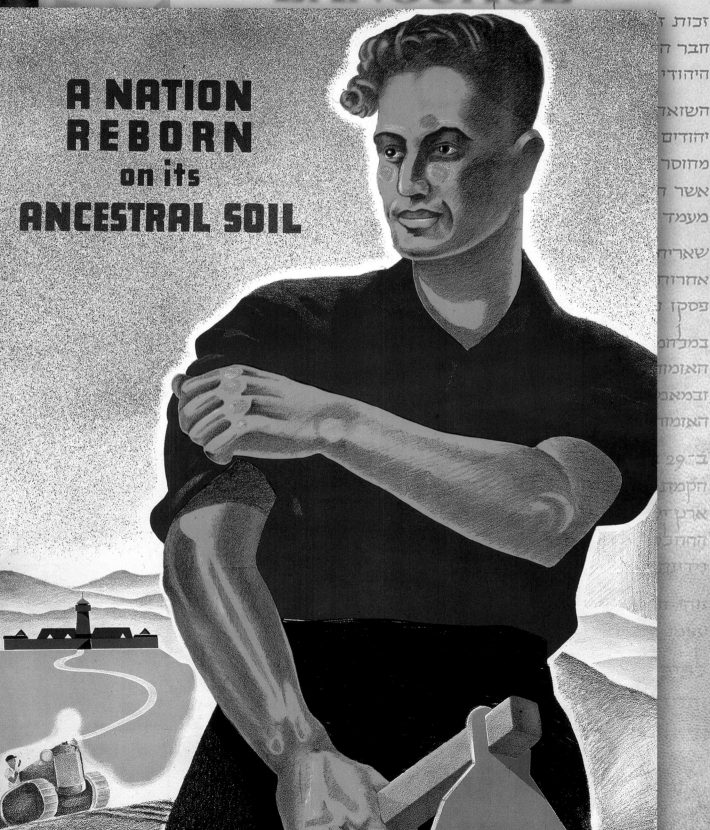

A NATION REBORN on its ANCESTRAL SOIL

Bear Aloft the Banner of Zion

Noah Rosenblum

Postage stamp, 2003 commemorating the founding of Nes Ziona in 1891.

Bear the standard high to Zion,
The standard of Judea's cohorts.
Mounted or on foot we come,
To create a mighty union

We will yet return together
To the land of our fathers,
To our beloved land,
The cradle of our childhood.

An orchard in Petach Tikva, 1925

The Rebirth of the Hebrew people

The Goals of BILU

The pogroms that broke out in Russia in 1881 led to a mass flight of Jews. Groups of youth conducted stormy discussions deep into the night as to where to go: America or Eretz Israel. "... Finally Eretz Israel was victorious" wrote Israel Belkind in his memoirs "and we established an association to promote the emigration of Jews from Russia to Eretz Israel." The name of the organization was BILU (acronym of the biblical phrase "House of Jacob come and let us go up." The association defined its aims as:

1. A national-spiritual and political-economic revival of the Hebrew people in Syria and the Land of Israel.
2. In order to achieve this aim, the association seeks to awaken people – regardless of status or religion – toward this worthy and sacred goal, that is: the settlement of the land for which there are good reasons, in the countries mentioned.

Articles of the Association of BILU, 1882

The Leibovitz family, one of the pioneering settlers of the BILU movement, Gedera, 1898. Postage stamp commemorating the First Aliya (wave of immigration)

New Year postcard from Rishon LeZion, early 20th cent.

A Small Group of Dreamers

On the 19th of the Hebrew month of Tammuz, 1882, a small group of 14 dreamers, most of them high school students, who had decided to become fighters, raised high the flag of BILU on the beach of Jaffa.

From Menashe Meyerovitz: *Mi-Bilu ve'ad ya'apilu* ("From Bilu to Illegal Immigration"), 1947

Look Around and See!

Zalman Chen

Look around and see
How great is this day.
This very day.
A flame blazes in our hearts,
As the plough slices through the fields again.

The hoe, the spade, the pitchfork,
Join in a stormy dance.
And we shall set the land alight again
With flames of green.

Merhavia, 1912

The Voice of the Lord Crying "Come up to Zion!"

Haim Nachman Bialik

From "The Blessing of the People" - the anthem
of the Zionist youth movements

Strength to the arms of our brethren as they till
The soil of our land wherever they may be.
Let not your spirit fail – exultant and joyous,
We stand shoulder to shoulder to aid our people.

And though you have but laid the foundations,
Enough, my brothers, your labor is not in vain!
Those who follow will build and plough
It is enough that we have drawn the line.

Do not belittle small deeds! Do not mock!
Redeem your people and wield your ploughshares.
Let us hear from the hilltops echoing
The voice of the Lord crying: Come up!

Nahalal Agricultural School

71

The Eyes of Israel are Upon You

Baron Edmond de Rothschild

In order to help the first settlements, which were fighting for their very existence, the French-Jewish philanthropist, Baron Edmond James de Rothschild (1845-1934) transferred substantial sums of money to cover their expenses. He was known by the sobriquet "The Well-known Benefactor" and his dream was to settle observant and Hebrew-speaking farmers on the land – who would be able to fend for themselves. In these Hebrew farmers the Baron saw "the hopes for our co-religionists throughout the world, their pride and their glory."

The eyes of Israel are upon you; all Israel watches you; you are the hopes of our co-religionists throughout the world and you are their pride and glory. You are the choicest of Israel, and that is why I wish that not even the slightest dust will fall upon you, and that Rishon LeZion will shine in the light without any shadow! I helped you from the outset, only because you were poor and a people imbued with idealism, but if you give up this idealism, I will have no place among you.

What am I doing here? Give work to your poorer brethren and strengthen all our co-religionists! At the time of extremist movements in the world; we have an obligation to the poor of our people. My brothers, my sons! When I see a downtrodden Jew, my heart is torn to pieces, I therefore say to you: "we must help each other."

From the words of the Baron addressing farmers in Rishon LeZion in 1899, quoted in A.M Linz "Calendar of Eretz Israel," 1899

Baron Edmond de Rothschild on a visit to Palestine

The Desire to Create and to Love

Avshalom Feinberg

A deep and radiant love for Eretz Israel burgeoned in the hearts of the young pioneers. Some of them were prepared to give up their lives for its sake. Such were the members of NILI (acronym for the Hebrew "The Eternal One of Israel will not Lie") a group that was established to spy against the Turks on behalf of the British during the First World War, even though the majority of the population in Palestine at the time did not support its activities. NILI is known primarily because of the Aharonsohn family who formed its nucleus, and especially through the heroism of Sarah Aharonsohn, who committed suicide rather than betray her friends after having been captured by the Turks. Aharon Aharonsohn, a distinguished botanist, was the leader of NILI activities. Another leader of NILI was Avshalom Feinberg (1889-1917), a life-loving, romantic youngster with extraordinary literary talents. Feinberg possessed an adventurer's charm and his life was cut short in a stormy adventure when he was killed by Beduin in the Sinai, on his way to British-controlled Cairo. Fifty years after his death, his bones were discovered (apparently after a date stone in his pocket germinated so that a palm had grown up, marking the site of his grave) and brought for reburial on Mount Herzl in Jerusalem. Feinberg's burning love for the homeland was expressed in a letter couched in romantic and fiery style, to his cousin Segula Backman, in which he sought to recruit all the young women in the country for the goal of the rebirth of the Jewish people in their homeland.

Avshalom Feinberg, romantic, daring and a lover of life

Hadera 8th February, 1911. To my beloved Segula, peace and blessing!
…Only those with thin-blooded, weak, and torn nerves are unable to understand what it is "to live" – to live simply without any meaning or cause, but simply because there is blood in one's veins and sun in the skies. But we, children of our land – we are neither from the Diaspora nor from the ghetto, nor do we suffer from depression. ...But why confuse the desire to embrace all of this great creation with the wish "to cry, to cry?" Be a Hebrew! Don't be a Jewess! Why cry? Why not embrace and laugh with a full-throated great laugh of joy and huge hope?...

If I had the great soul and the necessary skills to write this, I would produce a work of beauty. I would write a book for all the young girls of your age, between 13 and 18 years old. For all of them: the beautiful and the plain, the strong and the weak, as long as they are a part of our blood and our race, and that in their hearts they yearn for something indefinite...

"Sisters, I know what it is that tortures you: the desire to create and to love. The desire to sacrifice yourselves. Here, then, is your goal: from the Hermon to the Sinai, from the sea to the Lebanon and the desert, there lies a land which is the cradle of poetry, heroism and faith... Now the land has to be conquered, come what may! And we have to live in it as free people, and if not, we need to die the death of heroes. And in future the nations will say: "Two thousand years after its destruction, the ancient Hebrews gave birth again to a revived people who were heroes in the face of death." Here is the goal! And you, the young women! You should summon up the drops of blood from the remnant of those days and create for us a generation of giants about whom poets would sing, and strong-spirited young women who will free us from the chains of exile!

Girls of the First Aliya working in an onion field, Kinneret, 1914

"I Shall Stay Tonight on this Hill"

Yoram Teharlev

This song is based on a true story. Yoel Moshe Salomon (1838-1912) was a founder of Nahalat Shiva, one of the first Jewish settlements outside the walls of Jerusalem, and later the colony of Petach Tikva (Umm-Labbas in Arabic) the site of this ballad.

The Ballad of Yoel Moshe Salomon

In 1878, 'tis said,
One bright and sunny day
Five horsemen out of Jaffa rode
And set out on their way.

And Stemper came and
Gutman came
And Zerach Barnett
And Yoel Moshe Salomon,
A sword stuck in his belt.

And silver-headed Mizaraki,
The doctor, came along.
Along the Yarkon in the reeds
They heard the wind's soft song.

Beside Umm-Labbas they did halt
Among the swamps and trees
And climbed a little hill nearby
To see what they could see.

And as they stood and
gazed around
Upon that little hill,
Mizaraki said: I fear the worst,
This place is calm and still.

For if no birds here ever sing
Then death and sickness reign.
So let us flee it while we can
And never come again.

He turned to leave in
haste and fear
And three of them agreed
That it was time to ride away
To Jaffa at full speed.

But Yoel Salomon refused,
A light shone in his eyes.
No, I am staying here tonight
Until the sun shall rise.

And so he stayed there on that hill
And in the night, 'tis said
That Yoel Moshe Salomon
Grew wings just like a bird.

And where he went I cannot say
And if he really flew,
Perhaps it's just a fairytale,
Perhaps that story's true.

But when the dawn broke
in the morn
Above the hills so high
The barren valley echoed loud
With birdsong in the sky.

And to this day, so people say,
Along the Yarkon
The birds sing songs of praise
to Yoel Moshe Salomon

73

The Wonderful Story of the Grandson of Hertzenstein

Haim Gouri

Peretz Hertzenstein

Poet of the Palmach, soldier, author and journalist, Haim Gouri is deeply rooted in the Israeli experience. Generations grew up on his poems from the time of the War of Independence; on his spine-chilling descriptions of the trial of Adolf Eichmann in his book "The Glass Booth," and on his trenchant lectures on modern Israeli culture. As a fervent admirer of the giants of the spirit and of the deeds that marked the first settlers in Eretz Israel, Gouri reveals here a forgotten event from the past that contains within it a clear message for the future.

Some years ago, I visited the cemetery at Zichron Ya'akov, looking at the tombstones that tell the saga of the early days, their beauty and suffering, through names that gave this settlement a worthy place in the narrative of rebirth. I stood there opposite a grave of heavy stone, that had been eroded by moss and time. On the marble headstone I read the following words:

"Here lies:
A great man prematurely deceased
Weighed down with hardship most of his life
a faithful son of his country and people
to the last day of his life
When he died, to his children he did command
with much fervor, never to leave this land.
Mr Peretz the son of Rav Shmariyahu (of blessed memory) Hertzenstein
born in Russia on the 26th Kislev 1871
died in the Holy Land on the 29th Nisan 1909
May his soul be bound up with the soul of the Lord"

* * *

...Who wrote those lines? And what became of the man's last will? What did his widow and children do? Did they honor his will, or Heaven forfend, not stay in Eretz Israel and leave the country? If the words engraved on his tombstone are an indication, it seems that Peretz Hertzenstein feared that that might happen.

Time passed. One day I met the president of the State of Israel, Yitzhak Navon. Among other things, we spoke about emigration from Israel. He was about to deliver a speech to the Zionist Executive which was meeting in Jerusalem. I suggested that he relate to those who had come for the meeting, this story that encompasses the essence of the love for and connection to this soil. People will be there from the four corners of the earth, I said, maybe one of them knows something about Hertzenstein's children and their whereabouts.

And thus it was. Yitzhak Navon's remarks about Peretz Hertzenstein were published in several newspapers. Some while later, a letter arrived for him from the Galilee. The signature on it was a Dr Ovadiah Hartstone. The writer told President Navon that he is the grandson of Peretz and that he had immigrated to Israel and now lives with his family in one of the kibbutzim in the north.

I traveled north. ... the road passed through a landscape of vineyards, orchards and fields. Summer's land with all its wondrous fruits: peaches, apricots, persimmons, cherries and every variety of plum from the purple Santa Rosa to the golden Ogden. Piles of melons and watermelons on the sides of the road; these are the watermelons which have a reputation for their juciness,

Do not leave the Land!
Hertzenstein's plea engraved on his tombstone

74

honeyed taste and flavor. Soon, the mountain grapes as well as the figs would ripen, bringing joy to God and man.

I traveled the inhabited land on long wide roads filled with hurrying cars. I thought about that grandfather in those days, years of famine and deprivation and malaria that consumed whole families. You sometimes wish to salute the people of the first settlements, you return again and again to their stories and marvel at how they stood their ground... And thus I continued on my way towards Kabri junction, passing Kfar Yasif and shortly thereafter reaching Kibbutz Beit Ha'Emek. Dr Hartstone awaited me there. I greeted him using this name, but he asked me to call him Ovadiah - a mature, strong man, with a smiling face and a strong handshake. "I was born in New York in 1934," he said, "my father was Azriel Hertzenstein. My grandfather, Peretz, had three sons, my father was the middle one. There was also a sister, Naomi. She died seven years ago. All of them were born in Bat Shlomo. Grandfather had immigrated to Israel in 1887, from the region of Minsk. He was connected to the BILU settlers, though he arrived a little after them.

"Did he know he was about to die?"

"Yes, he knew. He summoned each one of the family, including the children, and made them swear never to leave the land. My father, Azriel, was then ten years old. Father told me about it. The oath made a profound impression on the children. All of them remembered it until their dying day."

(Peretz Hertzenstein himself composed the text that he wanted to appear on his tombstone, and made his family swear that they would have it cut in to the marble. His family was in dire economic straits and he was afraid that they would be unable to overcome the hardships and would have to leave the land.)

"My grandmother's family came from Gedera; the family name is Liss. Her sister Haya-Zippora married Hazanov, who was nicknamed "the Carpenter." My grandmother, Tchernia, had another three brothers who had left Palestine and were already in New York. Haya-Zippora and her husband Hazanov had a son called Amram who was 15 years old when my grandfather died. The aunt sent him from Gedera to Bat Shlomo, in order to take my grandmother to Jerusalem, to meet with Rabbi Kook, who was the chief rabbi of the city. The family believed that they were all going to die. Moreover, the brothers in New York tried to persuade her to join them in America.

"There was great distress. Grandmother was afraid to leave, because of her husband's will. The family sent Amram to take her to Rabbi Kook who knew the story. They were secular and she was a young woman. Rabbi Kook listened with great attention, and then stood in front of her, raised his hands and annulled her oath to the dead, and gave his sanction to her to travel to the United States. Otherwise they would all have died. There her brothers, who had beseeched her to come, were awaiting her.

Peretz Hertzenstein (right) and friends in Zikhron Yaakov. Left: David Ben-Gurion

(When he stood opposite her, dressed in his black robes, Rabbi Kook stretched out his arms. The woman was startled – he seemed to her like a huge bat. She accepted his words and traveled to the United States with her son and daughter. Ovadiah grew up on her stories. After the Six-Day War, a powerful Zionist spark was kindled in him and he immigrated to Israel with his family.)

"During the first month after arriving in Israel I visited my grandfather's grave. I knew the whole story. From a man of science I became a man of the soul. I communed with grandfather's spirit and I understood him even though by today's standards he had been a fanatic."

He searched for the right Hebrew expression and then repeated: "He was a *kanai* – a fanatic." Yes, he was a fanatic. You can find something of this fanaticism, without which there would have been no Hebrew revolution, in a letter he wrote to his cousin, Elkana Weisel, who had left for Egypt and returned in 1913, four years after the death of Peretz. In the letter he calls him "dear friend and brother in thought." This is a letter of deep friendship which, nevertheless, contains within it a hidden rebuke. He represses his weakness and writes to him in the name of "our elevated and holy idea," laying before him the fate of "our desperate people, the choicest of whose sons wander in alien fields and who sacrifice themselves for the nations who still seek our blood." He continues: "Were it only a tenth of the vital strengths of those who wander in alien fields, if it were only a tenth of our people, then we would not be an object of scorn and derision before the nations, for he who respects himself earns the respect of others."

In his vision he sees "many young people marching in orderly lines, like an army of pioneers in an organized manner: Forward!" Our duty is to recruit more and more members, "strong-hearted and energetic who will only know how to march forward." He adds that he is writing to him in Hebrew: "a living language in the mouths of my children who speak no other language and, of course, in this I am with them."

Peretz Hertzenstein - may his memory be blessed. Now I know more about this man, and the secret of the oath that he made his wife and children swear.

Ben Shemen Agricultural School, early 20th cent.

Ovadiah Hartstone and his wife Barbara arrived in Israel in 1969 with their three children. Here they changed their names: Barbara to Batya, Julie to Adi, Debbie remained Debbie, and Phyllis became Pnina. Their daughter, a "child of their old age," Galit, was born here, as was Ron-Amram, named after a cousin, Ron Hertzenstein, who fell in battle at Husniya on the Golan Heights in the Yom Kippur War.

"Before grandmother died she was confined to her bed. She grew progressively weaker. For a number of days she lost consciousness. Before that, she talked to herself, and to us and often repeated: "Oh! Oh! What will he say to me?" "We all realized she was talking about her husband, my grandfather. She had not fulfilled the promise that she had given to him before his death and here she was, now preparing to meet him in the Next World. What would he tell her, and what would she say to him? My grandfather died at the age of 37. For 55 years, my grandmother was a widow. She never remarried. Throughout all those years she wore a black dress and looked after the family."

I returned to Jerusalem. I thought about the story of Ovadiah Hartstone, grandson of Peretz Hertzenstein. I thought about the large numbers who leave the country today, and "wander in alien fields," in the words of the grandfather to his cousin Elkanah who had gone to Egypt.

I asked myself, how many fathers today make their children swear the oath of Peretz. "Do not leave the land!" I have not counted them. Some years ago I met in Rehovot a woman who reminded me in some way of the spirit of Peretz Hertzenstein. She gathered her sons together and told them that following their army service, they were free to travel abroad, to wander, or to study at university, whatever they wished. If they needed money she would do her best to help them. There was only one condition: that they had to return home to Israel after no more than three years. "Whoever does not return in that time, will no longer be my son. Take this in all seriousness. This is your mother talking."

But many leave and never return. Ovadiah returned after many years.

Maybe the story of Ovadiah Hartstone is one of closing the circle. I thought about the meeting between the grandfather and the grandson in the cemetery in Zichron Ya'akov, in the way that Ovadiah described it: "From a man of science I became a man of the soul. I communed with grandfather's spirit and I understood him, even though by today's standards he was a fanatic."

Yediot Aharonot, 21 July, 1989

Cover illustration of a volume dedicated to Theodor Herzl, Buenos Aires, 1901

There is Nothing Beside Eretz Israel
Aharon David Gordon

"Unseen, unnoticed, spreads over the Land
your wondrous dawn, the Second Aliya."

Thus did Nathan Alterman's poem immortalize the pioneers who had immigrated to Palestine during the Second Aliya, or wave of immigration, between the years 1904-1914, and who launched the social and ideological revolution in the Jewish community. Their untainted Zionist dream hung on a determination to build in the Land of Israel an egalitarian and just society, based on tilling the soil. The pioneers of the Second Aliyah built the kibbutzim and moshavim (collective settlements), the Worker's Trade Union (the Histadrut) and created medical and social services, as well as other frameworks which would eventually become the foundations for the State of Israel. The "prophet" of The Religion of Work was Aharon David Gordon (1856-1922) who arrived in Palestine at the age of 48 and transformed the concept of tilling the soil into a sacred value, without which the revival of the people of Israel in its own land would not be accomplished.

A.D.Gordon, pioneer ideologist of the concept of manual labor, in Kibbutz Degania, 1912. Above: commemorative postage stamp.

"The main thing is that in Eretz Israel…we can yearn - a yearning to the very roots of our nature – yearning to harness together all the strength of our body and soul to the task. There is no land other than the Land of Israel, in which a Jew can savor the taste of homeland, a true, natural homeland. Even though we were taken away from our land, and our land was far from our hearts while we are in exile, it is enough for a Jew with a soul to come to Eretz Israel to live and to work and to suffer here; the main thing is to work in Eretz Israel, to work in nature, and to live the nature of Eretz Israel, to feel the pain of the destruction and the heroism that is in its destruction, in order to taste and to feel what a homeland is to a human being...

Writings 1, 1925

On Guard
Shaul Tchernichowsky

Shaul Tchernichowsky (1875-1943) was a stormy, romantic poet who immigrated from Russia to Palestine in 1931.

Tonight again - no sleep for us,
In our hands we clutch our weapons –
The staff, the hoe, the pitchfork,
On guard, in the field, among the crops – in the cold.
Our ears will be deaf to our pulsing heartbeat
The voice of the bloodthirsty desert is silent.

Tonight again – no sleep for us,
For the sake of a mother and father grown old
Who sanctified the Name with body and soul,
Who blessed their daughter, who sent off their son
To the sacred battle with the ruthless foes
With the men of the desert, seeking plunder and blood.

Tonight again – no sleep for us
But our women can sleep in peace without fear.
The heart fears for their men at watch in the fields,
Stubborn and sturdy as the cactus plants.
On guard – with their weapons to hand –
For the sake of the children asleep in their beds.

Israel Shochat (center) with members of Hashomer - at the village of Mescha (Kfar Tabor), early 20th cent.

An Emissary from Eretz Israel to Yemen

Shmuel Yavnieli

In the Hebrew month of Kislev, 1910, Shmuel Yavnieli, a pioneer, writer, and childhood friend of David Ben-Gurion, was sent on a special mission: to bring a message of the renewed Land of Israel to the Jews of Yemen and Aden, and to try and persuade them to emigrate.

On the 15th of Kislev I embarked from Jaffa... The goal was to bring our Israelite brethren, in far off Yemen, tidings from Eretz Israel, tidings of renewal, tidings of the land and of the work. I spent two weeks in Aden. On the 12th of the month of Tevet I set out on my journey. I entered a narrow and dark tunnel, lit by discreet lights from small, scattered lamps, along a path of half a kilometer on a mountain above the city, on the road that led to the inner part of the country.

Shmuel Yavnieli (center) with two Yemenite rabbis, Aden, 1910

Above: Yemenite immigrants on their way to Israel
Below: Postage stamp commemorating the beginning of immigration from Yemen, 1881

I traveled around Yemen for four months, accompanied by a constant or temporary servant and by local Jews, on an ass that I had bought at the beginning of my journey. I went from village to village and from city to city. I visited these towns: Dalah, Ka'ataba, Ta'iz, Mavi'yah-Drach, Ib, Sedeh, Yerim, Demar, Sa'ana, Shiba'am, Imru'in and a large number of villages, altogether some 40 places during my travels.

In every place, when I was among the Jews, the local people would crowd around me and I would talk to them about Eretz Israel, about the new settlements, and the national movement of the people of Israel. They would listen to my words in joyful excitement and sometimes we – I and they – would become borne aloft on a high rung of elevation of the soul and the holy spirit. They would ask me about the Western Wall, the tomb of Rachel the Matriarch, the tomb of Shimon Bar Yohai. Instead of answering, I would say to them: "Why do you inquire about graves, about dead stones? Ask after the restored Zion; the well-being of the sons of Zion, who immigrated to it from the lands of exile, in order to live. I bear tidings of the redemption of our land. Every piece of the soil of our land, which has been worked on by Hebrew hands, has already been redeemed! The country has begun to give back fruits to its children, its workers, and this is a sign for us that the day of redemption is near. The time has come for you, too, to awaken! "Say to the north: give! And to the south... do not tarry!... They did not hear from me empty phrases and promises. In the letter that I sent from the centers to the surroundings villages, and which I read in almost every place before the community, I told them about life in the Land of Israel. In Zala there were Jews standing in the market place and selling off all that they possessed at half price. This was exit from exile, brazenly and in public. The king called the Jews and warned them that he would not permit them leave the city. But they replied that they were not beholden to him, that they were not slaves, but free men! Then the king commanded that a great feast be prepared for them, slaughtering flocks of sheep and oxen, if only they could be persuaded to stay, but they rejected this. No, they weren't concerned with the utterances of some Pharaoh! From Israel they had been called, and to Israel they were going! With the departure of the Jews from the city, the king lost the taxes that they had paid each year. In great anger the king issued an edict that no one was to buy a house belonging to a Jew. "Let them go however they wish, but not with our money. They should leave their houses and go." This was a hard blow. Many of the Israelites, especially the poorest of them, had pinned all their hopes on selling their houses and with the money leave for Israel. But this was to be the last blow. It is over! At last they are leaving!

Avraham Ya'ari: "Journeys to Eretz Israel," 1946

To Die for the Homeland

Joseph Trumpeldor

Joseph Trumpeldor (1880–1920) became a legend in his own lifetime. A hero of the Russo-Japanese war of 1904, where he lost his left arm but returned to battle; a founder of the Zion Mule Corps, a unit of the Jewish Legion of the British Army that fought in Gallipoli in the First World War, a founder of the Hehalutz pioneering movement, and tiller of the soil despite his handicap; a Zionist leader and activist. He immigrated to Palestine in 1912.

In the winter of 1919, he was sent to organize the defense of the settlements in northern Galilee. On 1st March 1920, he and his five comrades fell in the defense of the settlement of Tel Hai. His life and heroic death made him a symbol for Zionist youth in both Israel and the Diaspora.

Joseph Trumpeldor

9th February 1920

...the moment of truth has almost arrived. Possibly at this very moment the enemy is laying an ambush behind the house. Perhaps they are hiding in the darkness of the night... and in another hour, another minute, perhaps you will hear firing ...

A new generation, children of Eretz Israel, free, are standing at the frontier, prepared to sacrifice themselves in the defense of this border; while in the center of the country, people keep arguing, whether to approve the budget or reject it; whether to help those who are defending the homeland or not.

Hamara is no longer. Metulla has been almost wrenched out of our hands. A fearful danger hovers over Tel Hai and Kfar Giladi. We called for help for Hamara and Metulla in plenty of time, but our call was lost in the chaos, and for this mistake they have yet to atone, and for this indifference, a response has yet to be proffered. Now we again are asking: hurry up with help for Tel Hai and Kfar Giladi! The situation is more serious than at Metulla or Hamara. There were no victims there, and yet here there are already two graves. Forty young souls are in danger here. Will negotiations continue; will they continue to haggle; and will help be late in coming?

We offer them [our leaders] this opportunity, but they must know that the time for reckoning will come - either earlier or later, but it will surely come.

In the name of the Committee for Defense: Joseph Trumpeldor

From Avraham Ya'ari "Memoirs of Eretz Israel," 1947

The "Roaring Lion" Avraham Melnikov: Memorial in Kfar Giladi to Trumpeldor and his fellow fighters

On the 11th Adar, 1st March, 1920, Trumpeldor and five of his comrades were killed in the defense of Tel Hai after inflicting heavy casualties on their attackers. After having been hit, Trumpeldor transferred command to Shneersohn and then asked that someone push his intestines back into his stomach. Not one of us dared to take this duty upon himself. But he reassured us saying, "No matter: wash your hands and I will show you what to do." In wondrous silence and cold calm he watched us push his intestines back inside and wrap the wound with a towel. After we had finished dressing the wound, he said, "These are my last moments; tell everyone that we defended the place to the last for the sake of the honor of Israel..."

The day ended. On the way to Kfar Giladi Trumpeldor took his final breath. His last words in answer to the question how does he feel were, "It is good to die for the homeland."

D.Yeshaya, in "Kuntress" 22 Adar, 1920

Tel Hai Lies Under his Head

Joseph Haim Brenner

The writer, Joseph Haim Brenner (1881-1921), a member of the Second Aliyah, was the "Teacher of the Generation" of the nascent Labor Movement. In 1920, he delivered a eulogy in memory of Joseph Trumpeldor who had fallen at Tel Hai. Within a year, he too was dead: murdered in Arab riots in Jaffa.

Trumpeldor and his comrades are laid to rest, 1920

... There they stood. They stood against an enemy ten – twenty – times stronger than they themselves.

…and on this bitter, violent day they defended the place doggedly: some 30 Jewish workers facing hundreds outside, beyond the gate, and before the enemy officers, who penetrated inside armed with grenades – gaining access with stealth, behaving as if they owned the place, and talking words of peace – peace and treachery –

But this knowledge, knowledge that the heroism of despair has not departed from Israel; the knowledge that Tel Hai has brought us anew, has cost us losses which are far above what we can bear within the borders between Dan and Beersheba.

Joseph Trumpeldor, the fair and the pleasant, the bold and the chosen; a symbol of pure heroism, was slain on the high places. Before these wicked people his blood was shed. And with him another five souls: Benjamin Montar, Sarah Chizzick, Devorah Drekhler, Tauker, Sharf, who were never parted, neither in their lives nor in their deaths.

The best of our blood. Before wicked people the best of our blood was spilled. What we feared, or did not fear, happened to us. We sustained a mortal blow. Tel Hai was burned. But Israel's heart is alive. Our brothers and sisters there, both those who were killed and those who survived and reached us – showed us that the heart lives, for it was purified in fire. And we? We are the scattered, the weak. Will every weak person among us say henceforth, "I am a hero" and by so saying, become a hero?

Did we all hear the echo of the strong yet silent call of the one-armed hero: "It is good to die for the homeland?" Good! Happy is he who dies in this knowledge - and Tel Hai lies under his head.

Ha'Adama, year one, pamphlet 6, Adar, 1920

Tel Hai – the restored courtyard. Trumpeldor fell on the steps leading to the upper floor

The Establishment of the Haganah

In 1920, the Hagana was set up, replacing the Bar Giora and Hashomer defense and guard organizations. The Haganah had a clear political link with the "Ahdut Avodah" political party.

Kinneret, 12 June 1920.

Ahdut Avodah (the United Labor Party), conscious of the importance and historical responsibility, accepts the initiative that has been presented to it by the Hashomer organization, to undertake the arrangements regarding defense, to organize the workers in this endeavor, and to ensure that defense of the land will have a national and social content. This will be achieved by organizing a group of dedicated workers, who will stand on guard in every matter concerning the formation of defense units and participation in the police force.

The Convention (of the United Labor party) recognizes that the Hagana has to be organized so that it will be run entirely by its members, and will strive to incorporate in it every person who has experience in defense work and is prepared to take upon himself this burden.

The Committee obliges all members of Ahdut Avodah to adhere strictly to the Committee of the Hagana: instructions in all matters regarding defense.

The Hagana Archives

Jewish defender in the Valley of Jezreel

On the Hills of Sheikh Abreik

Alexander Penn

Alexander Penn (1906-1972) dedicated this poem to Alexander Zeid (1886-1938) – a pioneer and a founder of the Hashomer guard organization, who was killed by Arabs while on guard duty in the Jezreel Valley in 1938.

O land my land
Beloved till death.
The hot wind scorches your clods.
I am betrothed to thee
By blood, by red and silent blood,
On the hills of Sheikh Abreik and Hartiya.

There the dance is strong and joyful
And the circle spins around
In the place that I have chosen
For my days and nights.
Where I revel in my labor
On the hills of Sheikh Abreik and Hartiya

The olive trees murmur
This land is my home,
And each stone whispers: I know him,
To the hills, my dance,
Where our crops are ripening
On the hills of Sheikh Abreik and Hartiya.

We are linked evermore
By a passionate vow,
And the heart will be faithful for ever.
For it calls for the freedom
Of the common man
On the hills of Sheikh Abreik and Hartiya.

Alexander Zeid. Memorial at Sheikh Abreik

We will not Surrender our Blood!

David Shimoni

David Shimoni (1886-1956) was one of the leading poets of the Second Aliyah.

No! We will not surrender our blood!
The blood is sacred,
Human life is sacred,
But we will dedicate and sanctify our lives.
Let enemies know as they lurk in wait,
We will not surrender our blood!

Like water our blood has been spilled
throughout the universe,
But here we will not be like driven leaves,
Like leaves battered by the winds of heaven –
We will not face death like sheep!
Here they will not beat and whip us.
We shall confront death and we shall live!

And you shall not frighten us! What are knives and arrows
To a nation which has seen so much suffering?
It will not tremble or bow the head before the wicked,
This nation for whom there is one sole path,
Only one path: redemption in their land!
In their only land: Eretz Israel!

The Redemption of the Land of Israel

The Jewish National Fund

One of the famous slogans of Zionism was "dunam by dunam" (four dunams is one acre) that is to say that the settlement of Eretz Israel would be done gradually, step by step, as moshavim and kibbutzim were established on redeemed land. Obtaining additional dunams was the task of the Keren Kayemet le'Israel, known in English as the Jewish National Fund, (JNF) and each purchase of land was seen as an achievement and cause for a celebration.

The period between 1921-3 was one of the most productive practical periods of work until now in the annals of the Jewish National Fund. During this time, the purchasing of land by the JNF increased almost fivefold. At the end of 1920, the JNF owned 22,500 dunams; at the end of 1921, 73,044 dunams, and currently its area includes 98,101 dunams of agricultural land and 718 dunams of urban land; in all, 98, 819 dunams. It is already on record that in 1921, the JNF purchased two large parcels of land in the Valley of Jezreel , Nahalal and Nuris.

The exact measurement of the Nahalal parcel comes to 18,632 dunams, the area of the Nuris parcel is 29,425 dunams. Purchase of the second most important area of land in the Valley of Jezreel accounts for 17,697 dunams; this was realized at the end of the first half of 1923. Through these purchases of land, the area owned by the JNF in the Valley of Jezreel, along with the area acquired before, and together with the land in Yagur and Merhavia that were acquired in 1921, is roughly 75 percent of all its agricultural land.

Report of the Jewish National Fund to the 13th Zionist Congress, London, 1923

"The Promised Land"
Poster for a promotional Zionist film produced by Keren Hayesod, Paris, 1935

"Let us Redeem the Emek"
(Valley of Jezreel)
Poster of the Jewish National Fund, 1920s

Agricultural workers, 1930s

Like a Maharajah

Nathan Alterman

In his play "Kinneret, Kinneret" Alterman takes a wry look at Zerach, a pioneer of the Second Aliyah, who complains that the heroic era of pioneering is over because he has been allocated "a mud hut with a window" – unthinkable luxury!

Zerach: No good, Eliezer, no good. I came here and hoped
To start something, to take up a new burden
Which has never before been tackled,
To take all of it, all the weight of it,
To be a pioneer, Eliezer…yes, to be one who gives,
Not one who takes what's already completed and done,
 and now I'm here
And everything here is already…Oh… (a gesture of despair),
Better not to talk about it.

Eliezer: No, Zerach – you mustn't talk like that.
I've told you often before – you should be ashamed.
Nobody is entitled to ask for everything,
All the ills, all the problems and all the flaws.
You are worthy, I'm not saying you are not.
But what's to be done. First come first served.
But in fact, Zerach, all is not lost.
See, all this waste and expanse,
All the swamps, all these hills,
Everything from end to end, is steeped
In sulphur and stone and fumes of fever
And rot and mould – isn't that enough for you?

Poster exhorting people to speak Hebrew

Members of the "Labor Battalion," Kibbutz Ein Harod, 1921

Zerach: Eliezer, you don't understand.
You don't see how you are living. You came here and found
A courtyard and a hut and a mule and a cow,
And a dish of food waiting in the clay oven
And a place to lay your head – the first pioneers
Who came here before last winter
They were given nothing – but today, Eliezer –
Just imagine: today a pioneer comes to a settlement
And is given – just imagine – a mud hut with a window,
With first-class hay to sleep on and a bench,
And soon, I'm telling you
You'll have a special rush mat for the floor
Like a maharajah. No, Eliezer!
I must escape all this, flee to a place
Where there is still a little real pioneering spirit.

Tel Aviv 1962

To Return to the Tongue of our Ancestors

Eliezer Ben Yehuda

Eliezer Ben Yehuda (1858-1922) was a fervent Zionist, who believed that without a rebirth of the Hebrew language, there could be no rebirth of the Hebrew people in their own land. From the day he arrived in Palestine in 1881, he made a vow: from that day on he would speak only Hebrew. Ben Yehuda devoted his life to the revival of the Hebrew tongue and is considered the father of modern Hebrew speech.

I perceived that there were two things without which the Jews could not become a people: the land and the language. While the return to the land cannot be accomplished without the goodwill of those ruling it, the return to the language of our ancestors rests solely in our hands; there is no person who can prevent it if we only desire that it be so.

From the preface to Ben Yehuda's "Dictionary of the Hebrew Language," 1910

Eliezer Ben-Yehuda

Yaron London

Like the prophets with their zeal to serve their God,
He expended his zeal on nouns and adverbs too
And at midnight by his oil lamp in his room,
He jotted down stacks and stacks of words.
Fantastic words and words that flew,
Which tripped with ease off the tongue.
"Eliezer, it's time you went to bed,
You're bent and worn with all your labors.
Hebrew has waited two thousand years,
It can wait until morning."

Eliezer Ben-Yehuda,
A man of inspiration.
Words, words and words galore
He produced from his feverish brain.

So what if Hebrew has slumbered for 2000 years,
Let's wake it up and find new words like *yozma*,
Like *maghetz*, like *petsatsa* and like *rihut*
With quill and ink he wrote them down.
He thought up *glida* and *kruvit*.
Until his dictionary was done

Eliezer Ben-Yehuda

And added more and more new terms
And his quill pen never rested
And the language grew until
It didn't recognize itself,
Its very image in the morning.

His son was born, and Eliezer said,
This son of mine, I'll call him Itamar,
And from the day he speaks his first word
Till the day he dies
He'll be dedicated to the Hebrew tongue
And he will fight all other languages,
I swear.

And Itamar became a man
Tall and proud and handsome
And the language he spoke was Hebrew
Itamar Ben Avi
Whose father was a prophet,
A man after my own heart.

yozma – initiative; *maghetz* - iron; *petsatsa* – bomb; *rihut* –furniture; *glida* – icecream; *kruvit* – cauliflower. All these words and many others are neologisms coined by Ben-Yehuda.

Soil and Labor

Shalom Shapira

The pioneers of the Second Aliyah and those who followed in their footsteps, were inspired by a naïve vision of labor, fraternity, equality and peace, which would encompass all mankind.

From above descends a blessing,
Fruit is growing in the wasteland,
A nation has found its homeland,
Man has returned to the soil.

Soil, we will live your life,
Soil, we will celebrate you.
We will cling to your roots
And be woven into you.

All are fashioned in God's image,
Brothers to the world entire.
We will plough the soil together
For equality and redemption.

For equality of all mankind,
For redemption of a sinning world.
No child will be born to war,
And all swords shall be destroyed.

"Land, my Soil" Jewish National Fund poster, 1950s

Members of the Labor Battalion working on the Tiberias-Tabgha road

We Will Even Gnaw on the Stones

Malka Aharonsohn

The generation of the founders was a generation of giants. Peretz Hertzenstein, who made his children swear an oath not to leave the Land of Israel; the father of Moshe Barski, who sent his second son to replace the one that was killed and then immigrated himself with his family; Joseph Trumpeldor and Alexander Zeid; Aharon David Gordon; Yoel Moshe Salomon; Eliezer Ben-Yehuda; Shmuel Yavnieli who went to Yemen, and the tragic heroes of NILI. All of them were representatives of a generation of giants. Among them was Malka Aharonsohn, the mother of Aharon, Alexander, Sarah and Rivka of the NILI group: "With a will of steel – we shall not be moved from here."

...In the house of Ephraim Fischel Aharonsohn, there are a number of farmers, his brother Kalman Aharonsohn, Yaakov Grad, and Shmuel Ze'ev Bronstein, sitting, grim and depressed. With them is the mistress of the house - Malka Aharonsohn. By her side, holding on to her mother, stands her small daughter, Rivka. She is listening to the words of the adults And her eyes stare at their gloomy faces:

"Who would have ever thought 20 years later....

"Indeed it is very bitter. We have almost failed under the weight of evil and woe. Will the same fate befall us too? To leave? ...Where to?

"Who will return to us the years of our youth? Aha, if we still had our youth…"

While still busy serving glasses of tea to those sitting there, Malka Aharonsohn hears the words of the men and a storm boils up within her:

"What's happening to you that you've become so weak! Is it in vain that we experienced all the suffering and deprivation? Have we not stumbled seven times and yet arisen? Should we leave our land? Never! We will even gnaw on the stones but we shall not move from this place!" And they did not.

Aryeh Samsonov, "Zichron Ya'akov: Chapters in its History, 1882-1942"

We Shall Pass Over the Land with Ploughs

Nathan Alterman

In the hills the blazing sun has risen
In the vales the dew is glistening still
We will love you forever, our own homeland
With joy, with song, with labor too.

From the Dead Sea to the Lebanon slopes
We will drive our ploughs across the land.
We will plant for you and we will build you
We will make you beautiful again.

We will dress you in concrete and in mortar
And spread before you carpets of flowering green,
On the soil of your redeemed fields
The wheat, bell-like, will sing.

We will carve a path through the desert
All your swamps we will reclaim...
What else can we give to bring you splendor
Tell us and we'll do it right away.

In the hills, in the hills our light is glowing,
We will climb the mountain to the peak.
Yesterday is left behind us,
But the road to tomorrow is still long.

Though the road is hard and treacherous
Though more than one will die en route,
We will love you for ever, our own homeland,
We are yours in battle and in toil.

Ploughing the land – a stamp issued by the Jewish National Fund

85

Chapter 5

The Independence Day Torch

I, Peretz Hochman, son of Benjamin and Miriam who were murdered by the Nazis in the Warsaw Ghetto; a Holocaust survivor, who came to Israel in 1946, on the so-called "illegal" immigrant vessel "Biriya," in the teeth of the British coastal siege; am honored to kindle this torch to mark the 49th anniversary of the State of Israel.

In honor of the courage of those hundreds and thousands who ignored borders, hardships and deprivation, and took into their own hands the right to immigrate to the Land of Israel at any cost, by land, by sea or by air.

In honor of the striving of thousands from the early days of Zionism up to this day; to ensure that the gates of the Land remain open, whether by authority or without, for all Jews wherever they be in the world, who wish to pass through them.

In honor of the holy memory of my parents, my family and their friends and their communities, and all those of the slaughtered Jewish people who did not survive to witness the redemption.

And to the glory of Israel.

Eve of Independence Day, 1997

British army recruiting poster
Background: Prisoners in Auschwitz at the time of liberation

Written in Pencil in the Sealed Railway-Car

Dan Pagis

The poet Dan Pagis (1930-1987) was himself a Holocaust survivor.

here in this carload
i am eve
with abel my son
if you see my other son
cain son of man
tell him that i

Translated by Stephen Mitchell

Memorial at Yad Vashem, Jerusalem, (design: Moshe Safdie). A cattle car used for transportation of Jews to the death camps

In the City of Slaughter

Haim Nachman Bialik

"The sun shone, the acacia blossomed, the slaughterer slaughtered" wrote Bialik after the pogroms in the town of Kishinev in 1903. His frightening poem gave expression to the deep fears for the horrendous fate of the Jews during the years of exile. An extract:

Get up, go to the city of slaughter and you will come to the courtyards,
And with your eyes you will see and with your hands you will touch the fences
And the wood and the stones and on the plaster walls
The congealed blood and the hardened brains of the fallen.
From there you will come to the ruins and you will pass over the breaches
And you will cross over the perforated walls and the demolished ovens,
Into a place where the smashing deepened and crushed, widened, enlarged the holes,
Uncovering the black stones and exposing the burnt brick,
And they appear as open mouths of wounds mortal and black
Which no longer have a remedy nor will have a cure,
And your feet will drown in the feathers and stumble upon many heaps

Of broken splinters and tiny fragments and ruins of books and parchments,
Destruction of inhuman deeds and double fruit of rigorous act;
Do not remain at the ruin but continue from there on you way –
The acacias bloom opposite you and sprinkle spices into your nostrils,
Their buds half feathers and their odor like the odor of blood;
In spite of your anger and your wrath their strange incense will bring
The pleasure of spring into your heart – and you will not find it loathsome;
And with ten thousand golden arrows the sun will pierce your liver
And from every glass splinter seven beams will rejoice at your calamity.
For God called forth the spring and slaughter together:
The sun shone, the acacia bloomed and the slaughterer slaughtered.

Translated by Steven L. Jacobs

Let us not Go like Sheep to the Slaughter

Abba Kovner

Abba Kovner, a prominent leader of the partisans in the forests of occupied Europe, warned the Jews against the deceitful propaganda by which the Nazis tried to calm them down in order to prevent ferment and rebellion during the "Final Solution."

Jewish youth, give no credence to those who mislead you.
Of the 80,000 Jews in "The Jerusalem of Lithuania" [Vilna] only 20,000 remain. Before our eyes our parents, brothers and sisters were torn away from us.
Where are the hundreds of men that were seized for work by the Lithuanian kidnappers?
Where are the naked women and children that were taken from us on the horrific night of the provocation?
Where are the Jews of Yom Kippur?
Where are our brethren from the second ghetto?
No one who was taken out of the gates of the ghetto ever returned.
All the paths of the Gestapo lead to Ponar
And Ponar is death!
To the indecisive! Throw away your illusions! Your children, your husbands and wives are no longer. Ponar is no camp – there they shoot everyone.
Hitler intends to destroy every Jew in Europe... The Jews of Lithuania are to be the first in line.
Let us not go like sheep to the slaughter!
It is true we are weak and defenseless, but the only response to the enemy is resistance!
Brothers! It is better to die as fighters who are free men, than to live on the mercy of murderers.
Defend yourselves! To the last breath!

Vilna Ghetto, 1st January, 1942

Mass killing of Jews, Vinitza, Ukraine

Memorial to Janucz Korczak and the children of his orphanage, Warsaw

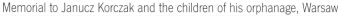

The Shtetl is Burning!

Mordechai Gevirtig

The Yiddish poet, Mordechai Gevirtig (1877-1942) was one of the most prominent Jewish writers in Poland.

A fire, brothers, a fire! Our whole shtetl is burning,
Raging black winds will fan the fire till the flames are blazing higher,
Till it becomes a funeral pyre,
Till our shtetl's gone and you stand by and watch the flames. You stand with folded arms... You stand by and watch the flames, as our shtetl burns.
Brothers, a fire! It's burning! Only you can save it from the fire. Come, make haste and lend a hand here
Come and help us save our shtetl.
Come and help put out the fire
With your very blood. Do not stand aside, my brothers
As the flames blaze do not stand with folded arms
The fire is raging greatly!

Cracow, 1938

Six Million Accusers

Gideon Hausner

Adolf Eichmann, one of the key figures behind the Nazi "Final Solution" for the Jews of Europe, was captured by agents of the Mossad, the Israeli secret service, in Buenos Aires, Argentina, in 1960. Gideon Hausner (1915-1990) was the legal advisor to the government and subsequently a member of the Knesset and a government minister. He served as chief prosecutor during the Eichmann trial. His opening speech for the prosecution received worldwide recognition.

When I stand before you here, Judges of Israel, to lead the prosecution of Adolf Eichmann, I am not standing alone. With me are six million accusers. But they cannot rise to their feet and point an accusing finger towards him who sits in the dock and cry: "I accuse." For their ashes are piled up on the hills of Auschwitz and the fields of Treblinka, and are strewn in the forests washed by the rivers of Poland. Their graves are scattered throughout the length and breadth of Europe. Their blood cries out, but their voice is not heard. Therefore I will be their spokesman and in their name I will unfold the awesome indictment.

The history of the Jewish people is steeped in suffering and tears. "In thy blood, live!" [Ezekiel 16:6] is the imperative that has confronted this nation ever since it made its first appearance on the stage of history. Pharaoh in Egypt decided to "afflict them with their burdens" and to cast their sons into the river; Haman's decree [in Persia] was "to destroy, to slay, and to cause them to perish"; Chmielnicki slaughtered them in multitudes; they were butchered in Petlura's pogroms. Yet never, in the entire blood-stained road traveled by this people, never since the first days of its nationhood, has any man arisen who succeeded in dealing it such grievous blows as did Hitler's iniquitous regime, and Adolf Eichmann as its executive arm for the extermination of the Jewish people. In all human history there is no other example of a man against whom it would be possible to draw up such a bill of indictment as has been read here…

At the dawn of history, there were examples of wars of extermination, when one nation assaulted another with intent to destroy, when, in the storm of passion and battle, peoples were slaughtered, massacred or exiled. But only in our generation has a nation attacked an entire defenseless and peaceful population, men and women, grey-beards, children and

The Eichmann Trial, 1961
Above: Adolf Eichmann in the glass defendant's box
Below left: the courtroom

David Olera: "The Package"
The artist, a French Jew deported to Auschwitz, painted himself against a background of the crematoria with a cache of food found among the belongings of those who died in the gas chambers

infants, incarcerated them behind electrified fences, imprisoned them in concentration camps, and resolved to destroy them utterly…

Murder has been with the human race since the days when Cain killed Abel; it is no novel phenomenon. But we have had to wait till this 20th century to witness with our own eyes a new kind of murder: not the result of the momentary boiling of passion or the darkening of the soul, but of a calculated decision and painstaking planning; not through the evil design of an individual, but through a mighty criminal conspiracy involving thousands; not against one victim whom an assassin may have decided to destroy, but against an entire nation.

It was [Eichmann's] word that put gas chambers into action; he lifted the telephone, and railroad cars left for the extermination centers; his signature it was that sealed the doom of thousands and tens of thousands. He had but to give the order, and at his command the troopers took the field to rout Jews out of their neighborhoods, to beat and torture them and chase them into ghettoes, to pin the badges of shame on their breasts, to steal their property – till finally, after torture and pillage, after everything had been wrung out of them, when even their hair had been taken, they were transported, en masse to the slaughter. Even the corpses were still of value: the gold teeth were extracted and the wedding rings removed.

We shall find Eichmann describing himself as a fastidious person, a "white-collar" worker. To him, the decree of extermination was just another written order to be executed; yet he was the one who planned, initiated and organized, who instructed others to spill this ocean of blood, and to use all the means of murder, theft, and torture.

Extract from the opening speech for the prosecution at the Eichmann trial

The Oath
Avraham Shlonsky

The renowned poet Avraham Shlonsky (1900-1973) was a pioneer, a member of the Battalion of Labor and a literary editor.

Because my eyes witnessed bereavement,
And burdened my heart with cries of anguish,
Because compassion commanded me – forgive!
Until days came too terrible for pardon,
I have sworn an oath: to remember it all
To remember- and to forget nothing.

To forget nothing – till the tenth generation -
Till the pain of the insult has waned
Till my moral outrage is exhausted..
I swear that the night of fury shall not be forgotten,
I swear not to return to old ways in the morning,
And once again learn nothing.

Another Planet
K. Tzetnik (Yehiel Dinur)

Yehiel Dinur (1909 or 1917-2001) called himself "K. Tzetnik" (concentration-camp inmate) 135633 to commemorate the letters and numbers tattooed on the arms and stamped on the clothing of camp inmates. He survived the horrors of Auschwitz and immigrated to Israel, where he devoted his life to writing books on the Holocaust. While writing, he lived in seclusion, without eating or washing, and in his mind reverted to being a nameless inmate of Auschwitz. When he discovered that a book of Yiddish poems he had written before the war had been found in a library, he burned it in order to demonstrate that nothing written before the war was of any importance. He testified at the Eichmann trial.

Presiding judge: What is your full name, sir?
Witness: Yehiel Dinur.
Presiding judge: You were born in Poland?
Witness: Yes.
Presiding judge: And you are the author of "Salamandra," "House of Dolls," "The Clock Overhead" and "They called him Piepel."
Witness: Yes.
Presiding judge: For what reason did you conceal your identity behind the pen name K. Tsetnik, Mr. Dinur?
Witness: It is not a pen name. I do not regard myself as a writer composing literature. It is a chronicle from the Planet Auschwitz. I was there for about two years. Time there

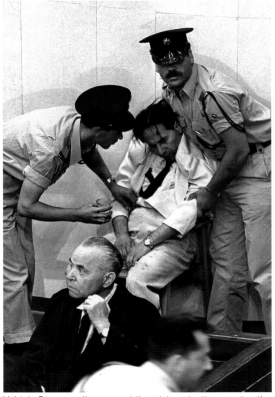

Yehiel Dinur collapses while giving testimony in the Eichmann trial

is not as it is here on earth, each fragment of a minute proceeds there according to a different time. And the inhabitants of that planet had no names; they had no parents and no children. They did not dress as we do here; they were not born and did not beget; they breathed according to different laws of nature, they did not live or die according to the laws of this world. Their name was the K. Tsetnik number. They wore, what shall I say...

Presiding judge: Yes, is this what they wore there? (Shows the witness striped garments from Auschwitz).

Witness: That is the clothing of the planet called Auschwitz. And I believe with all my heart that I must continue with that name as long as the world has not arisen after the crucifixion of a people, to wipe out the evil as it arose after the crucifixion of a single man. I believe with all my heart that just as in astrology the stars influence our fortunes, the star of ashes called Auschwitz overlooks this world and influences it.

If I can stand here before you today and relate what happened on that planet, if I, the fall-out of that planet, can be here now, I believe with all my heart that it is thanks to the oath I swore to them there. They gave me this strength. This oath was the armor with which I acquired the supernatural power... to endure it all. Because they always went away from me, they went away, they parted from me, and in our eyes was that oath. I see them. They are looking at me, I see them, I saw them standing in line...

(Dinur stands up, comes down from the witness stand and collapses).

Presiding judge: I think we will have to adjourn this session. I think we cannot go on.

Prosecutor: I did not anticipate this.

Presiding judge (after a pause): I don't think we can continue. We will adjourn this session now and Mr. Hausner will keep us informed of the witness's health and if he is capable of giving evidence today. Please do it soon.

The witness faints, and does not return to the stand.

Jerusalem, 1961

Left: A child in the Warsaw Ghetto
Right: Cover page of "Dror" a magazine published by the "Young Pioneer" movement, Lodz, 1947

Twenty-Five Years Since the Warsaw Ghetto Uprising

Yitzhak (Antek) Zuckerman

Yitzhak Zuckerman (1915-1983) was among the founders of the Jewish Fighters' Organization in Warsaw. Together with Mordechai Anielewicz, commander of the Warsaw Ghetto, he led the uprising in the ghetto. After heroic battles, he succeeded in escaping and eventually immigrated to Israel where he joined Kibbutz Lohamei Hagetaot ("Ghetto Fighters").

[After taking out the first Jews] there were 70,000 left in the Warsaw Ghetto... The first uprising broke out on 18th January, 1943, when the Germans attempted for a second time to take out the Jews from the ghetto on the personal order of Heinrich Himmler. In the ghetto were some scores of handguns, ten of which had been given by the Armia Krajowa and the rest had been bought through our representative on the Aryan side of Warsaw – and grenades. Several companies undertook the defense of the ghetto. After four days, the Germans were forced to

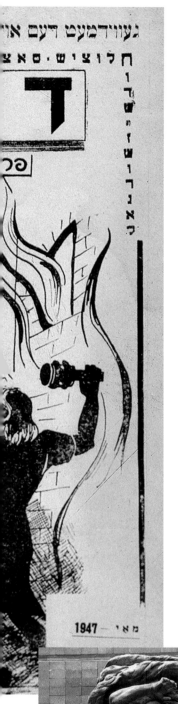

lift the siege... Obviously it was not our forces that had led to this: the Germans were worried that the uprising might spread to the Aryan side of Warsaw as well.

But the January uprising was the more important step in the development of the major uprising... Many bought weapons to defend themselves in the bunkers. On the same day that the Jewish cobbler mended free of charge out of his own goodwill, the holster of a fighter's revolver, that same day that the Jewish baker gave away with a good heart and without monetary reward, a piece of bread to a fighter, we knew thgat the people were with us. The community that had survived so far was transformed into a fighting community. A fighting people, meaning the identification of the masses with its fighters and its goal – an identity without bounds. The people and the fighters were mentally ready for the fight for life. The attempts by the Germans by peaceful means to bring out the Jews from the ghetto to the concentration camps which had been established in the area of Lublin, broke down in the face of the proud stand of the Jews, in the face of the Jewish fighters. The Germans were left with one option only: to bring out the Jews by force. That is to say, a struggle of life and death. In the midst of the days of blood, the few remaining individuals on the Aryan side of Warsaw, had written to their friends in Eretz Israel:

"When you read this letter do not think that our spirit was broken, or that we despaired. We can only look with open eyes at our inevitable fate. We know that you are doing everything you can in order to save us. We also know that you are powerless. It is easy for us to die with the knowledge that a free world will arise, and from a belief that in Eretz Israel, a homeland for the Jewish people will be created."

This letter was dated November 15, 1943.

Their fiery vision was realized. We have now had a Hebrew homeland for 20 years, and this gathering of the Jewish resistance organization is taking place in a united Jerusalem.

Jerusalem, 1968.

Deportation of Jews from the Warsaw Ghetto

Benno Rapoport:
Memorial to the Warsaw
Ghetto fighters, Yad
Vashem, Jerusalem

Listen! Listen!

A broadcast from the Warsaw Ghetto

We are making an announcement for the entire world to hear: the Warsaw Ghetto is dying, the Warsaw Ghetto is dying in battle! For these past two weeks, battles between unequal forces have been continuing, during these two weeks the ghetto has been convulsed by flames and blood.

Thousands of Jews are fighting heroically throughout Warsaw against the German murderers. Young and old are fighting. The Germans are using tanks and heavy cannons. One after the other the fighters' positions are falling. Airplanes bomb the ghetto. Every road, every house, every threshold – has turned into a site of resistance and battle.

Honor and glory to the heroic fighters! Honor to those who have fallen in battle!

With ever-weakening strength they call to the world: Give us help! Give us weapons!

Listen! Listen! The Warsaw Ghetto is dying! The Warsaw Ghetto is dying in battle!

Warsaw Ghetto, April-May, 1943

93

Song of the Partisans

Hirsch Glick

Statue of Mordechai Anielewicz, commander of the Warsaw Ghetto fighters; Kibbutz Yad Mordechai

In 1943, in the Vilna Ghetto, Hirsch Glick wrote the "Song of the Jewish Partisans" which became one of the best-known songs of the Second World War and the anthem of Jewish partisans everywhere.

From lands of palm-trees to the distant lands of snow,
See, we are here despite our suffering and our woe.
And in the places where our blood has soaked the earth
Tis' there our courage and resolve will blossom forth.

The morning light then once again will cast its glow,
The pain of yesterday will vanish with the foe,
But if the coming of the light should be delayed,
This song will fortify our hearts from day to day.

Because our song's inscribed in blood and tears and lead,
It's not the boundless song that birds sing overhead.
Our people sang it as they manned the barricades
And in their hands they clutched their pistols and grenades.

So never say: "Our final hour must be nigh,
The clouds are black and hide the sunlight and the sky."
Because the day for which we yearn will soon appear,
The ground will echo to our tread: "Yes, we are here!"

Do We Know How to Remember?

Elie Wiesel

Professor Elie Wiesel, a Holocaust survivor, author and philosopher, won the Nobel Prize for Peace in 1986.

It was almost 60 years ago, immediately after Passover. Posters in two languages - German and Hungarian – announced the establishment of a ghetto in a very small town, somewhere in the Carpathian mountains. All Jews were commanded to move into the ghetto with all their possessions, within three days. The consequence of disobedience was death. Almost 60 years ago.

What happened to our memories? Where is it possible to find them? What happened to the pain that saturated them? The sadness was likely to leap over a generation or two. Is our sadness yet to come? Has it reached us incomplete? In a certain way we do not know how to mourn. Do we know how to remember?

We know nothing but this: Exactly as the murderer was intent on wiping out Jewish life and the Jewish memory, so we have to preserve it.

The German oppressor and his local assistants choked, burned, murdered, and killed in every conceivable way their Jewish victims, and afterwards concealed the evidence. Thus were the Jews murdered twice. Never in the history of our people have so many Jews been deprived of their right to be buried in a Jewish grave. Now our memories are their cemeteries.

We believe there is a precious virtue in memory but also a deficiency. It is difficult for memory to absorb more than a certain amount. It is selective. At the very best we retain what

A delegation of Israel Defense Forces officers salute facing the mound of ashes at the site of the Majdanek death camp, Poland, 2003

was known and was experienced directly. But what of that which was not known? How many families and communities were destroyed without leaving behind even one shred of memory? Who will pass on their stories, and who will bear witness for them?

These questions pursue many of us year after year before the Holocaust Memorial Day ceremonies that take place in Israel and many places in the Diaspora. Yet there is another question, no less important: Did we and the world learn anything from these memories? And if we learned, did we all learn exactly the same lesson?

What will happen when the last witness has gone? Our only response is that the listener to a witness must himself become a witness.

Yediot Aharonot. Holocaust Day, 9th April, 2002

At Least Let us Fulfill our Historic Task

Ruzhka Korczak

Ruzhka Korczak fought the Nazis in the Vilna Ghetto and in the forests. Against all odds, she survived, emigrated to Israel and became a member of Kibbutz Ein HaHoresh.

It's easier to die knowing that there [in Eretz Israel] authentic Jewish life stills pounds, because in that one corner of the wide world we are not unwanted, wandering, lonely. There would have been no meaning to our death if not for the feeling that after we are no longer here, they would be the only ones who would think of us with true emotion. Every action of ours is a step on the way to liberating and advancing the building of an independent national homeland.

Since it is not vouchsafed us to participate in the creative work of building the homeland, we can at least fulfill here our historic task : we must raise the banner of the lost people, rid ourselves of the mark of slavery and thus place us alongside the nations who are free in spirit...

From "The Fighting Pioneer," the underground newspaper of the fighters of the Jewish Pioneer Youth, Vilna. Issue 29, 13th August, 1943

Israeli delegation at the annual "March of the Living" from Auschwitz to Birkenau, on Holocaust Remembrance Day, 2003

Martyrs and Heroes Memorial Law – Yad Vashem, 1953

19 August, 1953

The Yad Vashem Memorial Authority is hereby established in Jerusalem to commemorate:

  1) The six million members of the Jewish people who died a martyr's death at the hands of the Nazis and their collaborators;

  2) The Jewish households annihilated and destroyed by the enemy;

  3) The communities, the synagogues, the movements and organizations, the public, cultural, educational, religious and charitable institutions destroyed in a heinous attempt to erase the name and culture of Israel;

  4) The heroism of Jews who gave their lives for their people with purity and sanctity;

  5) The heroism of Jewish servicemen and of underground fighters in towns and forests who staked their lives in the battle against the Nazi oppressors and their collaborators;

  6) The heroic stand of the besieged and fighters of the ghettos, who rose and kindled the flame of revolt to save the honor of their people;

  7) The sublime and constant struggle of the Jewish masses in the face of oblivion to preserve their humanity and Jewish culture;

  8) The incessant efforts of the besieged to make their way to the homeland and the heroism of their brethren who came to the rescue of the survivors and liberated them;

  9) The righteous gentiles who risked their lives to save Jews.

The task of Yad Vashem is to preserve in the homeland the memory of all those sons and daughters of the Jewish people who gave their lives, fought and rebelled against the Nazi enemies and their henchmen and to perpetuate their names and memories, and those of communities, organizations and institutions which were destroyed because they were part of the Jewish people...

Yad Vashem, Jerusalem
Above: Valley of the Lost Communities. Right: Hall of Remembrance

The Millstone of Guilt

Haim Gouri

The poet Haim Gouri, who covered the Eichmann trial, agonizingly examined accusations that the Jews of Palestine had not done enough to save their brethren in Nazi-occupied Europe.

...After this trial, people will cease, at least, to deal with the behavior of the Jews there, they will cease to judge them. They said everything to us. One day we will be obliged to talk.

  I am afraid.

  There is something close to us that there is no running away from. Just a moment – a repeated interjection - and you? [you – the Jews of Eretz Israel] and you – for heaven's sake !? And you!?

  You accuse us [the allies who fought the Nazis] with cynicism, with numbness, indifference. You say that we did not offer help, that we just watched from afar how the last Jews were being massacred.

  And you!?

  We return to those years.

בחום שלושה חדשים של אפס-מעשה

זעקת הישוב מול שתיקת העולם

אספת הנבחרים נותנת בטוי לכאב, לזעם לאבל ולאכזבה

Article in Yediot Aharonot, 22 February, 1943. The headline reads, "The Jewish community of Palestine cries out in the face of the world's silence"

So, what do you say? I say that there the Jewish people was destroyed, and here (after El-Alamein and after we were spared the danger of another Majdanek) the brethren of the murdered ones did not do what might have been expected of them in the light of the news coming from there...

From a lack of a psychological ability to bear a millstone of guilt on our shoulders, we now attempt to shift it to the shoulders of the leadership.

"But they knew more." "They were responsible, the leaders, the guides." "You have to admit that they were responsible for telling us what to do." "There are different levels of responsibility, aren't there?"

It is difficult not to agree with the man who said that the leadership of today is obliged to give an accounting to the people.

No. I am not making comparisons. There exists a crucial difference that cries out, isn't that true? Between the leadership of the martyred people, crying and pleading and sending cries for help, standing in the waiting rooms of the McMichaels, the Edens and the Moynes, [British leaders during and befor World War Two] and between those who commanded victorious armies, the bombers and the warships.

But ...and with this sentence witnesses have been interrogated at length: why didn't you resist? Or why didn't you kill Eichmann? And why, why didn't you flee?

These questions return like a wounding splintering boomerang in our faces: Why didn't you say anything? Why didn't you shout? Why didn't you demonstrate? Why didn't you start a hunger strike? Why didn't you drive the world crazy? What will we reply to the questioner – are you able to say that you did everything in your power in order to help?

What shall we do then? Search for the guilty? Why not? Are we permitted? We, who received garlands of flowers and praise, must be ready for a stone to be thrown at us. But we didn't answer the question that also connects us, in the first person plural.

They knew more. That is true. But we also knew. In May 1943, we knew that Jewish Warsaw no longer existed. We heard the broadcast on Radio London. Before this we also knew that the Jewish tribe in Europe was being extinguished, day by day.

We went to fight Nazism. Thousands enlisted, marched to battle. Yet simultaneously life continued here, and death continued there, as in a bad dream of helplessness.

I'm not venturing in these few lines to offer an answer. Perhaps there is an explanation for everything: knowing – not knowing – the numbness, the too fast pace of events, the strangeness, the world that had no time to listen, the thought that somehow we are doing something ... the short-handedness, the helplessness of being without a state or an army.

The more I think about these concerns, the more fear overcomes me. The questions today are too cruel to flee from and too dangerous to attack. Yet they fall upon us continuously.

"Did you ever try to douse a burning city with a cup of water?" a friend asked me and buried his face in his hands. Since then, I ask myself again and again – why wasn't all our life then like one more cup of water on the burning city? ... But it is too late to pose this question.

2 June, 1961. From "Opposite the Glass Booth – Judgment in Jerusalem," 2001

The Crime of Genocide (Prevention and Punishment) Law, 1950

In this Law, "genocide" means any of the following acts committed with intent to destroy, in whole or in part, a national, ethnic, racial or religious group (hereinafter referred to as "group"), as such:

1. Killing members of the group;
2. Causing serious bodily or mental harm to members of the group;
3. Inflicting on the group conditions of life calculated to bring about its physical destruction, in whole or in part;
4. Imposing measures intended to prevent births within the group;
5. Forcibly transferring children of the group to another group.
   A "child" means a person under 18 years of age.
   A person guilty of genocide shall be punishable with death.

Responsibility for Genocide

Those found guilty under the provisions of this law will receive due punishment whether if they bear legal administrative responsibility or if they are members of a legislative body; whether they are civil servants or private individuals.

Place of the Crime

A person found guilty under the provisions of this law for a crime committed outside the State of Israel may be brought to trial and convicted in Israel just as if the crime had been committed in Israel.

Yediot Aharonot, 15 December 1991. "Eichmann Sentenced to Death by Hanging"

Above: Holocaust survivors arriving at the port of Haifa.
Right: Jewish youth from all over the world participate in the "March of the Living," Poland, 2003

The Shoah ("Holocaust") – Past and Present

Yehuda Bauer (A reply to a teacher)

Professor Yehuda Bauer is one of the world's leading scholars of the Holocaust period. From 1996 to 2001, he directed the International Institute for Holocaust Research at Yad Vashem – the Institute for Holocaust Remembrance in Jerusalem. Since his retirement he has served as academic adviser to Yad Vashem.

There was an argument between us... You responded to my claim that the Holocaust and the establishment of the State of Israel – are not events that happened and ended, died as it were, but are part of an on-going process in which we are still involved. I said that the background that allowed the Holocaust (and not the destruction), that is to say our isolation in the world, the special relationship of the world toward us, the animosity toward the Jews – are still conditions of our existence today, as the Yom Kippur War [of 1973] again demonstrated. We have allies, and we have more today than we did then, and, of course, we are much stronger. Yet our existential situation is a continuation of that of almost two generations ago.

On these things you rebelled. You claimed that you as a teacher are unable to teach according to this view of reality. A student of yours approached you, you related, a student who is also a soldier...and threw at you the sentence: "Why did you teach me humanism and yet afterwards to kill enemy soldiers? You said that you have conversations with students who are not yet soldiers – and that you clarify the problems and yet still insist on the brotherhood of nations in a world with a better future, while observing reality as it actually is. And that the concept of the Holocaust as a process cannot be correct. You cannot raise people on this.

There might be an answer to all this for a young person: Let us travel to New Zealand or to Brooklyn, and we can be normal people there - not Jews: except that those among us who have tried this, and others who tried it have found out that it just doesn't work. We thought that the individual at least could escape from his existential situation. But only a few manage it and the price is sometimes psychological self-alienation that is a much higher price to pay than the suffering involved in the identity with which to achieve spiritual and emotional satisfaction. There also exists a minute problem of ethics. One might be able to find mice that climb on to the deck of a ship and see if it is sinking,

Israeli youth at the Majdanek death camp, Poland, 1991

and whether it is worthwhile jumping. Are you also among the mice? Your 12th grade students will not wish to identify with mice.

The whole point is that the ship is not sinking at all. In Auschwitz we had no tanks or cannons, and no one invited us for peace talks. The allies refused to bomb the railway lines that led the Jews to destruction. Despite all the initial mistakes, peace talks [between Israel and her neighbors] became possible, for the first time since 1948, and the chance – perhaps not soon, although a change like this is a revolution in our enemies' thinking – to establish more or less normal relationships between nations. The new existential situation could bring about new relationships.

We have not escaped our Jewish fate by establishing the State of Israel. We shall escape from it only by exhausting it. Only by walking proudly on the paths of that fate until we are recognized for what we are and not according to how someone else wishes us to be, can we raise and teach young people. Do you not agree?

From a lecture, 1974

A Voice Called and I Went

Hannah Szenes

Hannah Szenes (1921-44) immigrated to Israel from Hungary and after joining Kibbutz Sdot Yam, volunteered to parachute into Nazi-occupied Europe. She was captured, sentenced to death as a spy, and after refusing to divulge details of her mission, was executed by firing squad in Budapest shortly before the liberation of the city by the Red Army. Her poems give expression to the deep sense of mission that she had felt since childhood.

A voice called and I went.
I went because the voice called.
I went lest I fall.

But at the crossroads
I blocked my ears with the cold whiteness
And I wept
Because I had lost something.

Caesarea, December, 1942

Above and opposite: Recruiting posters calling on Palestinian women to join the British army. More than 4,000 joined the ATS (Women's Army Territorial Service)
Above: A daily newspaper published for "Hebrew soldiers in Europe," announces the formation of a Palestinian infantry brigade
Center: A parade to encourage recruiting, Tel Aviv, 1941

I was Accepted by the Army Fighting Hitler

Rivka Guber

A small woman who became a legend, Rivka Guber (1902-81) was one of the first Palestinian volunteers to join the British Army in the Second World War. A married woman with three children, she nevertheless volunteered out of a total belief in her duty to contribute to the struggle against Hitler. She became known as "the mother of the sons" when her two sons, Zvi and Ephraim, were killed in the War of Independence. She was among the founders of the Lachish area in the northern Negev and aroused admiration among new immigrants and veterans alike.

A letter to Shlomo Lavi, Ein Harod

2 January, 1940
Dear Friend!
During the last days I have felt depressed, following the argument regarding the mobilization of the Jewish community. Now that I have read your article "Pioneers in Volnteering" I am relieved. It is easier to bear the indifference and numbness of the surroundings, if I know that there is someone greater than me who thinks like me.

Your call found a powerful echo in my heart. "How envious I am of youngsters who can

get up and go!" I too, like you, am strongly envious of those women, whose husbands are young or whose sons have already grown up. I felt myself impoverished by comparison with them: I have nothing to offer...how can I prove that I wish to take a part in the struggle? But what can a mother with three children and responsibility for a farm do – on top of what she already does?

All those who oppose the government's White Paper seem to have completely forgotten that we are engaged in a sacred war against the enemy.

I am ashamed. There are surely other people and nations in the world who are intelligent and clear thinking - what will they think about us if even in our homeland we do not know how to fight back against an enemy who has arisen to destroy us?

A letter to Sarah Kafri

10th January, 1942
Dear Sarah!

Two weeks ago I underwent a medical test and was accepted by the army fighting Hitler...

The news that spread in the village about my volunteering apparently amazed people. When I meet them they fall silent. But the silence is like a sentence. My son Ephraim told me that my friends in the village stop him in the street, shaking their heads and telling him: "If I were your mother I wouldn't do this" without thinking that their words are like hot lead on the youngster's sensitive heart. H.P was the only one brave enough to come to me and tell me with a candidness that deserves praise, that she sees in my action a negative phenomenon and a lack of responsibility towards my family. I have no intention of abandoning my family – I am not a person for whom the idea of "abandonment" is conceivable. I would hope to leave my family in a supportive environment that understands the sacrifice my children have made and appreciate it. My children are also

British army recruiting poster. The text calls for "Revenge and Redemption"

proud, and will not accept a gift of charity from the community that maligns their mother.

I leave a man who was my teacher and mentor; who has given me 22 years of love and endless devotion. I leave a farm, which we have worked on for many hard years; I leave children whom I have nurtured faithfully and in whom I began to see signs of blessing; in my house my beloved young daughter will be an orphan. My first child died during the depression and famine that was our lot after the last war. I could not be comforted over her death until the birth of Hayaleh, the most loved of the children. I hope to raise an honest, strong woman, a woman who does not shed tears in front of a man and does not weaken his hand. All this I leave without mercy – and for what? I never sought to travel in foreign countries. I have not even seen the Valley of Jezreel; I have not visited the Galilee, I have not seen the Plain of Sharon. I have yet to walk along all the paths of Israel. One narrow path brought me from the coast of Jaffa to Rehovot, and from there to my village. Yet in the place I lived, I was there completely. I have never left my house. I never went to any other place. I did not take a holiday. When I read the notice calling on women to volunteer, signed by the Committee of Working Women, the leadership of my movement, I felt my moment had come...

I am no heroine, I am no Joan of Arc, but when I am called on to help my brothers who defend me – how can I not answer?

From" Mother of the Sons," 1953

Soldiers of the Jewish Brigade meet Holocaust survivors in a camp in Italy

Survivors

Hanoch Bartov

The writer Hanoch Bartov, joined the Jewish Brigade of the British Army and fought in Europe. In his autobiographical work "The Brigade," Bartov describes his first encounter with Holocaust survivors.

Blessed is the Match

Hannah Szenes

Hannah Szenes composed the poem "Blessed is the Match" (below: in her own handwriting) after she had parachuted into Europe, on her way to Hungary. Did she feel that she was writing about herself? When she was captured and sentenced to death, it was hinted that if she would beg for mercy, her life would be spared, but she refused.

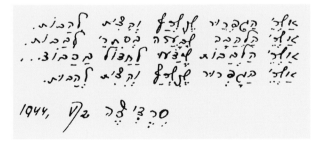

Blessed is the match, consumed in kindling flame.
Blessed is the flame that burns in the secret places of the heart.
Blessed is the heart with strength to stop its bleating for honor's sake.
Blessed is the match, consumed in kindling flame.

Szenice, 2 May, 1944

I don't know what the place at the foot of the mountain could have been used for before they made it a way-station. Maybe it had been a lumber mill or a small work camp. One two-story building stood there, together with a number of long black barracks, German style. Between the building and the barracks stretched a yard of sorts that was bustling with people.

At first my eyes took in the soldiers, a cross section from all units. A few of them were from the corps; you could spot them by what they were doing. At the entrance to the building they were dishing out lunch to a long line of people...

I stood to the side so as not to get in the way, already sorry I had rushed to a place where I had nothing to do. I had no one to search out, no one to rejoice over me.

And that was not all. I began to look closely at the survivors. Not at the mass of tattered refugees, but at one tall man, at one living head; I couldn't tear my eyes from him – maybe because he loomed over all the others. Though he was unshaven, his hair consisted only of scattered clumps, as though he had just emerged from the fire. What a bald pate, what ears! And his lips: they were covered with rusty scales rather than flesh. His gigantic fingers, which seemed nourished by the very sores they bore, gripped a cold bowl of soup that from time to time, he drew to his scaled lips, before circulating among the soldiers once again. He would ask everyone the same question and when they started in horror at his appearance he would walk on to repeat that question, which I couldn't make out. Only his fingers curled about the bowl of soup showed that the man was alive.

I was terror-stricken at the thought of his coming over to me and ashamed of that terror. Goddamit, why was he allowed to walk around like that, why wasn't he being taken care of, hospitalized, given clothing fit for a human being, I thought.

A woman, young it would seem, though you could only guess at her age and her figure too. She was swollen and ugly. Her puffed feet scarcely squeezed into the army boots without shoelaces. A black satin dress was stretched over her distended belly and the seams were split open the length of her thigh. Over her dress she wore an American

fatigue jacket, the insignia and buttons ripped off, and her head was completely covered by an American workcap, an olive sailor hat of sorts whose wide brim fell over her forehead and her ears. The woman – or girl, perhaps – stood in one spot, sleeping. Her cheeks, puffed up like dough, all but covered the slits of her eyes.

Suddenly, for no reason whatever, that frozen face broke into a smile. Had she seen someone or was that smile but a remnant of the body she once had? She lifted her hand to her hat, and her sleeve, which no longer had a button, slid down to her elbow. Her fingers stroked the hat as if it were a hair-do. I wanted to run away. I was afraid of bursting out in tears or crumpling at her swollen feet. Ah, she was only a girl, a little girl at that! Should I crush her to my chest with her innocent smile, that coquettish hand movement? I couldn't bear looking at such faces. Why didn't they take her somewhere, find a bed for her in some quiet spot so she wouldn't have to stand there on her swollen feet? I'll take her place in the afternoon line, I thought, find her something to wear instead of that tight party dress somebody got her during the long journey.

Translated by David S. Segal. From "The Brigade," 1988

First meeting of Palestinian solders of the Jewish Brigade with survivors in a displaced persons' camp

The Brigade has Arrived!

Ya'akov Margalit

Ya'akov Margalit edited a book "Here I am: Send me" a compilation of letters and reports by Palestinian soldiers who fought in the British Army during the Second World War, among them a letter sent by him to his friends.

Jewish Brigade soldiers with children who survived the Holocaust, Florence, Italy, 1945

Lodz, Poland

When we reached Lodz, the morning was already at its peak...Yosef, who drove the car, pressed on the accelerator and drove all over the place noisily, as though pursued by anger. Without our speaking I knew that he had turned into Zabedska Street. Both of us were born and grew up there: and, as we had heard, it was the location of a cluster of survivors

We broke into the street... There was not much movement, and the street was silent as though in a deep Sabbath sleep. The silence was broken by the jeep whose brakes were screeching. We stopped between the two houses in which we had been born and grew up. Two youths came out from the gate of the house, drew near in curiosity and looked at the jeep and at us. The youths detected something strange in our style and outward appearance. Something lit up in their eyes and one of them asked in a hoarse voice: "Where are you from?" Without thinking I spat out an answer in Hebrew, "First unit, the Jewish Brigade." The two were completely confused. Yosef added in Yiddish *Fon der Yiddische Brigada* ("From the Jewish Brigade.") The youths clapped their hands and began calling in hoarse voices and a strange lilt: *Yiden, di brigada iz gekumen.* ("Jews, the Brigade has arrived.") The quiet street filled with tumult. Windows opened, unkempt heads looked out calling with joyous blessings. Around us an excited crowd began to form surrounding the car, with us still sitting inside, dumbfounded and shocked, stretching out their hands to touch us, speaking all together simultaneously, as the word Brigada went back and forth. Yosef was completely confused and switched on the jeep's engine. One of the youngsters who had "discovered" us, leapt on the hood and began shouting with all his might *Ich loz aych nisht faren un mir.* ("I won't let you go without me!").

From "Here I am: Send me; Volunteers in the British Army Write Home," 1985

103

Chapter 6

 ## The Independence Day Torch

I, Yehoshua, son of Bluma and Yaakov Cohen, from Kibbutz Sde Boker, a member of Lehi -Lohamei Herut Yisrael ("Freedom Fighters of Israel") am honored to light this torch on the 36th anniversary of the State of Israel.

In honor of my fellow members in the ranks of Lehi.

In honor of the fighters who struggled to throw off the foreign yoke from the Land of Israel.

I, Ziva Arbel-Halevy, a graduate of Youth Aliya, a member of the Palmach, am honored to kindle this torch on the 36th anniversary of the State of Israel.

In honor of my fellow members of the Palmach, the striking force of the Haganah.

In honor of those who conducted the struggle at sea prior to the establishment of the state.

And to the glory of Israel.

Eve of Independence Day, 1984

"Illegal" Immigration: poster, 1947
Background: Zionah Tagger: Kibbutz Maoz Haim

THEY CONTINUED TO IMMIGRATE

שארית הפליטה שניצלה מהטבח הנאצי האיום באירופה ויהודי ארצות
אחרות לא חדלו להעפיל לארץ-ישראל, על אף כל קושי, מניעה וסכנה, ולא
פסקו לתבוע את זכותם לחיי כבוד, חירות ועמל-ישרים במולדת עמם.

במלחמת העולם השנייה תרם היישוב העברי בארץ את מלוא-חלקו למאבק
האומות הדוגלות בחירות ובשלום נגד כוחות הרשע הנאצי, ובדם חייליו
ובמאמצו המלחמתי קנה לו את הזכות להימנות עם העמים מייסדי ברית
האומות המאוחדות.

ב-29 בנובמבר 1947 קיבלה עצרת האומות המאוחדות החלטה המחייבת
הקמת מדינה יהודית בארץ-ישראל. העצרת תבעה מאת תושבי

War Against Hitler – War Against the "White Paper"

David Ben-Gurion

On the eve of the Second World War, Great Britain turned its back on Zionism. In order to placate the Arabs, the British government published a "White Paper," a document that delineated its official policy, in which it seemingly detached itself from the Balfour Declaration of 1917, and placed severe limitations on immigration and Jewish settlement in Palestine. The leadership of the *Yishuv* (the pre-state Jewish community) engaged in a struggle against the British, by means of "illegal" immigration, by enlarging the settlements, and by the acquisition of arms. But, at the same time, the heads of the Yishuv were determined to join in the much larger struggle of the Jewish people – the fight against the Nazis and Hitler. David Ben-Gurion declared two parallel struggles:

We must help the British in their war against Hitler as if there were no White Paper, and fight against the White Paper as if there were no war.

2 September, 1939

Poster opposing the British "White Paper" May, 1944

Between Borders

Haim Hefer

Haim Hefer, poet and lyricist, was one of the founders of the Chizbatron, the Palmach's light entertainment troupe. His verse and limericks were published for many years inr Yediot Aharonot

Between borders, among hills, on winding tracks
On nights without stars –
Convoys of brothers, without cease

We bring in to the homeland.
We will open the gates
For the infant in arms,
The weak and the old
We will protect and shelter.

If the gate is locked and barred,
We will break it down,
We will shatter every wall,
Break through every breach.
Convoy, no tears and no sorrow!

Lean on my arm, old man,
And for those who have barred your way
The day of reckoning will come.

Left: The Haganah ship "Exodus" packed with new immigrants, Haifa, March, 1947
Opposite, above: British soldiers boarding the Haganah immigrant ship "Jewish State," Haifa, October, 1947
Opposite, below: Poster issued by the Histadrut trade unions association honoring "illegal" immigration, 1946

If They Beat Us

Yaakov Orland

If they beat us,
They can't defeat us.
From each Patria and Struma
we'll arise.
They may banish,
We won't vanish,
We'll return, yes, we'll return.

For this is our land and there is no other,
And here we'll live and here we will not die, brothers
Our eyes are open, never more to close,
Because Israel lives, it lives
Am Yisrael Hai.

If they surround us,
They will not confound us,
Barbed wire fences we'll tear down
And pass through!
If they beat us,
They can't defeat us,
We will never more retreat.

They Did Not Stop Coming

Mordechai Na'or

At the worst possible time, with the threat of destruction hanging over European Jewry, Britain, the mandatory power, closed the doors to Palestine. Thousands of desperate Jews risked their lives by attempting to reach the shores of Palestine in fragile boats. Many of them found their death in disasters at sea, such as the sinking of the "illegal" immigrant vessels, "Salvador," "Patria" and "Struma." Most of those who survived and reached their destination were imprisoned or exiled by the British authorities. Dr. Mordechai Na'or is a writer, historian and researcher of the history of Eretz Israel.

During the 14 years of mass emigration from Europe (1934-1948) some 120,000 souls reached Palestine by way of the sea. In this operation, that was marked by great courage, were many great days, but also days of tragedy and disaster. The "Patria" and the "Struma" were among the small number of ships (out of over 140) that were involved in disasters at sea in which many victims drowned.

At the end of 1940, there arrived in Palestine during a short period, three blockade-running immigrant ships; "Milos," "Pacific," and "Atlantic" with some 3,500 Jewish refugees from Germany, Austria and Czechoslovakia aboard. The British determined to banish these refugees far away from Palestine, to the island of Mauritius in the Indian Ocean. With this intent, they began transferring the refugees to a French ship, ironically named "Patria."

The assumption of the British was that an expulsion of this nature would make it clear to potential blockade runners in Europe that they had no chance of entering Palestine, and that by such means, they could bring to a halt, or at least, a drastic reduction in the number of illegal immigrants.

The leadership of the Yishuv decided to confuse the British operations. Haganah members in Haifa were ordered to scuttle the "Patria" and thus prevent the expulsion of thousands of potential immigrants. One of the commanders of the Haganah in Haifa, Munia Mardor, dressed as a port worker. He joined a group of builders who were repairing the ship's boilers and succeeded in smuggling an explosive device aboard. This was made known to the immigrants, who were supposed to place it as far away as possible from the places were they were concentrated.

The first attempt failed. The second attempt was set for the morning of the 25th

Group of Holocaust orphans, Atlit, 1944

Immigrants

Yitzhak Shinhar

In secret a ship sails onward
The night is black, and fierce the storm.
Listen, homeland to our message,
Your weary sons are coming home.

In secret a ship sails onward,
Hopeful hearts there beat as one.
Listen, homeland, to our message,
Homeward sails your dreaming son.

In secret, my brothers come,
To the soil of the homeland
And in their ears the secret is whispered,
Welcome home, welcome home!

November, 1940. The assumption was that the small device would cause slight damage, but no more. But that is not what happened… The explosion made a huge hole in the side of the vessel, and in seconds large amounts of water poured inside, causing it to capsize.

At the time, on board the "Patria" were some 1,800 refugees destined for expulsion and tens of British police and soldiers. Within minutes, 250 of the refugees had drowned. The rest were transferred to the British detention camp in Atlit.

… In February 1942, another disaster struck the blockade runners who were desperately attempting to reach the coasts of the country. The "Struma'" was an old ship that in 1941 had sailed from Romania with 796 refugees and crew aboard. The British discovered the ship immediately as it was departing and announced explicitly that they would not allow its passengers to enter Palestine. Under conditions of extreme hardship, the ship reached the port of Istanbul where the Turkish authorities detained it for some ten weeks. The Mandate authorities were adamant in their refusal to allow the ship to enter the country. The Turks decided to return the ship to the heart of the Black Sea. The morning after, a huge explosion was heard. Within minutes the "Struma" sunk into the depths and all the passengers except one, drowned. Many years later, it transpired that a Russian submarine, failing to identify the ship, had sunk it with a torpedo.

The sinking of the "Struma'" triggered massive anti-British sentiments in Palestine. It emerged that the Mandate authorities after prolonged negotiations with the organizers of the "Struma" voyage, had been prepared to allow youths aged 11 to 16 from among the immigrants into the country, and only after more pressure, also agreed to allow in younger children. Their opposition to the entry of adults among the immigrants remained unchanged. While negotiations were still in progress, the ship sunk. The sinking of the Struma was the worst catastrophe that blockade-running operations experienced. Nevertheless, the tragedy did not prevent hundreds and thousands of additional illegal immigrants from setting out in the following years.

From "Aliyah Bet 1934-1948," 1988

Preparing to establish Kibbutz Hanita, March, 1938

Hanita – Stockade and Tower

Yitzhak Hinberger

In the first stage of The Arab Revolt (1936-1939), constructing the so-called Stockade and Tower settlements was the Yishuv's response to the problem of setting up communities in far off and dangerous locations. This was an unambiguous declaration along the lines of "We are Here!" The concept was to construct a prefabricated settlement, from elements prepared in advance, in order to stand up to an Arab attack should it come. The settlement consisted of a wooden wall or stockade, filled with gravel, a high watch tower and a number of huts. Everything was transported to the chosen destination at night and erected by the following dawn. Up to the publication of the British White Paper in May, 1939, 35 such Stockade and Tower settlements were built by this method. Thereafter the main aim of the activity, directed mainly against the British Mandate which sought to limit Jewish settlement, was to add another ten such settlements. Despite attempts by the Arabs, and afterwards by the British, to limt the Jewish communities, during the years of the Arab Revolt, 6o new settlements were set up, of which some 45 were of the Stockade and Tower type. To a large extent ,they determined the borders of the State of Israel in 1948. The above account is of the establishment of Hanita, a Stockade and Tower settlement on the Lebanese border, which is now a kibbutz.

Guard tower at Kibbutz Maoz Chaim, 1938,
(see also painting on page 104)

In keeping with the policy during the period of the Arab Revolt, and because of the unstable security situation, the move to Hanita was prepared like that of a "conquest," calling for exact planning and precise co-operation between the Jewish Agency, the Jewish National Fund and the Haganah.

The day for the move was set, after several postponements, for 21 March, 1938. For the purposes of this enterprise some 400 people were recruited, among them 110 armed guards, from all over the country. On the day of the operation, the guards were under the command of Yitzhak Sadeh and his deputies, Yigal Allon and Moshe Dayan.

Because of topographic problems and the lack of a suitable road for vehicles, the transportation of equipment was effected by camels, donkeys and on the shoulders of the participants. At the same time, a group of Solel Boneh [the Histadrut construction company] builders began paving a road from Beza-Kadesh [Betzet] to the site; and the laying of a water pipe from the spring of Ein Bida was also begun. An airplane from the Aviron company carried out reconnaissance flights over the area to prevent unexpected surprises.

The operation was planned with military precision in order to complete the establishment of the camp before nightfall. Despite the planning and the recruiting of so many people, the work of building the fortifications did not finish until the evening hours. The construction of a wire fence around the camp was completed, however, as was the erection of the watch tower and a lookout post, but they did not complete the building of the stockade, and even the gravel fill did not arrive in time. This fact was an impediment to the "Conquest Group" in the first attack (from local Arabs) on Hanita, which took place already on the first night of their stay in the camp.

The security conditions made an impact, too, on the organization of land settlement, on its planning, and even on the external form of the settlement. The Stockade and Tower settlements were planned so that they could serve as a means of defense for this problematic region.

From "Hanita - Stockade and Tower Settlement," 1978

A group of the founding settlers, Kibbutz Hanita, 1938

Jewish auxiliary police approaching Hanita, March 1938

We Are Standing Guard

Avraham Shlonsky

Here we stand on guard
Stars above our heads
On guard together, men and women,
Our rifles ready in our hands.

Softly, softly, to our dugouts
The enemy crawls forward.
Softly, softly on their guard
The enemy sharpens his weapons.

The heart trembles, but why fear,
The fate of each is the fate of all.
We stand here awaiting the moment,
Ready to defend lives and toil.

Creation of the Palmach

19 May, 1941
Haganah High Command

Emergency Command no.2
Creation of the *Plugot Machatz (Palmach)* [Literally - Shock or Strike Companies]

1. In view of the deterioration in the security situation, the Haganah High Command in its meeting of 16 May has determined to create and set up in a state of preparedness, a number of Palmach companies according to the following allocations:
   3 companies in Northern Galilee
   3 companies in Central Galilee
   3 companies in Lower Galilee
   1 company in the Jerusalem area
2. These companies will be made up of members of existing Haganah brigades on the basis of volunteers and personal willingness.
   a. To report for active service within 24 hours from the issuance of this order by the High Command.
   b. to serve in any capacity required in any place and at any time as shall be determined by the High Command.
3. The Palmach companies will serve as a fighting reserve both countrywide and in the Galilee. Training and organizational maintenance will be under each regional commander in the area to whom they belong. For operational purposes they are solely subject to the orders of the High Command.

Head of the General Staff, Haganah High Command

From the History of the Haganah," 1973

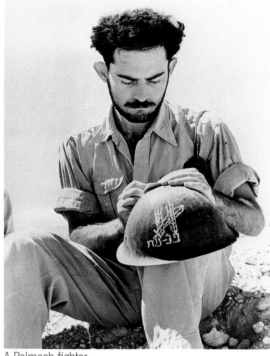

A Palmach fighter

The Song of the Palmach

Zerubavel Gilad

Though the storm is ever raging
Still our heads remain unbowed.
We are ready to obey all commands,
We are, we are the Palmach.

From Metulla to the Negev,
From the desert to the sea,
All our youth will take up arms,
All our youth are on guard.

In the eagle's path we follow,
Over mountain tracks we go,
Among stony heights and caverns
We are seeking out the foe.

We are always first in battle,
By daylight or darkest night,
We are ready the command to obey,
We are, we are the Palmach.

Briefing a group of Palmach members

Voice of the Bonfire

Moshe Tabenkin

The poet Moshe Tabenkin (1917-1979), son of a prominent labor leader, Yitzhak Tabenkin, was a fighter in the Palmach elite strike force. He dedicated the following poem to his fellow-members of the Palmach who broke into the Atlit detention camp on 9th October, 1946, released hundreds of illegal immigrants who were Holocaust survivors, and concealed them in different kibbutzim.

Demonstration against the restrictions of the British "White Paper," Tel Aviv, 1940

With the liberators of Atlit

He who contains a tempest,
Whose blood rages within,
Whose skin is caressed by rough winds,
Let him come to us!

He who contains a void,
Whose blood is leaden with sorrow,
Who gazes blankly at the dark horizon,
Let him come to us!

He who contains a shudder,
Who has forgotten laughter,
Who thirst to rejoice but cannot,
Let him come to us!

The pathways of vengeance lead to us,
Sorrow and loss burn in their trails,
The path of the strong.
Their gaze is shadowed by their fury.

To the gate of our camp
Their path will lead them.

A group of Palmach commanders, 1948. Center: Yigal Allon; second from left: Yitzhak Rabin

Open Appeal for Military Revolt

Irgun Zva'i Leumi, 1944

To the Hebrew nation in Zion!

We have reached the final stage of this world war. Now that each country is conducting its own national reckoning: what are its triumphs and its defeats? What path should a country follow in order to achieve its objectives and fulfill its mission? Who are its friends and who its enemies? Who is a true ally and who a traitor? Who is going to take part in the decisive battle?

Four years have passed and all the hopes which filled our hearts in 1939 have been dashed. We have not been granted international recognition, no Jewish army has been established, the gates of our country have not been opened, the British regime has carried out a shameful treachery against the Hebrew nation and there is no moral basis for its continued presence in Eretz Israel.

We must draw the conclusion fearlessly. An armistice no longer prevails between the Hebrew nation and its youth and the British administration in Eretz Israel, which hands over our brethren to Hitler.

And this is our demand: [British] rule over Eretz Israel must immediately be handed over to a provisional Hebrew government!

We will fight, all the Jews of the homeland will fight – the God of Israel, the God of hosts, will aid us. There can be no retreat. Liberty – or death!

Build a wall of iron around your fighting youth. Do not abandon them. Cursed be the traitor and shame on the coward!

Hebrews! The fighting youth will not shrink from sacrifice and tribulations, blood and suffering, we will not surrender and we will not rest until we have restored our past glories, until we have assured a homeland for our people. Liberty, honor, bread and justice! And if you extend your help to them, your eyes will soon behold the return to Zion and the rebirth of Israel. May God be with us.

From Menachem Begin, "The Revolt," 1969

Poster of the Herut movement, 1948
(which succeeded the Irgun – Etzel)

The Beitar Anthem

Ze'ev Jabotinsky

Beitar. From the pit of
decay and dust.
With blood and with sweat
We shall build up a race
Proud, generous and
fierce.
Captive Beitar, Yodfat,
Massada, will rise up in
force and splendor.

Splendor -
Even in poverty – a Hebrew
is a prince.
Whether slaves or nomads

You were born the sons
of kings, adorned with the
crown of David.
In light and in darkness,
Remember that crown
The crown of pride and
defiance.

Of every obstacle and
boundary.
If you rise up or falter
In the heat of revolt
Pay no heed – carry the
flame.

Silence is an abomination,
Let us dedicate blood and
soul for the sake of the
hidden glory.
To die or to capture the
mountain -
Yodfat, Massada, Beitar

Paris, 1932

Wall poster in memory of Meir Feinstein, a member of Etzel, and Moshe Barazani, a member of Lehi, both sentenced to death by the British for their underground activities. The two of them committed suicide by exploding a grenade that had been smuggled into their cell on 21 April, 1947. Before their death, together with the rabbi attending them, they sang the prayer *Adon olam* - "Master of the Universe"

Unknown Soldiers

Ya'ir Stern

Avraham Stern – known in the underground as "Ya'ir" – (1907-1942), writer and poet, was one of the leaders of the *Irgun Zva'i Leumi* (Etzel). When the Etzel decided to cooperate with the British authorities against the Nazis in 1940, Ya'ir seceded and established *Lohamei Herut Yisrael* (Lehi), known to the British as the "Stern Gang." He was killed in controversial circumstances in Tel Aviv in 1942 after having been captured by British police.

Avraham Stern (Ya'ir), 1942

Unknown soldiers are we, no uniforms have we,
We march in the shadow of death,
We will fight for the cause to the end of our days
Death alone from the ranks will release us.

Through the days of destruction, red with our blood,
Through the nights that are black with despair,
Over village and town still our standard we raise:
With its message: defense and conquest.

Not as browbeaten slaves were we brought to these ranks
To spill our blood in distant lands.
Our desire to be free brought us here to the fight
We have vowed to die for our people.

Many pitfalls and snares lie in wait all around,
And a cruel fate lurks on our path
But the foes and the spies and the dark prison cells
Can never stop our advance.

And if we should fall as we fight in the streets
And be buried in secret by night,
Many thousands of others will rise in our stead.
To defend and to guard evermore.

"Wanted" poster issued by the British Mandate police force, announcing a reward for anyone providing information leading to the apprehension of those named in the poster, 1947

Emblem of the Haganah

The Haganah Oath

I hereby declare that I enter the Haganah - the Hebrew organization for the defense of Eretz Israel voluntarily and from my own free choice.

I hereby swear to be faithful to the Haganah all my life; to its rules and duties as defined by the High Command.

I hereby swear to abide by the authority of the Haganah all my life, and to accept without condition or limitation, the burden of its discipline, and to heed its call to report for active service at any time and in any place, to submit to its commands and fulfill its orders.

I hereby swear to dedicate all my strength and even to sacrifice my life for the defense of my people and for my homeland, for the freedom of Israel and the redemption of Zion.

The National Organization of Members of the Haganah.

The Etzel Oath

Emblem of the Irgun (Etzel)

I hereby swear to be a faithful soldier in the army for liberation that is struggling for the immediate and complete freedom of all of Eretz Israel.

I hereby recognize the highest authority of the *Irgun Zva'i Leumi* (Etzel) [In English – the National Military Organization] and swear to obey its orders without question or refusal.

In fulfilling my role in the organization in the Diaspora or in Eretz Israel, I hereby swear to observe stringently the secrecy and clandestine nature of the underground army.

In full awareness and with prior agreement I hereby accept the heavy responsibility that is a result of all the foregoing.

I hereby dedicate my life to the war for national liberation and I swear to fight until complete victory is achieved.

I am ready to fulfill my tasks and in accordance with the instructions of my commanders, to dedicate my health, my property, and my life to the purpose of the war of liberation.

May the Guardian of Israel grant me this.

Memorandum of the Movement of Hebrew Resistance

Jerusalem 2nd Adar 5706 – March, 1946

At the end of 1945, after the heads of the Yishuv despaired of the hostile policies of the Labor government that had come to power in Britain, they decided to intensify the struggle against the British. With this in mind the "Movement of Hebrew Resistance" was set up with the participation of the three underground quasi-military organizations - Haganah, Etzel and Lehi. The Movement of Hebrew Revolt lasted for less than a year - from October 1945 through August 1946. Among successful operations were the "Night of the Railways," "Night of the Bridges," the breakout at the internment camp for illegal immigrants at Atlit, the attack on British airfields, and attacks on police stations and the British Criminal Investigation Department. The movement broke up because of differences of opinion between the three groups. One of the main causes for its disbandment was the blowing-up by the Etzel of an entire wing of the King David Hotel in Jerusalem, in July 1946.

Saluting the flag: members of the Beitar movement

1. The Movement of Hebrew Resistance does not set itself any specific political goals, and does not come before you with any separate demands. The claim that Eretz Israel should immediately be opened to free Jewish immigration and become a Hebrew state –is also our claim.

2. In this land there exists a secret, armed Jewish force. This force has one fixed aim – to defend the Jewish Yishuv and the restoration of Jewish independence. The force exists, because no authority in Eretz Israel – formerly the Turks and latterly the British – has been able to defend us to the degree necessary. The existing force is clandestine, because no authority is prepared to recognize it, and to leave its leadership and development in our hands. The ultimate goal is defense...

3. Ours is not the way of terror. During the three years of Arab riots that preceded the [Second World] war, Arab terror rampaged against us, and we defended ourselves with determination and even pursued the terrorist groups to their places of concealment; yet we maintained the highest ethical standards with respect to our weapons lest innocent Arab blood be shed. We have not attacked any Arab just because he is an Arab. The elevated concept of restraint has guided us. Thus we restrained ourselves during the six years of

The Lehi Oath

Emblem of Lehi

I hereby swear an oath of loyalty to the homeland, to the people, to freedom.
I swear to sacrifice conscience and life;
to obey, to fight, and to die!
…In my blood I will defend the Land of Israel
And in my life, the life of Israel;
And to bless its name among the nations.
So help me and protect me, Guardian of Israel!

פוצצו גשרים בכל רחבי הארץ

בסביבות עכו, מתולה, משמר הירדן, הכנרת, עמק בית־שאן, עזה.־ ג יהודים נהרגו—נאסרו פצועים—הפעולה בוצעה ע״י תנועת המרי

הופסק שרות הרכבת בין ארץ ישראל, סוריה ועבר הירדן

בחיפושים בבית־הערבה, חניתא ומצובה פצעו עשרות ונעצרו רבים

war, a time when the gates of our country were locked while our brethren in Europe were being massacred . And when, during the last year of the war, two of our constituent groups lost patience and split from the general defense forces, and started to engage in acts of sabotage and individual retaliation against the British, then we and not the country's authorities – we, the Jewish community led by the Haganah – put a stop to these acts, since they were carried out when the struggle against Hitler was still raging, and when there was still hope that justice would triumph through appropriate political action.

4. We have clear knowledge of plans by various organs of the British authorities in Eretz Israel to suppress the resistance movement and wipe us out. This is just a short-term blunder by the administration of Eretz Israel that is unable to comprehend the issues that are before them. In order to destroy the resistance movement, or even just the Haganah, it would be necessary to wipe out the entire Hebrew Yishuv in Eretz Israel, and to uproot the eternal love of Zion from world Jewry.

The Jews are a people: Eretz Israel belongs to the Jewish people! Jewish emigration will continue; a Hebrew state will surely arise.

"Night of the Railways," November, 1945

Youth, Listen!

Yitzhak Sadeh

Yitzhak Sadeh (1890-1952), legendary leader and courageous fighter, was one of the founders of the Labor Battalion and a fighter in the *Plugot Sadeh* ("Field Companies"). He was appointed first commander of the Palmach in 1941.

Youth, listen!
Someone out there is holding the scales of our lives in his hands,
And they rise and fall, rise and fall.
On one scale – Israel's Holocaust, Israel's rebirth and battle;
On the other: the intrigues of commerce and politics,
And the weight of those intrigues is very great.

Youth, remember!
When the hour arrives, cast yourselves on the scale,
Cast yourselves with force and courage!
That will resolve the problem and shift the balance
Youth, listen!

Left to right: Moshe Dayan, Yitzhak Sadeh, Yigal Allon before the establishment of Hanita, 1938. On the back of the photograph, Chaim Weizmann wrote "L'Etat Major" – the General Staff.

Story of a Fighting Woman

Geula Cohen

Geula Cohen, who would in time become a member of the Knesset and a deputy minister, was a courageous fighter in the Lehi underground movement. She described her role as a broadcaster for the clandestine Lehi radio station in her book "The Voice of Valor 1943-1948."

... I hear the sound of a yearning song, and it comes from over the hill.

Up to that point I had never heard our men singing like this. It is impossible to sing in the underground, not just because it is in the nature of a voice to be heard, but also because everything sang within us, and the voice if it wished to rise would return and be swallowed in the great storm that was raging. I know within myself that I sang thus. All the day long. Even when I was pasting up a poster, when I followed a British detective, when I dismantled a pistol, even when I tried to persuade someone with words to come and join us. Everything was singing.

Now, far away and in the sand, they sing with the voice of young men, they sing of yearning. The sand has no ears for the bad, the voices return to me in a dim echo.

We prepared in the dark of the underground
In holy blindness, dream: a puddle on the floor – Kinneret,
a light of a lamp – the glow of the sun high in the sky ...
The song of Ya'ir [Avraham Stern, the founder of Lehi)
...We of Lehi stood and saluted a dream of yearning and went enchanted towards it,

We were like every other soldier, even without a uniform, saluting his officer and following him with eyes closed. Facing Michael [Yitzhak Shamir, later to become prime minister] I turned for the first time in my life consciously into a soldier, and I felt that even without raising my hand, my whole body was saluting. Beams broke upon him and returned to me concentrated and united as one. Each of us refracted on Michael but did not return exploded, but rather assured that there was something of the rock in Michael...

Geula Cohen was appointed a newscaster at the Lehi clandestine broadcasting station. The news bulletins were broadcast each time from another place because of the danger that the broadcasters would be seized by the British authorities.

Evenly, deliberately, I spoke each word:

"For every murderous British law the Hebrew underground will enact an opposite and equally cruel law of its own. There will be quick justice and no mercy for all British criminals. The foreign regime has decided that prima-facie evidence is no longer necessary in order to condemn a man to death. We have decided the same! The foreign regime has decided that membership in an enemy organization is punishable by death. We have decided the same!

"Henceforth, in accord with the laws of the Hebrew underground which have been enacted as an antidote to the British terror, all officials in the illegal foreign regime will be dealt with as accessories before the fact as will members of the following criminal organizations:

The British administration
The British army of occupation
The British police
The British Criminal Investigation Department.

"Wanted for Murder" poster directed against the British High Commissioner, Sir Harold Macmichael, protesting the sinking of the immigrant ship "Struma," 1942

I did not raise my voice; I did not raise my hand. But each word was connected to its fellow, sentence by sentence:

"Belonging to any one of the above-mentioned terrorist organizations will henceforth be considered sufficient evidence to call down the death sentence upon the guilty party. It will be unnecessary to conduct an investigation into the actions of particular individuals. Any individual who continues to serve in a criminal capacity and to help execute British laws or terror has sentenced himself and will be accordingly dealt with by the Hebrew underground.

"Listen, Sir Allan Cunningham, hangman and High Commissioner—attention! While you are so busy preparing for the execution of our people, do not neglect to prepare the burial grounds for your criminal henchmen. British general, British commissioner, British hangman, attention! You too will be paid in kind."

It was the last broadcast that I will remember.

Geula Cohen and another broadcaster were arrested by the British. After failing in an attempt to escape from prison, she was arraigned before a British judge who pronounced sentence...

...Perhaps this was why the voice of the presiding judge as he announced my sentence seemed so insignificant:

"For illegal possession of a radio transmitter, you are sentenced to two years. For illegal possession of weapons, you are sentenced to seven years. All together, nine years."

"The offenses were committed at the same time. The court recommends that the sentences be served simultaneously, over a period of seven years. The court feels that the defendant should be given this much special consideration."

Someone in the audience had begun to sing "Hatikvah." It was my mother. I felt like crawling into a hole in the ground.

But if I had known then what I learned later — that at the moment my mother began to sing, my five year-old brother was lying at her feet having fainted from hunger or exhaustion — I would have looked at her with wonder and admiration, instead of staring embarrassedly at the floor. If I had known that then, I would have understood that "Hatikvah" was an outlet for the cry of pain which she restrained herself from uttering in the presence of her daughter for fear of seeming weak and undignified. And yet the pain was there; her little son was slumped unconscious on the floor, and if she didn't do something she would choke. So she stood up and sang "Hatikvah."

Little by little other voices joined in. The policemen made no attempt to interfere.

Geula Cohen, a member of the Lehi underground group, with Sheikh Abu Ghosh who saved her from a Jerusalem prison

While in prison a slip of paper was smuggled in to her cell from a member of the Etzel, Dov Gruner, who had been arrested by the British after a raid on the Ramat Gan police station. The mandatory court sentenced him to death and Gruner was incarcerated in a death cell, awaiting the carrying out of the sentence.

...We had channels of our own: the nurses, the doctor, the rabbi, and occasionally even secretly smuggled letters. One had reached me just the day before. It was addressed from the death cell and written by a doomed man – Dov Gruner.

Gruner did not have to die. He had just lived through combat against Nazi armies in the ranks of the Jewish Brigade, had lived – despite a fractured jaw – through the Etzel assault on a police station during which he was captured and, had he cared to ask the British High Commissioner for mercy, he could have gone on living now. But he hadn't asked, so he was going to die. With him were four others. Three of them, Dresner,

Kashani and Elkachi, were Etzel members who had been found guilty of flogging British soldiers in retaliation for acts of violence against Jews. The fourth, Moshe Barazani, was a member of Lehi who had been caught one evening in Jerusalem trying to throw a grenade into the headquarters of the British Sixth Division.

Gruner's note was only seven words: "Greetings to Geula from the death cell — Dov."

With the aid of an Arab family, Lehi members managed to rescue Geula Cohen from prison, and she resumed her role as the underground voice of the movement. However, on the evening of 29 November, 1947, she felt deep disappointment:

"This is the Voice of the Hebrew underground! This is the radio station of the Freedom Fighters of Israel!"

My voice had lost its timbre, its fight. I stood before the microphone as before, only my voice was weaker, and each time I broadcast it grew less powerful. One night, on November 29, 1947, it was drowned out completely. I stood with my friends on a rooftop in Tel Aviv and empty-heartedly watched the delirious crowds dancing in the streets below. Over Kol Israel, soon to become the official government radio station, an announcer was victoriously reporting the news that the General Assembly of the United Nations had approved by the necessary two-thirds majority, the partition of Palestine and the creation of a Jewish state — a Jewish state without Jerusalem, without Hebron and Bethlehem, without the Gilead or the Bashan or the lands beyond the Jordan.

For a moment I failed to understand why I felt so apart from it all, why I did not wish it was I who was broadcasting the historic decision, but then I knew. My voice could have nothing to do with it. The announcer's words could never have been my own. My own words remained integral, they could never have been partitioned. The joy of the crowds below could not be shared by me, for I felt only the infinite grief of a slaughtered dream, a dream that could not be divided without being mutilated at the same time.

Translated by Hillel Halkin

Geula Cohen broadcasting from a Lehi clandestine studio, June, 1948

When Geula Cohen's memoirs were published, they created a storm of support and objection at one and the same time. The controversy found impressive expression in a letter written to her by the prime minister, David Ben-Gurion. The following are extracts:

The Prime Minister

Jerusalem, Tu Bishvat 5722, January 20, 1962

Dear Geula,

This morning at 9:15 I arrived with bated breath at the final page of your "story" – with you feeling "the infinite grief of a slaughtered dream", following the announcement of the partition of the Land of Israel and the establishment of the State of Israel, "a State of Israel without Jerusalem, without Hebron and Bethlehem, without the Gilead or the Bashan" and you are standing outside the circle while "the delirious crowds are dancing in the streets below."

...I read your book out of an internal decision to forget during the time of reading all that I know of that period and to ignore my own political outlook of those days (and now I recognize even more how right it was) and to see the things that you retell through your eyes and to relive your experiences as if I were in your place. I was successful in this while reading most of the book. I became one of the members of Lehi in those days, dazzled as you by the great and faithful love and the deep and mistaken hate. Not through my merit did I become while reading as one of you but through the merit of the "fighting woman" who tells "her story" with amazing strength, with the exuberance of internal truth, burning, lighting and igniting, branding all experience as if in tongs of electrified steel. I experienced those things that you retell as if they occurred to me, as if I was one of the group. But there are portions – though not many – of your book, that prevented me from identifying with your emotions and all my efforts to disregard my opposition did not help. The secret of our people's reestablishment and its foundation-stone was not the liquidation of the foreign regime but the Return to Zion – that is to say immigration, settlement, Hebrew labor, guard duty, defense, reviving the Hebrew language and the accumulation of strength in all conditions and with all means. In our land many foreign regimes were replaced or done away with: Roman, Byzantine, Persian, Arab, Crusader, Seljuk, Mameluk, Turkish – and no Jewish state arose. In 1948 also, when foreign rule left here, we were a minority. Without partition, an Arab state would have been established through the length and breadth of Eretz-Israel.

...I read your book with pounding heart, excited and stirred, proud and admiring, and in several instances it appeared to me that I was a partner to the acts and the perpetrators. The storm of the soul of those leading themselves to sacrifice carried me away too, and I bowed my head with honor and respect before the death of the heroes, the two Eliyahus in Cairo, Moshe Barazani, Meir Feinstein and others. And I deeply felt what was for you the little note that contained the words: "Greetings to Geula from the death cell – Dov."

It is impossible to read your book – and it matters not who the reader is – without a shiver of sanctity and awe. Even those who disagreed and still disagree to this day with the political views of Yair and his comrades, as I do, and who thought that it was limited, short-sighted and ignored the main element, will share the feelings that you succeeded in expressing so powerfully, even cruelly – the complete dedication to your mission.

I did not know Yair personally and I am not sure if the image that I conjure up from reading the memoirs of Lehi members and the two volumes of his collected writings is correct, but I have no doubt that he was one of the finest personalities to emerge during the Mandate period. And I honor and respect with all my heart the poetry and the steel of his tempestuous soul and his unending commitment to the redemption of Israel – even if I completely negate his mistaken path.

I have no doubt that "A Story of a Fighting Woman" will be a proud memorial to the fearless fighters that sacrificed themselves out of faith in Israel's salvation.

It is also a supreme testament to the nobility of the storyteller herself.

Sacred is the pen that wrote this book.

With deep appreciation
David Ben-Gurion

The "Night Squads" led by their British commander, Captain (later Brigadier) Orde Charles Wingate

Faced with the stubborn resistance of the Jewish community to the British Mandate, the authorities rounded up and arrested the leaders of the Jewish Agency and the Haganah on Saturday, 29 June, 1946, an event which became known as the "Black Sabbath"

The Trenches of our Lives

Nathan Alterman

In his poem, the "Song of the Companies" Nathan Alterman formulated a vital summons to the people of Israel, that stressed the fateful character of its struggle. "No nation can retreat from the trenches of its life." The sentiments remain valid to this day.

Let us sing the song of the companies
The wadi is dark, dark. Fighters! On
your guard!
A company moved out into the night,
A company moved out to fight and
defend their land.

Await us, my country, on your mountain
paths,
Await us in the broad fields of grain.
Once your boys brought you the peace of
the plough,
Now they bring you peace on their arms.

Company – climb, climb the mountain,
Company – rise up and conquer.
By distant and untrodden tracks
There the field companies will pass.

Wrongly they said: daytime alone is ours,
Wrongly they said: the night is for fire and
plunder.
Both night and day were given us for life,
Night and day are Eretz Israel.

You do not plough and build in vain my
brother.
We battle for our souls and for our homes!
Juara, Tel Amal, Kinneret and Hanita.
You are our flags and we are your wall.

For we will not retreat, there is no other
path.
No nation can retreat from the trenches of
its life.
As the company moves out tonight in single
file,
your face, my homeland, accompanies it
to battle.

For the sake of mother, father, son,
We will erect our ramparts.
Company, the battle is not yet over,
Company – march onward!

For Three Things we are Prepared to Die

David Ben-Gurion

This speech by David Ben-Gurion is known as his "Reply to Bevin." Ernest Bevin was the British foreign minister, and known for his anti-Zionist policies.

While six million of our people are still lying before us in Europe, our blood is already being spilled anew here on the soil of the homeland; in a Jewish village, in a Jewish town, in Tel Aviv, in the Sharon, in Samaria; the blood of our children, our youth, our workers, our farmers, is being spilt by those who are carrying out the orders of Bevin and his friends.

Over the graves of our fallen soldiers in Tel Aviv, and in the Valley of Sharon, over the graves of our dear brothers and sisters, I wish to say a few words to Bevin and his friends.

We, the Jews of Eretz Israel, do not wish to be killed; we wish to live. We believe, in contrast to the teachings of Hitler and his disciples in various countries, that we Jews also have a right to live as individuals and as a people, just like the British and all the others. Yet we too, like the British, cling to something that is more precious than life. I wish to tell Bevin and his friends that we are prepared to die but not to relinquish three things: freedom for Jewish emigration, our right to build up the arid soil of the homeland; and the political independence of our people in its own land.

28th November, 1945

David (Ben-Gurion) and **Goliath** (Ernest Bevin)
– cartoon in a Swiss paper

121

Chapter 7

The Independence Day Torch

I, Benjamin Levine from Jerusalem, am honored to kindle this torch to mark the 36th anniversary of the State of Israel.

In honor of the youth of Israel which day after day takes upon itself the tasks of generations to ensure the unity of our people.

In honor of the feelings of brotherhood that beat in the breasts of so many of us. In honor of the striving for togetherness and unity that we have inherited from our forefathers and which we in turn will pass on to our children and our children's children.

And to the glory of Israel.

Eve of Independence Day, 1984

A JEWISH STATE TO BE CALLED "ISRAEL"...

Prime-Minister David Ben-Gurion reads the Declaration of Independence of Israel, Tel Aviv, May 14, 1948
Background: The candelabrum (menorah) outside the Knesset building, Jerusalem

Crowds in Tel-Aviv celebrating the UN partition resolution, 29 November, 1947

To Establish a Jewish State

The Biltmore Program

Raising the flag,
29 November, 1947

On 11 May, 1942, David Ben-Gurion, Chairman of the Jewish Agency, faced the 603 delegates of the National Conference of American Zionists at the Biltmore Hotel, New York. It was not an especially important conference, but Ben-Gurion's speech was destined to change the course of political Zionism. It was at the height of World War Two and it seemed that no one cared about the Zionist movement and about the fate of the Jews of Europe who were being systematically murdered by the Nazis. Ben-Gurion, however, assumed that at the end of the war a new order would emerge, nations would disappear from the map and others would rise in their stead; old borders would be erased and new ones drawn. This was the moment when the Zionist movement had to raise its voice, and demand that the world do justice to the Jewish people.

The Conference declares that the new world order that will follow victory cannot be established on foundations of peace, justice and equality, unless the problem of Jewish homelessness is finally solved. The Conference urges that the gates of Palestine be opened; that the Jewish Agency be vested with control of immigration into Palestine and with the necessary authority for upbuilding the country, including the development of its unoccupied and uncultivated lands; and that Palestine be established as a Jewish Commonwealth integrated in the structure of the new democratic world. Then and only then will the age-old wrong to the Jewish people be righted.

Declaration adopted by the Extraordinary Zionist Conference at the Biltmore Hotel, New York City, 11 May, 1942

Partitioning Palestine

29 November, 1947

The struggle of the Jewish community in Palestine, with the support of the Diaspora Jews and many world leaders, eventually bore fruit. After years of "illegal" immigration, settlement in areas fraught with danger, armed struggle and diplomatic efforts, the Zionist Movement had finally achieved its goal. On 29 November 1947, the United Nations General Assembly decided by a majority of two-thirds to partition Palestine in two – an Arab and a Jewish state. The Arab nations rejected the plan outright and declared they would destroy the newly-born Jewish state.

The Partition Plan

Part I – The Future Constitution and Government of Palestine
A. Termination of the Mandate: Partition and Independence

1. The Mandate for Palestine shall terminate as soon as possible but in any case not later than 1 August 1948.

2. The armed forces of the mandatory power shall be progressively withdrawn from Palestine, the withdrawal to be completed as soon as possible but in any case not later than 1 August 1948. The mandatory power shall advise the Commission, as far in advance as possible, of its intention to terminate the mandate and to evacuate each area. The mandatory power shall use its best endeavors to ensure that an area situated in the territory of the Jewish state, including a seaport and hinterland adequate to provide facilities for a substantial immigration, shall be evacuated at the earliest possible date and in any event not later than 1 February 1948.

3. Independent Arab and Jewish states and the Special International Regime for the City of Jerusalem, set forth in Part III of this Plan, shall come into existence in Palestine two months after the evacuation of the armed forces of the mandatory power has been completed, but in any case not later than 1 October 1948. The boundaries of the Arab state, the Jewish state, and the city of Jerusalem shall be as described in Parts II and III below.

4. The period between the adoption by the General Assembly of its recommendation on the question of Palestine and the establishment of the independence of the Arab and Jewish states shall be a transitional period.

UN General Assembly Resolution 181 (Partition Plan), 29 November, 1947

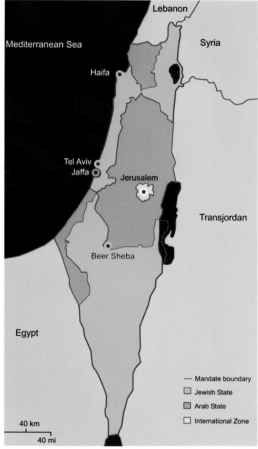

Partition Map of Palestine, 1947. Accepted by Israel, but rejected by the Arabs.
©Koret Communications

The State of Israel is Born!

Ze'ev Sharef

Ze'ev Sharef (1906–1984) was the secretary of the provisional government in 1948, and later a government minister. In his book "Three Days" he describes the ceremony of the proclamation of Israel's independence, 5 Iyar 5708, 14 May, 1948.

We hurried along Rothschild Boulevard toward the Tel Aviv Museum Hall, the precious document – the Declaration of Independence – in hand …

The guard around the building was strict, cordon within cordon, and pressing against them a multitude of people hastening from all directions. Below the steps leading to the Museum entrance stood an honor guard of young soldiers, the cadets of the Jewish Army's officers' school, their white belts gleaming from afar.

The hall was packed from wall to wall. It was still, and the heat was intense. Movie

David Ben-Gurion arriving for the Declaration of Independence ceremony, 14 May, 1948

Declaration of Independence. Moshe Sharett, future minister of foreign affairs, and later prime minister, affixes his signature to the Scroll of Independence

The crowd celebrates Israel's independence outside the Tel-Aviv Museum

Opposite: Newspapers announce: "The State of Israel is born. A Yiddish newspaper rejoices in the establishment of a "Jewish Kingdom"

cameramen and newspaper photographers from other countries added to the mounting temperature with their arc-lamps and flash-bulbs. There were so many newspapermen and reporters that they seemed to fill the hall...

Beneath Herzl's likeness sat the members of the National Administration and the [government] secretary. The other members of the National Council, facing each other, were at a table in the center, forming the pillar of a T. Ranged in a semi-circle were members of the Zionist General Council, mayors and party leaders, rabbis and elders of the Yishuv [pre-state Jewish community of Palestine] writers, artists, newspaper editors, members of the Haganah high command, representatives of the national funds and economic organizations, district representatives, municipal councilors and others.

Exactly at four o'clock Ben-Gurion rose, rapped the gavel on the table, and the gathering rose to its feet.

Ben-Gurion said: "I shall now read to you the Scroll of the Establishment of the State which has passed its first reading by the National Council."

"Eretz Israel was the birthplace of the Jewish people" – here came Joshua Bin-Nun and King David, Nehemiah and the Hasmoneans.

"Here their spiritual, religious and political identity was shaped. Here they first attained to statehood, created cultural values of national and universal significance.

Here came the Prophets and Ezra the Scribe and the men of the Great Assembly – "and gave to the world the eternal Book of Books."

A profound sigh seemed to well up out of the words: "After being forcibly exiled from their land, the people kept faith with it throughout their Dispersion, and never ceased to pray and hope for their return to it and for the restoration in it of their political freedom," and one remembered the prayers – "for our sins and iniquities were we banished from the land... O Almighty Father, gather us in from among the gentiles... and bring us unto Zion Your city in gladness..."

"Impelled by this historic and traditional attachment, Jews strove in every successive generation to re-establish themselves in their ancient homeland" – the manifesto of 18 hundred years of exile and wandering, 18 centuries of ceaseless striving to return to the Holy Land and become a people once more; Israel's staunch struggle against the pressures of the Christian Byzantine Empire; the fugitives from Mahomet's sword fleeing from Arabia to the land of their origin, and the others coming after the Arab conquest to found in Jerusalem a home for their sages; the merciless destruction of the Jewish community by the Crusaders and the victory of Saladin over the Crusaders' empire inaugurating a new epoch of settlement; the Rambam [Maimonides, the pre-eminent Jewish spiritual leader of the Middle Ages] comes to the land and with his disciples enters Jerusalem; the persecutions in Western Europe and the expulsion from Spain bringing new streams, and Don Joseph Nassi's experiment in Galilee – to what great disappointment; and then the Polish Hassidim, the vicissitudes and the abysmal poverty.

"But a new spirit sweeps through the Diaspora; the urge to return assumes practical shape and the new epoch of *Shivat Zion*, the Return to Zion, is born amid travail – In recent decades they returned in their masses... They made deserts bloom, revived the Hebrew language, built villages and towns... These were the builders of Petah Tikvah, the men and women of the BILU movement from Russia, the founders of Rehovot and Hadera, the pioneers of the Second Aliya and the stalwarts of Hashomer, the earliest watchmen, the builders of Tel Aviv and Mount Carmel and the New Jerusalem.

" ...The First Zionist Congress convened and proclaimed the right of the Jewish people to national rebirth in its own country. This right was recognized in the Balfour Declaration... and was reaffirmed in the mandate of the League of Nations..."

Ben-Gurion continued reading the Resolution of the General Assembly of the United

Emblem of the State of Israel. Postcard marking the first anniversary

Nations adopted on 29 November 1947, requiring the establishment of a Jewish state in Palestine... After reading the ten paragraphs of the preamble, setting forth the background and reasons for the Declaration, he paused for a moment, and then in a raised voice continued: "Accordingly we, members of the People's Council, representatives of the Jewish community in Eretz Israel and of the Zionist Movement, are here assembled on the day of the termination of the British Mandate over Palestine; and by virtue of our natural and historic right and on the strength of the Resolution of the United Nations General Assembly, hereby declare the establishment of a Jewish state in Palestine, to be known as *Medinat Yisrael* (the State of Israel)."

As he pronounced these words the entire audience rose to its feet and burst into prolonged hand-clapping. All were seized by ineffable joy, their faces irradiated...

And the concluding paragraph:

"Placing our trust in Almighty God, we affix our signatures to this proclamation at this session of the Provisional Council of State, on the soil of the homeland, in the city of Tel Aviv, on this Sabbath eve, the fifth of Iyar, 5708, the fourteenth day of May, 1948."

He added:

"Let us stand to adopt the Scroll of the establishment of the Jewish State."

The gathering again stood up and remained standing for a few moments. They were fleeting moments yet pregnant with glory...

The Proclamation was adopted by acclamation. Then the secretary of the National Administration, or now of the Provisional Government (the chairman, by a slip of the tongue, referred to him as "Secretary of the National Governmen") called the roll-call of Council members, beginning with David Ben-Gurion and then in alphabetical order. There had not been time to inscribe the Declaration on parchment – this was only done a few days later - and so the signatures were appended to a separate sheet of parchment, to be joined later to the completed text.

As the signing of the document ended, "Hatikvah" was struck up by the Philharmonic Orchestra situated on the upper floor; and with the music resounding from above, it seemed as if the heavens had opened and were pouring out a song of joy on the rebirth of the nation. The audience stood motionless, transfixed, listening to the poignant melody coming from nowhere as it were – and as the violins sobbed away the last note the chairman declared:

"The State of Israel is established! This meeting is ended!"

It had taken 32 minutes in all to proclaim the independence of a people who, for 18 hundred and 87 years, had been under the servitude of other nations, monarchy after monarchy, Roman and Byzantine, the exile of Edom, the exile of Ishmael, of West and of East.

Ze'ev Sharef: "Three Days," 1962

An extract from Ben-Gurion's diary, 14 May, 1948

At four pm Jewish independence was proclaimed and the state was established. Its fate depends on our armed forces. Right after the ceremony I returned to Headquarters and we reviewed the worsening situation. Disturbing news on armored columns of the Legion and concentrations of enemy forces in Mafraq, in Syria. Some say also around Lydda. On the other hand our forces have reached several isolated settlements in Galilee... We also captured the Police Academy in Jerusalem and some other important positions in the capital...

Swearing-in of Israel's first president, Dr. Chaim Weizmann, 1949

Song of the Morning
Amir Gilboa

Amir Gilboa (1917-1984) was a leading poet, a soldier, a pioneer, and an Israel Prize laureate

Suddenly a man wakes in the morning
He feels he is a nation and starts walking
And he bids peace to all those he meets along the way.
Wheat stalks sprout before him from cracks in the sidewalk
And the trees shower their rich fragrance on his head.
The dewdrops sparkle and the mountains are a multitude of rays
And he smiles, drawing centuries of courage from the mountains.

Right: Independence Day poster commemorating the centennial of the First Zionist Congress, 1997
(Design: Gideon Sagi)
Below: The first meeting of the Israeli cabinet, 1949

"Ben-Gurion was Chosen by the Almighty"
Shmuel Yosef Agnon

The 1966 Nobel Prize laureate for literature and world-acclaimed author, Shmuel Yosef Agnon (1888-1970) spoke of David Ben-Gurion's crucial role in establishing the State of Israel in a speech delivered on the occasion of Ben-Gurion's 80th birthday.

… David Ben-Gurion was chosen by the Almighty to establish the State of Israel. I know that all of you, to the very last one, desired more than anything else to renew the State of Israel. But when I look into my heart I remember that if I were asked – do you want us to establish a State? – I would have said – of course; but if I were told that today we would be declaring the establishment of the State, I would have said, let us wait another 20, 30 years. All this I am saying about myself. David Ben-Gurion did not wait, but arose and did it, and the Lord was with him, because even before the deed itself, the Almighty agreed with him, and David Ben-Gurion chose that moment that had been ordained by the Almighty for the renewal of the State of Israel…

And my mind tells me that each one of us would have been afraid to complete this task. Ben-Gurion, whom I did not appreciate before, and I was wrong about him, understood and completed the task.

From "From Myself on Myself," 1976

An End to Underground Warfare

Menachem Begin

With the establishment of the State of Israel, the most prominent leader of the underground warfare against British rule emerged from the shadows. This was Menachem Begin (1913-1992), the commander of the Irgun, or Etzel, who was later to become prime-minister. On Saturday, 15 May, 1948, he emerged from his place of concealment and delivered an emotional speech over the hitherto clandestine Etzel broadcasting station.

Menachem Begin reviews the last honor guard of Etzel fighters, 1 July, 1948

After many years of underground warfare, years of persecution and moral and physical suffering, the rebels against the oppressor stand before you, with a blessing of thanks on their lips and a prayer in their hearts. The blessing is the age-old blessing with which our fathers and our forefathers have always greeted the Holy Days. It was with this blessing that they used to taste any fruit for the first time in the season. Today is truly a holiday, a Holy Day, and a new fruit is visible before our very eyes. "The State of Israel has arisen. And it has arisen "Only Thus:" [The motto of the Etzel.] Through blood, through fire, with an outstretched hand and a mighty arm, with sufferings and with sacrifices. It could not have been otherwise. And yet, even before our state is able to set up its normal national institutions, it is compelled to fight – or to continue to fight satanic enemies and blood-thirsty mercenaries, on land, in the air and on the sea...

Our one-day old state is established in the midst of the flames of battle. And the first pillar of our state must therefore be victory, total victory, in the war which is raging all over the country. For this victory, without which we shall have neither freedom nor life, we need arms; weapons of all sorts, in order to strike at our enemies, in order to disperse the invaders, in order to free the entire length and breadth of the country from its would-be destroyers.

But in addition to arms, each and everyone of us requires another weapon; we also need, each and everyone of us, a spiritual weapon, the weapon of unflinching endurance in face of attacks from the air; in the face of grievous casualties; in the face of local disasters and temporary defeats; unflinching resistance to threats and cajolery.

And within our homeland, justice must be the supreme ruler, the ruler over all rulers. There must be no tyranny. The ministers and officials must be the servants of the nation and not their masters. There must be no exploitation. There must be no man within our country – be he citizen or foreigner – compelled to go hungry, to want for a roof over his head, or to lack elementary education. "Remember ye were strangers in the land of Egypt" – this supreme rule must constantly light our way in our relations to the strangers within our gates. Now we have Hebrew rule in part of our homeland. And as in this part of the homeland, Hebrew law will prevail - and that is the only rightful law in this country – there is no need for a Hebrew underground. In the State of Israel we shall be soldiers and builders. And we shall respect its goverment, for it is our goverment.

But for the time being let us think of the battle, for only the outcome of the battle will decide our fate and our future. We shall go on our way into battle, soldiers of the Lord of Hosts, inspired by the spirit of our ancient heroes, from the conquerors of Canaan to the rebels of Judea ...

Menachem Begin:"The Revolt," 1951

Translated by Shmuel Katz

The Great Powers Recognize the State of Israel

Immediately after the proclamation of Israel's independence, the United States and the Soviet Union recognized the Jewish State of Israel *de jure*. At first, the Soviet Union warmly supported the state, evidently hoping that Israel would join the Communist bloc and provide Moscow with a foothold in the Middle East. Soon after, however, the hope was shattered, and the Soviet Union turned into a bitter adversary. Nevertheless, during the dramatic struggle for independence in 1947-8, the Soviet Union still stood by Israel. It provided the young nation with weapons via Czechoslovakia, and the Soviet ambassador to the United Nations, Andrei Gromyko, made a fiery speech in support of the establishment of a Jewish state.

David Ben-Gurion and Abba Eban present a gift of appreciation to President Truman

President Harry S Truman's note, recognizing the State of Israel, 14 May, 1948

The experience gained from the study of the Palestinian question, including the experience of the UN Special Committee, has shown that Jews and Arabs in Palestine do not wish or are unable to live together. The logical conclusion follows that, if these two peoples that inhabit Palestine, both of which have deeply rooted historical ties with the land, cannot live together within the boundaries of a single state, there is no alternative but to create, in the place of one country, two states – one Arab and one Jewish. That is, in the view of our delegation, the only workable solution. The opponents of the partition of Palestine into two separate, independent, democratic states usually point to the fact that this decision would, as they allege, be directed against the Arabs, against the Arab population in Palestine and against the Arab states in general. This point of view is, for reasons that will be readily understood, particularly emphasized by the delegations from the Arab countries. But the delegation of the USSR does not concur with this view. Neither the proposal to partition Palestine into two separate, independent states nor the decision of the Ad Hoc Committee that was created at that session and which approved the proposal which is now under discussion, is directed against the Arabs. The decision is not directed against either of the two national groups that inhabit Palestine. On the contrary, the USSR delegation holds that this decision corresponds to the fundamental national interests of both peoples, that is to say, to the interests of the Arabs as well as that of the Jews.

The representatives of the Arab states claim that the partition of Palestine would be an historic injustice. But this view of the case is unacceptable, if only because, after all, the Jewish people has been closely linked with Palestine for a considerable period in history. Apart from that, we must not overlook... the position in which the Jewish people found themselves as a result of the recent world war. However, it may not be amiss to remind my listeners again that, as a result of the war which was unleashed by Hitlerite Germany, the Jews, as a people, suffered more than any other. The solution of the Palestine problem based on a partition of Palestine into two separate states will be of profound historical significance, because this decision will meet the legitimate demands of the Jewish people, hundreds of thousands of whom, as you know, are still without a country, without homes, having found only temporary shelter in special camps in some western European countries. A great deal has been said on this subject by representatives who share the USSR delegation's point of view in this matter, and which support the plan for partitioning Palestine into two states.

Andrei Gromyko, Soviet foreign minister, at the United Nations General Assembly, 26 November, 1947

The Israel Defense Forces (IDF) Are Created

On 26 May, 1948, 12 days after the proclamation of Israel's independence, David Ben-Gurion signed an ordinance establishing the army of the State of Israel. The army was named "Defense Army of Israel" (later changed to IDF – Israel Defense Forces). The word "Defense" became a part of the army's name for two reasons. First, to define the primarily defensive character of the army; and second, to infer that the Israeli army was the natural successor to the former Haganah underground organization (*Haganah* is the Hebrew word for "Defense"). Following the promulgation of this ordinance, the Defense Army of Israel was established on 1 June, 1948.

Defense Army of Israel Ordinance

No. 4; 5708-1948

An Ordinance establishing the Defense Army of the State of Israel

By virtue of section 18 of the Law and Administration Ordinance, 5708-1948, the following Ordinance is hereby enacted:

1. There is hereby established a Defense Army of Israel, consisting of land forces, a navy and an air force.

2. In a state of emergency, there shall be introduced compulsory enlistment for all the services of the Defense Army of Israel. The age of those liable for enlistment shall be as prescribed by the Provisional Government.

3. Every person serving in the Defense Army of Israel shall take an oath of allegiance to the State of Israel, its constitution and its competent authorities.

4. It is forbidden to establish or maintain any armed force other than the Defense Army of Israel.

5. Orders, declarations, regulations and any other directives concerning matters of national service which were published by the Jewish Agency for Palestine, the General Council (*Va'ad Leumi*) of the Jewish community in Palestine, the People's Administration, the Provisional Government or any of their departments between 29 November, 1947 and the date of publication of this Ordinance, shall remain in force so long as they have not been varied, amended or revoked.

6. Any act done in accordance with the provisions of this Ordinance shall be legal, even if it appears as contradictory to any other provision in the existing law.

7. The Minister of Defense is charged with the implementation of this Ordinance.

8. This Ordinance shall be known as the Defense Army of Israel Ordinance, 5708-1948.

17 Iyar, 5708 (26 May, 1948)

The Provisional Government
David Ben-Gurion
Prime Minister

Poster commemorating the swearing-in of the army, June 1948

Above: Headline of an article in Yediot Aharonot on the creation of Israel's army, marking the ceremony of taking the oath of allegiance, 28 June, 1948

Independence Day parade in the Hebrew University stadium, Jerusalem, 1967

Prime-Minister David Ben-Gurion and the Chief-of-Staff, Lieut. Gen. Yaakov Dori, review the first IDF parade, 1948.

A Prayer for the State of Israel

The Chief Rabbinate composed a special prayer for the newborn State of Israel.

Our Father in Heaven, Rock and Redeemer of Israel, bless the State of Israel, the first manifestation of the approach of our redemption. Shield it with Your loving kindness, envelop it in Your peace, and bestow Your light and truth upon its leaders, ministers, and advisors, and grace them with Your good counsel. Strengthen the hands of those who defend our holy land, grant them deliverance, and adorn them in a mantle of victory. Ordain peace in the land and grant its inhabitants eternal happiness. Lead them, swiftly and uprightly, to Your holy city Zion, to Jerusalem, the abode of Your Name, as is written in the Torah of Your servant Moses: "Even if your outcasts are at the ends of the world, from there the Lord your God will gather you, from there He will fetch you. And the Lord your God will bring you to the Land that your fathers possessed, and you shall possess it; and He will make you more prosperous and more numerous than your fathers." Draw our hearts together to revere and venerate Your name and to observe all the precepts of Your Torah, and send us quickly the Messiah son of David, agent of Your vindication, to redeem those who await Your deliverance.

Manifest yourself in the splendor of your boldness before the eyes of all inhabitants of Your world, and may everyone endowed with a soul affirm that the Lord, God of Israel, is king and his dominion is absolute. Amen.

Independence Day poster, 1963 (Design: Paul Kor)

133

"After Two Thousand Years." Poster of Keren Hayesod, based on a painting by Nahum Gutman, 1937

Every Jew has the Right to Immigrate to Israel

The most important law legislated by the State of Israel is the "Law of Return." It states the basic raison d'être for the creation of the state – the ingathering of all Jews, wherever they may be, to a free and sovereign Jewish country. Israel is the only place on the globe which can be considered by the Jewish people as its land, and the Law of Return stipulated that all Jews have the right to return to their homeland.

Law of Return 5710-1950

1. Every Jew has the right to come to Israel as a new immigrant.
2. (a) Aliyah (immigration) shall be by means of a new immigrant's visa.
   (b) An immigrant visa shall be granted to every Jew who has expressed his desire to settle in Israel, unless the Minister of Immigration determines that the applicant:
   (1) is engaged in an activity directed against the Jewish people; or
   (2) is likely to endanger public health or the security of the state.
3. (a) A Jew who has come to Israel and subsequent to his arrival has expressed his desire to settle in Israel may, while still in Israel, receive an immigrant's certificate.
   (b) The restrictions specified in section 2(b) shall apply also to the grant of an immigrant's certificate, but a person shall not be regarded as endangering public health on account of an illness contracted after his arrival in Israel.
4. Every Jew who has immigrated into this country before the coming into force of this Law, and every Jew who was born in this country, whether before or after tcoming into force of this Law, shall be deemed to be a person who has come to this country as an immigrant under this Law.
5. The Minister of Immigration is charged with the implementation of this Law and may make regulations as to any matter relating to such implementation and also as to the granting of immigrant visas and immigrant certificates to minors up to the age of 18 years.

Jerusalem, 5 July, 1950

Yosef Sprinzak	David Ben-Gurion	Moshe Shapira
Acting President of the State	Prime Minister	Minister of Immigration

"On the way to the Land of Israel." New Year card, Rosh Hashana, 1920

Jerusalem, Capital of Israel

Israel was determined to promulgate Jerusalem as its capital, despite the United Nations Resolution that the city should be placed under international control as a *corpus separandum*. In November, 1949, the United Nations General Assembly decided to hold a debate on the internationalization of Jerusalem. Prime Minister David Ben-Gurion responded by making a statement in the Knesset, that Jewish Jerusalem is an inseparable part of the State of Israel. In December, 1949, Ben-Gurion ordered the immediate transfer of the capital to Jerusalem. The Knesset decided that after the festival of Hanukkah, most government offices and the Knesset itself would be transferred to Jerusalem, where they remain to this day.

Ben-Gurion's speech

As you are aware, the United Nations is currently discussing the issue of Jerusalem and the holy places. The State of Israel is a member of the UN... and this membership obliges us to proclaim from the podium of Israel's First Knesset, to all the nations assembled at the United Nations, and to all those who love peace and justice in the world, that the city of Jerusalem has been in Israel's heart since it became a united nation under King David three thousand years ago, and that we regard it as our holy city, while respecting the places which are holy to other religions.

When we proclaimed the establishment of the renewed State of Israel, on 14 May, 1948, we declared that the State of Israel "will guarantee freedom of religion, conscience, language, education and culture. It will safeguard the Holy Places of all religions; and it will be faithful to the principles of the Charter of the United Nations."

Accordingly, our delegation to the UN announced that Israel would honor all the existing rights regarding the holy places and sacred buildings in Jerusalem, assure freedom of worship and free access to all the holy sites under its control, recognizing the rights of pilgrims of all religions and nations to visit their holy places and assuring freedom of movement for clergy. We agreed to allow effective UN supervision of the holy places and the existing rights in a way that would be agreed upon. At the same time we see fit to declare that Jewish Jerusalem is an organic, inseparable part of the State of Israel, just

A session of the first Knesset, 1949

Celebrating 3,000 years of Jerusalem

as it is an integral part of Jewish history and belief. Jerusalem is the heart of the State of Israel. We are proud of the fact that Jerusalem is also sacred to other religions, and will gladly provide access to their holy places and enable them to worship as and where they please, cooperating with the UN to guarantee this. We cannot imagine, however, that the UN would attempt to sever Jerusalem from the State of Israel or harm Israel's sovereignty in its eternal capital.

Twice in the history of our nation we were driven out of Jerusalem, after being defeated in bitter war by the larger, stronger forces of Babylon and Rome. Our links with Jerusalem today are no less deep than in the days of Nebuchadnezzar and Titus, and when Jerusalem was attacked after 14 May, 1948, our valiant youngsters risked their lives for our sacred capital no less than their forefathers did in the time of the First and Second Temples.

A nation that, for two thousand and five hundred years, has faithfully adhered to the vow made by the first exiles by the rivers of Babylon not to forget Jerusalem, will never agree to be separated again from the city. Jewish Jerusalem will never accept alien rule after thousands of its youngsters liberated their historic homeland for the third time, redeeming Jerusalem from destruction and vandalism...

Had we not been able to withstand the aggressors who rebelled against the United Nations, Jewish Jerusalem would have been wiped off the face of the earth, the Jewish population would have been eradicated and the State of Israel would not have arisen. Thus, we are no longer morally bound by the UN resolution of 29 November, 1947, since the UN proved unable to implement it. In our opinion the resolution of 29 November regarding Jerusalem is null and void.

Statement of Prime Minister David Ben-Gurion in the Knesset, concerning the transfer of the capital to Jerusalem on 5 December, 1949

The Knesset in session

The Knesset building and the candelabrum (a gift of the British government) opposite the main gates
Opposite: Jerusalem vistas
Top to bottom:
The Western Wall beneath the Dome of the Rock;
The neighborhood of Yemin Moshe, the first Jewish settlement outside the walls of the Old City;
The Shrine of the Book at the Israel Museum;
The President's Residence;
The downtown pedestrian mall

Laws Concerning Jerusalem

With the liberation of the Old City during the Six-Day War of 1967 and the reunification of the city, the Knesset promulgated several laws on the status of Jerusalem.

Protection of Holy Places Law, 1967

The Holy Places shall be protected from desecration and any other violation and from anything likely to violate the freedom of access of the members of the different religions to the places sacred to them or their feelings with regard to those places....

The Minister of Religious Affairs is charged with the implementation of this Law, and he may, after consultation with, or upon the proposal of, representatives of the religions concerned and with the consent of the Minister of Justice, make regulations as to any matter relating to such implementation.

Levi Eshkol, Prime Minister; Zerach Warhaftig, Minister of Religious Affairs; Shneur Zalman Shazar, President of the State

Jerusalem, 27 June 1967

Basic Law: Jerusalem, Capital of Israel, 1980

1. Jerusalem, entire and united, is the capital of Israel.
2. Jerusalem is the seat of the President of the State, the Knesset, the Government and the Supreme Court.
3. The Holy Places shall be protected from desecration and any other violation and from anything likely to violate the freedom of access of the members of the different religions to the places sacred to them or their feelings towards those places.
4. a. The government shall provide for the development and prosperity of Jerusalem and the well-being of its inhabitants by allocation of special funds, including a special annual grant to the Municipality of Jerusalem (Capital City Grant) with the approval of the Finance Committee of the Knesset.

   b. Jerusalem shall be given special priority in the activities of the authorities of the state so as to further its development in economic and other matters.

   c. The government shall set up a special body or bodies for the implementation of this law.

Jerusalem, 30 July, 1980

Menachem Begin   Yitzhak Navon
Prime Minister   President of the State

Nobody Questions India About the Right of Return

Amnon Rubinstein

Amnon Rubinstein is a professor of law, a former Knesset member and minister in Israel's governments. He presently serves as Dean of the Law Faculty in the Herzliya Interdisciplinary Center. He brings forward an unexpected argument against the demand of the Palestinian refugees to return to the State of Israel.

A delegation of Liberal Democrat parliamentarians from the United Kingdom recently toured Israel on a study visit. Within a very short while, the discussion between the members of the delegation and their Israeli hosts focused on an issue that is often raised in such meetings: The argument that Israel's refusal to recognize the right of return of the Palestinian refugees of 1948 is a human rights violation and that Israel is making its offense all the more serious by granting citizenship to Jews from the former Soviet Union who were not born in Israel and who knew nothing about this country before arriving here. I tried to explain to these guests from Great Britain both the meaning of our Law of Return and Israel's character as a Jewish and democratic state. I also pointed out to them that, of the tens of millions of refugees on the face of the earth in the late 1940s and early 1950s, only the Palestinian refugees were not fully integrated into the societies in which they found themselves, the reason being that the Arab host countries preferred to confine them to refugee camps.

As I offered these explanations and tried to deal with the usual list of accusations hurled at Israel, one of the parliamentarians, who was of Indian origin, burst out, attacking my attackers. He asked his colleagues whether any of them could possibly imagine India ever agreeing to repatriate and grant citizenship to the millions of Moslems who sought refuge in Pakistan during the civil war of 1947-48. Surely none of them would ask India to commit suicide. Thus, if they would not demand that India accept these Moslems, why, he questioned them passionately, were they demanding that Israel open its gates to Palestinian refugees?

In the vast majority of instances, the attacks on Israel stem from a basic refusal to regard it as a legitimate state whose existence expresses the right of the Jewish people to self-determination – a right that entails a concomitant obligation to observe democratic and universal values. No one is demanding that the Czech Republic welcome back the German refugees from the Sudetenland, who were so cruelly banished from Czechoslovakia after the Second World War. Interestingly enough, advocates of the repatriation of these refugees are instantly accused of being warmongers.

However, the critical sociologists have decided that a special law applies to Israel and that the same laws that apply to all the other democracies of the world do not apply to Israel. Anyone who attacks the critical sociologists with this line of reasoning is immediately branded as an anti-liberal who has no regard for human rights.

Ha'aretz, 20 June, 2000

Israel's Flag in Space

Ilan Ramon

Colonel Ilan Ramon, a pilot in the Israeli Air Force and the first Israeli astronaut, perished in the crash of the space shuttle "Columbia" on 1 February, 2003. Col. Ramon regarded his mission not only as a personal achievement and a major scientific endeavor, but also as an event of great symbolism, as he set out on his voyage in the name of the State of Israel. He took with him on the space flight a miniature Israeli flag, a copy of the Scroll of Independence, a memento from the Holocaust and a ritual wine goblet. In an email from space to the president of Israel, Moshe Katzav, Ilan Ramon wrote:

Dear Mr. President,

It is an honor and a great privilege for me to write you this letter from space…

This morning – Saturday, 26 January – we flew over Israel… From space I could easily spot Jerusalem and while looking at our capital I prayed just one short prayer – *Shema Israel adonai elohenu adonai ehad.* ("Hear, O Israel, the Lord our God, the Lord is One")…

In our mission we are undertaking a variety of international scientific experiments, including those of scientists from Arab states. We are working on this mission for the benefit of all mankind, and from space our world seems as one unit with no borders. So let me call from up here in space – let us work our way for peace and a better life for everyone on earth.

Quoted in Yediot Aharonot, 2 February, 2003

Human Dignity and Liberty

Israel's Basic Law, "Human Dignity and Liberty," adopted in 1992, has become one of the most progressive and important foundation stones of contemporary Israeli society. It confirms several basic human rights, such as the protection of life, the human body, human dignity, individual property, and personal liberty.

1. Basic human rights in Israel are based on the recognition of the value of the human being, and the sanctity of his life and his freedom.
2. There shall be no violation of the life, body or dignity of any person as such.
3. There shall be no violation of the property of a person.
4. All persons are entitled to protection of their life, body, and dignity.
5. There shall be no deprivation or restriction of the liberty of a person by imprisonment, arrest, extradition or by any other manner.
6. All persons are free to leave Israel, and every Israel national has the right of entry from abroad.
7. (a) All persons have the right to privacy and to intimacy.
   (b) There is no entry into the premises of a person who has not consented thereto.
   (c) No search shall be conducted on the private premises or body of a person.
   (d) There shall be no violation of the secrecy of the spoken utterances, writings or records of a person.

Jerusalem, March 17, 1992

Above: Israel, as photographed from the space shuttle "Columbia" on its last mission
Below: Ilan Ramon, the first Israeli astronaut

"To the Glory of Israel"

"You have such a small country," former Secretary of State Henry Kissinger once remarked to an Israeli friend, "and you already have succeeded to develop a tank, a plane, a missile – and who knows what you've got down there in Dimona..."

Indeed, until the day when the Children of Israel will beat their swords into ploughshares, they have no other choice but to devote some of their best talents to the development of arms for their defense. In its research institutions, Israel has developed the "Arrow" anti-missile missile and the satellite "Ofek" (illus. 1), the supersonic jet fighter "Lavi" (illus. 2) and the "Merkava" tank (illus. 3), whose major contribution to the strength of the IDF is precisely in the protection of its crew's lives. In Dimona, under the leadership of David Ben-Gurion and Shimon Peres, Israel established a powerful nuclear reactor (illus. 4).

But Israel has excelled in other fields as well. During its early years, the young state drew pride from its achievements in agriculture that also symbolized the return of the Jews to working on the land. The nation, much of which is arid desert thirsting for water, mobilized huge resources for the construction of the National Water Carrier, a giant irrigation project that brings water from the lush north to the center of the country and the Negev Desert (illus.5). Nevertheless, Prime Minister Levi Eshkol was right in declaring, in the mid-1960s: "We shall not be able to remain an agricultural people as we thought scores of years ago... therefore we must dedicate our efforts to the development of industry." Israel turned to high-tech projects, aimed mostly at export (illus. 6). The pioneer of sophisticated industries in Galilee, Steff Wertheimer, built the Iskar Blades plant in the small town of Tefen and called his vision of high-tech; "Zionism Stage Three" (illus. 7).

A symbol of the Jewish people's renaissance was its eager exposure to all kinds of sport, which reach their peak every four years in the Maccabiah Games, (the "Jewish Olympics" - illus. 8). After 2,000 years of exile the Jewish people learned to excel in the art of basketball, and several times won the European Championship "We are on the map!" declared Tal Brody, the American-born captain of the Maccabi Tel Aviv basketball team, as he raised the trophy above his head (illus. 9).

The Children of Israel even learned to sing. They proved to the world that they were worthy descendants of King David, referred to in the Bible as "the sweet psalmist of Israel" by winning the Eurovision song contest three times (illus. 10).

And yet, the main source of pride for many were the Nobel Prizes awarded to several Israelis; the Nobel Prize for Literature, which was bestowed upon writer S.Y. Agnon; other Nobel awards won by Israelis engaged in scientific or medical research; and Nobel Peace Prizes, that crowned the achievements of Menachem Begin, Yitzhak Rabin and Shimon Peres. Maybe that is a modest fulfillment of the biblical vision describing the unique character of the nation of Israel and its dream for the future: "Not by might, nor by power, but by my Spirit, says the Lord of hosts." (Zechariah: 4: 6).

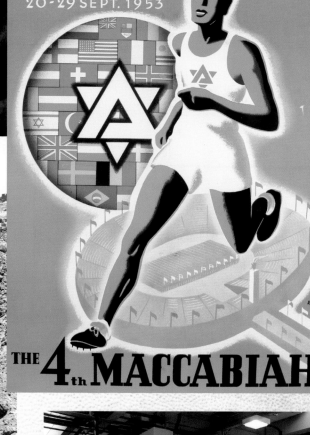

המכביה הרביעית
יא - כ תשרי תשי"ד
20 - 29 SEPT. 1953

R. Blass

THE **4**th **MACCABIAH**

This Land

Ephraim Kishon

Hungarian-born Ephraim Kishon (1915-2004) was undoubtedly Israel's greatest satirist and humorist. The following piece of gentle irony was penned to mark Israel's 50th anniversary in 1998.

Israel is a country so tiny that there is no room to write its name on the world map.

It is the only country in the world, which is financed by taxpayers abroad.

It is a country which consumes its inhabitants, and yet does not grow fat.

It is a country of boundless boundaries.

It is a country where mothers learn the mother tongue from their sons.

It is a country where the fathers ate sour grapes, and the children's teeth are excellent.

It is a country where one writes Hebrew, reads English, and speaks Russian.

It is a country where everybody has the right to speak his mind, but there is no law forcing anybody to listen.

It is the most enlightened country in the region, thanks to the Arabs.

It is a country where all the capital is concentrated in Jewish hands – and there is much grumbling because of it.

It is a country where one can get anything in the world for his money – except a Jaguar, which is very expensive.

It is a country where any babe in arms may contradict his father's political views.

It is a country of elections, but no choice.

It is a country, which is an organic part of its trade unions.

It is a country where nobody wants to work, so they build a new town in three days' time and go idle the rest of the week.

It is a country where paper can move mountains, but all the mountains beget are speeches.

It is a country, which produces less than it eats, and yet, of all places, it is here that nobody dies of malnutrition.

It is a country where nobody expects miracles, but everybody takes them for granted.

It is a country where one calls ministers simply "Moishe" – and then almost dies with the excitement of it.

It is a country whose survival is permanently endangered, and yet the upstairs neighbor causes you ulcers.

It is a country where every human being is a soldier, and every soldier is a human being.

It is a country that is fifty years old, but as smart as a twenty year-old.

It is the only country in which I could live.

It is my country.

Ma'ariv, Independence Day issue, 1998. The little boy – the artist Dosh's symbolic caricature, representing Israel – is holding a banner with the words "Happy End"

"Viper" January 17, 1991

Pinhas Sadeh

In this poem, written many years after the establishment of the State of Israel, the poet Pinhas Sadeh (1929-1994) describes the tremendous change that the creation of Israel brought about for the Jewish people. It is no more a people whose blood is free for the shedding, but a nation dwelling in its own land, willing and able to defend its existence and its borders. The following poem was written during "Desert Storm," the Gulf War of 1991, when the words *Nahash Tsefa* ("Viper") were broadcast on radio and television indicating a warning that an Iraqi Scud missile was about to hit Israel.

Night is falling on the town, on deserted streets.
The winter skies are darkening.
Blackness envelops the trees by my window; birds fall asleep in their nests.

I read once, somewhere, that when he stood at the foot of the pyramids, Napoleon said to his soldiers:
Four thousand years are watching us now.
Today, we are watched by something else: loftier than pyramids.
We are watched by the eyes of our fathers and our mothers.
Countless eyes, from the ghettos of Worms and Mainz, Toledo, Nemirov and Kishinev, Vilna, Warsaw, Treblinka.

And what do their eyes say? They say: our sons, our grandsons, how fortunate you are.
That you don't dig your own graves in the snow, and you don't burn in fired ovens, like us.
That you are not devoured by dogs' teeth, and are not stabbed in your mother's womb.
That you are not helpless in this world, as we were.
That you have the power, and you dwell in your own land.
You are our consolation, if there can be any.

Translated by Michael Bar-Zohar

Never Again! Three fighter aircraft of the Israel Air Force overfly the Auschwitz death camp, Poland, September, 2003

Chapter 8

The Independence Day Torch

I, Sarah Shimoni from the town of Lod, daughter of Esther and Shmuel Gaon, mother of Avraham who fell in the Yom Kippur War, am honored to kindle this torch to mark the 35th anniversary of the State of Israel; in the name of the families of the fallen – parents and spouses, brothers and sisters, sons and daughters.

And to the blessed memory of those who fell in the defense of the country, both before and after the establishment of the State of Israel.

And in honor of the Hebrew mother.

I, Moshe Kravitz, son of Naomi and Israel, and an IDF officer, holder of the Award for Valor in Operation "Peace for Galilee," am honored to kindle this torch to mark the 35th anniversary of the State of Israel.

In honor of the Valorous, the Courageous and the Distinguished in Israel's military campaigns from the War of Independence and up to Operation "Peace for Galilee."*

And to the glory of Israel.

Eve of the Day of Independence, 1998

*Israel has three military awards; they are: Gevura (Valor), Oz (Courage), Mofet (Distinction)

THE ONSLAUGHT LAUNCHED AGAINST US

Paratroopers at the Western Wall, June, 1967
Background: "Follow me!" In the Israeli Army, the officers traditionally lead the attack, and the order: "Follow me!" has become an IDF slogan.

On a Silver Platter

Nathan Alterman

"No state is given to its people on a silver platter"

Chaim Weizmann

The Earth grows still.
The lurid sky slowly pales
Over smoking borders.
Heartsick, but still living, a people stand by
To greet the uniqueness
of the miracle.

Readied, they wait beneath the moon,
Wrapped in awesome joy, before the light.
- Then, soon,
A girl and boy step forward,
And slowly walk before the waiting nation.

In work garb and heavy-shod
They climb
In stillness.
Wearing yet the dress of battle, the grime
Of aching day and fire-filled night.

Unwashed, weary unto death, not knowing rest,
But wearing youth like dewdrops in their hair,
- Silently the two approach
And stand.
Are they of the quick or of the dead?

Through wondering tears, the nation stares.
"Who are you, the silent two?"And they reply:
"We are the silver platter
Upon which the Jewish state was served to you.

So they speak, before falling in shadow at the nation's feet.
Let the rest in Israel's chronicles be told.

Avraham Adan ("Bren") hoists a hand-inked improvised Israeli flag at the newly captured Um Rashrash (today, the town of Eilat), March, 1949
Opposite: An armored car at Sha'ar Hagai – the road up to besieged Jerusalem, now a war memorial

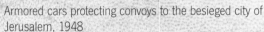

Armored cars protecting convoys to the besieged city of Jerusalem, 1948

By His Own Hands

Moshe Shamir

Moshe Shamir (1921-2004), author and playwright, served in the Palmach. He was editor of the army magazine *Bamahaneh* and a member of the Knesset. The first line of this story has become a paradigm for Israeli-born youth.

Elik was born of the sea.

That's the way father used to tell it when we would be sitting down to supper on the verandah of our little house on summer evenings. Father and I – the big brother who was already old enough to tell the difference between a bit of tomfoolery and the truth – would suddenly feel like teasing the lovable little fellow...

Father used to say: "We found you in a barrel that the sea washed ashore." I also remember the version: "Actually we found you among the Bedouins in the desert," which smarted worst of all...

146

It was invariably part of the game that whenever any of these aspersions were cast on the birth of one of the little ones, he would stamp his feet and bawl indignantly at the top of his voice till father hastened to mollify him. With a smile for the joke-that-came-off, father would murmur affectionately into the little one's ear:

"No, no, no. You're ours, you're our little boy. You're ours!"…

The above is the beginning of the book, "By His Own Hands" that Moshe Shamir wrote in memory of his younger brother Elik, who fell in the early stages of the War of Independence. The chapters on Elik have become over the years a central element of remembrance of those fallen in war.

…Three minutes later, on the highway approaching Yazur…

Watch out now, you're getting near. The lads out there in the back are getting their guns ready. For the last few days, they've been deprived of the protection of the armored pick-up on the clear-cut orders of the British, who found that the armor was proving too effective, while the open, unprotected pick-up would certainly restore the balance: one side shoots and the other gets shot. Since then you've gone out on the job in the light, exposed green pick-up. Since then, you've gone out on the job with only your khaki shirt between the bullets and your breast. Let us never forgive what the British have done to us, never forget, and never forgive!

But a humble row of almond trees whose white buds have burst into blossom overnight drains the angry heart of all oaths, opens it wide to the sheer joy without, to the green and yellow, the white and red, the gold, the saffron, the brown and black.

On the highway, approaching Yazur.

One minute later, inside the village, every fiber alert.

At once you see the solid barricade, the heaviest yet, thrown across the road. No choice but to fight.

Can't stop the pick-up. The only way is to break through.

And at once – the shots. A hail. All hell is let loose. Can't get through that, and you naked and exposed.

The pick-up flails back, full blast.

A mine or a grenade. The petrol tank's caught fire. The pick-up screams to a stop.

Jump! Into the ditch!

A bullet.

Is this it?

A numbness between each gasp of breath – from the pain. Or is it the pain itself? Where are the others?

Is this it, then?

To fight, fight on, to win! As long as the scorching barrel will fire. You haven't finished me yet! We'll hold out under fire. God of – my boys are getting killed! Our men will hear this and come. You haven't finished me – with all the hatred, with all the compassion, with all the outrage, with all the longing, with all the pain, with all the amazement and wonder. God – my boys are getting killed!

Is this it? With all the wonder…

No more.

Translated by Joseph Schachter

From "By His Own Hands," 1973

Bab el-Wad

Haim Gouri

In his poem "Friendship" Haim Gouri described his comrades who had fallen in the War of Independence, as the boys "with rebel locks and handsome visage." He swore "to remember them all." Several of them fell while attempting to break the siege of Jerusalem in the narrow ravine of Sha'ar Hagai ("Gate of the Valley" – Bab el-Wad in Arabic), leading up to the capital.

Here I pass by, standing by the stone.
A black road, rocks and ridges.
Day goes down, slowly, sea-wind blows
Light of a first star, over Beit Machsir.

Bab el-Wad,
Remember our names forever,
Convoys broke through, on the way to the City.
Our dead lay by the sides of the road.
The iron skeleton is silent like my comrade.

And I walk, passing by silently,
And I remember them, one by one.
Here we fought together on cliffs and boulders
Here we were one family.

A spring day will come, the cyclamens will bloom.
Red anemones on the mountain and the slope.
You who walk on the road we followed,
Do not forget us, those of Bab el-Wad.

Translated by Daniel Shalev

If Only I had a Girl...

Moshe Rashkes

"Days of Lead" is a novel by Moshe Rashkes about the War of Independence, the story of one young soldier. Rashkes, a novelist and journalist,was chairman of the Association of Wounded IDF Veterans.

"You're going out there tonight," said the company commander. He said it casually, as if we were discussing a football match. "You're going to take Cedar Hill." His expression changed slightly, his tone became more serious. "It's going to be a very tough job," he added.

Do we really have to go?... Is there no way we can refuse?... Maybe? And maybe I just don't have the courage to do it, the strength to say no. I nodded, although something within me rebelled. No. I don't want to do it. Cedar Hill! It's a slaughter-house. I've heard all about it. It's changed hands several times – and everyone on it comes to a bitter end...

"You're moving out at ten PM." the CO summed up. "With all your gear. Till then you can go into town for a break," he added casually.

... I soon found my way to the soldiers' club...I went inside. It was filled with square tables. Cheerful groups of soldiers were sitting around them. Someone was playing the accordion, a hard, loud sound. He was hitting the buttons hard. Why didn't he play with more emotion? Only his body was swaying enthusiastically to the beat. I found myself a vacant chair. The soldiers around the table glanced at me and immediately returned to their conversation. I saw dozens of faces. Sun-tanned, tousle-headed, smiling, laughing, slapping one another on the shoulder with an encouraging soldierly slap. I didn't know a soul. There were girls here and there, but very few.

How nice it would be to have a girl here. I could rest my head on her shoulder and press

On leave from the fighting, 1948

A convoy with essential supplies entering Jerusalem, 1948

my hungry lips to the hollow of her soft neck. I could breathe in the fragrance of her skin. Her hair would tumble down my face and slide over my burning forehead. Silken threads, a young girl's hair, silken threads....And that nurse I saw in the hospital! I don't even know her name. Perhaps I'll pass by the hospital and try to see her, as if by accident. I don't have much time, only two hours till we set out. Only two hours. I remember her clearly, as if it was only a moment ago. I've been thinking about her for the last few nights, in bed, gaping into the dark. I yearned for her in those hours of arousing images, which left me with nothing but a dull and nagging pain in my loins. How lovely her eyes were, with a slight downward slant, as if they were trying to blend with the hollows of her cheeks. If she were here with me, I'd stroke her long fingers, how long they are, curving with seductive delicacy. What am I to her? She may well have forgotten me. I was probably only a passing figure for her, one face among hundreds in the hospital corridors. But I remember her well, and I want her desperately.

It's good to know that you're remembered, who remembers me now?... my parents... they certainly remember me.

Is there a girl who remembers me? I don't think so. Oh, if only she were sitting here now. She'd probably throw me a sad, pleading glance, and sob: "Don't go, don't go!" Then I'd feel like a man, a man leaving a weeping woman behind him; leaving and going out to battle... but I'm not a man yet. If only I had a woman, a woman.

At ten PM the unit assembled. Each man picked up his rifle and took his place in the armored car. They sat hunched over their weapons, sunk in thought...

I called to the driver, "We're ready. You can move off."

The armored car set out. Dark streets, dense blocks of buildings...Then the dark

landscape, glimpsed through the apertures, began to change. Silhouettes of hills…we sat in silence, nobody said a word. My brain was emptied of all thoughts. Something in my consciousness was dormant, dulled. I was sunk in melancholy and I wanted to sleep.

Just before the pumping station, the armored car came to a halt. "All off!" the driver broke the silence.

….I peered around me – Sha'ar Hagai – the gateway to the valley! The valley was a narrow, steep fissure, closed in on both sides by giant walls. Only a thin, clear strip of sky hung over it. A deathly-pale moon was visible on the rim of the sky, like the heavy water-logged prow of a sinking ship.

And so I came back here. It was here that my journey to war started…the convoy…the cries of battle…the ruined building…there it is, a vague dark silhouette.

Beside it is the hill where for the first time I took the life of a human being, an enemy…

From "Days of Lead," 1962

An Arab mob attacks a Jewish relief convoy on the way to Jerusalem

The Battle of Harel

Haim Hefer

Boom bu bu boom boom boom
The universe is dark.
The mountain is dark, the street is black,
The city is dying, besieged,
No bread there, nothing!

Boom bu bu boom boom boom
We shall not sleep tonight,
We will slip quietly across the road
With forty bullets each.
Merciful God, preserve us.

Boom bu bu boom boom boom
Our hearts are already dulled.
Thirty died at Nebi Samuel,
Seventeen on Mount Castel,
The convoy of Nebi Daniel,
But we shall rise again!

The dark night up here
Conceals a knife in its blackness.
If we return from this night
We will have aged by twenty years.

But you will see, you will see
That the way is free
You will see, yes, you will see

The way that is free
Your lover went off to the fight
Your lover went off to the fight
But where is he now
He has not returned from the path.

From the journey he did not return
The dirt covered his eyes
His comrades dug his grave
For he did not live until morning.

If we return, if we come back,
Then you will wear a dress of

black
In memory of all the boys.
For only ten of us were left
Of our company by morning.

Boom bu bu boom boom boom
Our hearts are already dulled.
Thirty died at Nebi Samuel,
Seventeen on Mount Castel,
The convoy of Nebi Daniel,
Ginger, Moishe, Michael,
Menahem, Zvika and Shmuel
And Moti, Gad and Bezalel
But we shall rise again!

Bereavement

Rivka Guber ("The Mother of the Sons")

Rivka Guber

In her letters to her son's comrades and her own friends, Rivka Guber writes about the death in battle of her two sons, Ephraim and Zvi.

3 April 1948
Dear Beatrice,

A week has gone by since we buried our beloved son, our main hope for the future. We are not the only ones who have made such a heavy sacrifice. The blood of our best and finest has been spilled like water; the best of the sons born in the homeland are fighting for our honor and our very national and human survival. Nonetheless many people were shaken by Ephraim's death. This is not on our account: it is not thanks to us that he grew up here so faultless and so honorable. We were privileged to raise one of the young Jews whose like has not been seen for generations. Only when we returned here and put down roots, could the land once again produce a yield such as Ephraim and his comrades.

…Now Zvi is leaving the farm to take Ephraim's place because the struggle continues and we cannot abandon the fight.

12 October 1948
To Yitzhak Levanon, who is like a brother to me,

Three months have passed since I fell silent in the face of my sons' fate. Yesterday I opened Zvi's drawer, which was always locked. He did not even leave us the key when he left the house. I read page after page for the first time in my life, everything written by Zvi, my beloved son, who was so inspired, who was such a wonderful blend of the ardor of youth and the wisdom of age. But I cannot describe to you how stirred I was by reading your letters to him, which he kept in that drawer. No words of mine can express my gratitude to the hand that wrote them.

You were the first herald of the recognition he would have won some day. Zvi was destined for greatness. I have also seen the note you wrote to Shazar when you sent him Zvi's poem "Mother:" "If the grim reaper, now reaping the best of our crop, spares him – Zvi Guber will be one of the most important writers of the third generation." A cruel condition!

President Chaim Herzog at the ceremony marking Remembrance Day for the Fallen, Western Wall, Jerusalem 1990

2 November 1948

To Rivka Alper

The day before yesterday we drove down to the Negev, to the place where Zvi fell. We drove along narrow roads and tracks, only recently cleared of mines. Even the fresh breeze in the fields, bearing the fragrance of plants, could not disperse the stench of corpses rotting beneath the ground. A large number of letters written in Arabic were scattered around the bunker. Perhaps they were written with love and desperate concern by mothers, just as I wrote letters to Zvi when there was no longer anyone to receive them. I collected the letters and burned them, because they deserved a worthy burial.

Zvi himself has no grave. I remembered the elegy he wrote on the night we sat and waited for Ephraim's body to be brought home:

Come, my child, night will darken
The fires of life and the sources of pain.
In a quiet grave, voiceless, soundless,
You will rest tranquil for ever.

Around you the world will spin on dizzily
In the tumult of war and of loss.
Only you, in your frozen sleep of death
Will not suffer the ruin and pain.

In the quiet of the grave you will lie motionless
In the eternal darkness of night.
Only the spring rain will stir your clods
And patter on them joyfully.

Even this rest was not to be his lot. And once again his father recited kaddish [the mourners' prayer for the dead] in the open field over his second and last son.

From "With the Sons," 1953

Yitzhak's Last Kit Bag

Yehuda Amichai

Yehuda Amichai (1926-2000) served as a soldier in the Jewish Brigade and the Palmach. He was one of the best-loved poets of Israel.

Towards the end of the war, I brought from the Negev to the wine cellar
The last military bag of Yitzhak from Rishon LeZion.
For the line of defense of the wine cellar passed through the Negev
Where he fell. I brought the kit bag to his father, a veteran wine cellar man.
For I was told not to go to the women's house, to mother and sister,
But to the man's place, to the father. In a rubber apron
Up to his chin and rubber boots up to his knees
He stood in the fermenting of the wine and the raging of his life.
He called his colleagues from between the barrels,
In a loud voice in the dark cellar;
Here is his friend who was with him when he died,
Here is his last kit bag, here is the towel,
The big striped towel we gave him on his way to the Negev.

Oh, Yitzhak, you fell in the Negev
And your father cries in a wine cellar,
I remember the silly song
By Ibn-Gabirol: "At the end of the wine, The eyes of mine,
Run streams of water. Streams of water," Here,
The wine did not end, but the eyes ran out of tears.

In the cellar's ceiling, yellow lamps burned
In cages, like trapped souls,
And in the big, dark barrels
The fermentation began that will never cease.

Translated by Benjamin and Barbara Harshav

Samson's Foxes

Uri Avneri

Uri Avneri is a journalist and former member of the Knesset. In the War of Independence he fought on the southern front in the jeep reconnaissance unit known as "Samson's Foxes."

Four of them, four, on the jeep as it speeds
And their song bursts out of the heart.
And the road dances under the wheels,
The road which to the enemy leads.

Samson's foxes
Are on the attack again,
Bearing the flaming torch by night.
From Gaza to Gath
The battle rages again
The battle for Israel's liberty.

Listen, Egyptians, to Samson's song,
Once it augured the Philistine's end.
Listen closely to the machine guns, the grenades,
The song of death to the invaders.

Four of them, four to the fierce battle,
And the engine hums slowly.
Yes, the gun which spits fire is new
But the fire itself is old.

Hirbet Hiz'a

S. Yizhar

Together with the acts of heroism of the War of Independence, there were also dark and controversial incidents, such as that described by S. Yizhar (the pen name of the writer Yizhar Smilansky.) The State of Israel never tried to whitewash or conceal these incidents and the story of Hirbet Hiz'a has been taught in schools to emphasize that Israel is a state governed by democratic and moral principles.

It did indeed occur long ago, but it continues to haunt me.

…It might of course be better to start by mentioning what was from the outset the purpose of that day, that "Order of the Day" number so and so, which noted specifically that we were "to assemble all the inhabitants from point X (see enclosed map) to point Y (see the same map) – load them onto vehicles and transport them across our lines; blow up the stone houses and burn the huts; arrest the young men and the suspects and cleanse the area of 'hostile forces,' etc, etc" – since it will now be clear what great expectations were pinned on those who went, who were charged with this mission of "burn-detonate-arrest-load-transport" and sent to burn and blow up and arrest and load and transport in respectful fashion and with civilized moderation, and this is a reflection of the prevailing mood, of a proper upbringing and perhaps also of the Jewish soul, of its greatness.

…We reached a certain hill, where we huddled under a cactus hedge and prepared to eat some of our rations, but then we were gathered together by Moishe, the platoon commander, who explained matters to us, and briefed us on the terrain and the mission. It transpired from what he said that the few houses visible on the slope of another hill was a village called Hirbet Hiz'a, that all the groves around and the fields belonged to that village, and that its abundant water supply, its fertile soil and excellent crops had won almost as much renown as its inhabitants who were, it was said, scoundrels who aided the enemy. Always ready to commit evil actions when the occasion arose or, for example, to vent their wrath on Jews if they should come across them and wipe them out – that is their nature…then someone returned with oranges and we ate them.

[When the soldiers approached, the Arab inhabitants fled their homes].

…When we approached the groves near the village, there were signs in the courtyards and houses that they had been abandoned shortly before. The beds were still made up and the fires on the cooking stones were still smoking, and the hens scratching through the garbage as if nothing had happened fled instantly, squawking as if about to be slaughtered. Dogs sniffed at us suspiciously, approaching then shrinking back, barking hesitantly. And the utensils in the courtyard seemed to be still in mid-activity. The silence was still nothing but a kind of amazement and astonishment, as if nothing had yet been decided and everything could still recover and return to normal.

…Then there was the sound of an explosion, loud and reverberating, and immediately afterwards the wailing began. At first it seemed as if their cries would die down and fall silent as soon as they saw that there was no killing; but the wailing, the sharp, high-pitched, stubborn and rebellious cries, which sent a shiver down the spine, continued to rise and you cannot evade them, cannot turn away; impatiently you shrug your shoulders, glance at your comrades and want to move on; now it was no longer like the squawk of a trapped and terrified hen – but the scream of a she-tiger whose pain maddens her, augments her evil strength, like the scream of the condemned man filled with hate who struggles against his executioners, a scream which is a defensive weapon. I shall not move, I won't permit it, I will die before I let you touch me, until even the stones cry out with it – a terrible scream,

swelling at brief intervals, in gasps, and soon it was even possible to make out words but they were not intelligible.

"Why are they screaming like that, eh?" Our wireless operator could not contain himself.

…Because who was actually there, apart from women with babes in arms (snotty-nosed Arab babies wrapped in rags and covered in amulets), and other women who were wringing their hands, their lips moving soundlessly, and several old men walking silently and ceremoniously as if on their way to the Judgment Day. And there were others there, middle-aged, who did not feel old enough to be safe from inflicted rage and they were marked by the need to explain and occasionally by a rebellious spark revealed in a glance or two. And there was a blind man led by a boy, his grandson perhaps, who walked, his eyes darting in bewilderment and curiosity, forgetting the hand on his shoulder and the calamity which hung over them, so that even the fact that he stumbled from time to time, scarcely diverted his attention from us. And the blind and the crippled, the old and the weak and the women and infants seemed all together to belong to some chapter in the Bible where all this was related – I cannot recall where, and in addition to this biblical scene, which already lay heavy on our hearts, we reached an open space where a wide-boughed sycamore tree grew, and beneath it, sitting huddled together, all the villagers were assembled, silent, a large multicolored mass gathered together, a silent crowd whose eyes followed what was happening, and from time to time one of them sighed and said *Akh-ya-rab*.

…And from among the women there rose soft, monotonous almost aimless weeping, and from time to time it turned into sobs and was choked off.

…And then a stone house exploded suddenly, with ear-splitting noise and a cloud of dust, and from a distance its roof seemed to float upwards almost peacefully, flat and entire, and suddenly on high, disintegrated and split and fell lump by lump, crumb by crumb, in a hail of debris and stones. The woman whose home it apparently was leapt up and shrieked wildly, and began to run in that direction, carrying one infant and with a pitiful toddler clutching the hem of her dress, and she was screaming and gesturing with one hand, and talking and choking, and then another woman rose,

Right: IDF soldiers entering the village of Tur'an in the Galilee during the War of Independence
Opposite: A jeep of the reconnaissance unit "Samson's Foxes"

and another, and a very old man, and others stood up and she began to run, the toddler attached to her dress dragging behind her and falling down and bursting into wails, his tanned buttocks exposed...

Moishe said: "Firstly we need to check all the Arabs down there and identify suspicious young men. Secondly, trucks will be here soon and we'll load them and leave the village empty. And third, we have to finish burning and detonating. Then we can go home."

...I gazed around me, uneasy. Where did it come from, this feeling that I was being charged with a crime? And why this urge to apologize? The calm demeanor of my colleagues merely increased my disquiet. Don't they know? Or are they pretending not to know? They will not believe me if I say anything, and apart from that, I don't know what to say; and if I only knew how to express what I feel, my discomfort.

...Then we saw a woman standing in a group of three or four. She was holding the hand of a boy of about seven. There was something special about her, she looked resolute, restrained, stiff with grief. Tears, which seemed unconnected to her, trickled down her cheeks. And the little boy was sobbing a kind of tight-lipped, "what have you done to us?"

....We saw that something was happening in that child's heart, which when he grew to manhood could be nothing but a viper, but that something was now the weeping of a helpless child. Something came to me like a flash of lightning. Suddenly everything sounded different, truer: exile, this is exile. This is what it is. This is what exile looks like.

"Why are you looking at me like that," said Moishe.

"It's a dirty war," I said, my voice strangled.

"Come on!" said Moishe, "so what is it you want?"

There was something I wanted, and I had something to say.

..."Now you listen to me!" said Moishe, trying to trap my gaze: "As for this Hirbet-whatever its called, immigrants are going to come here, do you hear me, and they'll take over this land and cultivate it, and this place will be great!"

Of course. What else! Quite so! How did I fail to see it from the beginning? Hirbet Hiz'a is ours. Questions of housing and absorption problems! Hurray, we will house and absorb: we'll open a village store, set up a school, perhaps a synagogue as well. There will be political parties, people will argue about all kinds of subjects. They will plough fields and sow and reap and expand. Long live Hebrew Hiz'a! Who could ever imagine that once it was Hirbet Hiz'a; that we banished people and inherited. We came, we shot, we burned, we detonated, we shoved and pushed and exiled.

In God's name, what are we doing in this place?

...I wanted to do something. I knew I was not going to cry out. Why, why in hell, was I the only one who was so affected. What was I made of? I had complicated things this time. There was something rebellious in me, something iconoclastic. Who would listen to me? They would only laugh at me. I felt a stunning sense of collapse. There was a single conviction planted in me, like a hammered nail; I knew that I could not reconcile myself to all this, as long as tears glinted in the eyes of a child departing with his restrained mother in a fury of soundless tears, going into exile, carrying with him his howl of injustice and a scream of such intensity that it cannot be that there is nobody to hear it when the time comes – so I said to Moishe: "Moishe, we have no right to take them out of this place!" and I did not want my voice to shake.

And Moishe said: "Oh you, you're starting again!"

And I knew that nothing would come of it.

And I felt nothing but regret, choking regret.

May, 1949

A reprisal raid in Kalkiliya

Mordechai Gur (later Lieut. Gen and commander-in chief of the IDF), briefing a unit of the Nahal Parachute Division before a reprisal raid, (bearded, fourth right future Maj. Gen Danny Matt)

How Cruel is War

Meir Har-Zion

"Meir Har-Zion was a true fighter, the greatest fighter we ever had," wrote Ariel Sharon, founder of Unit 101, commander of the paratroopers and future prime-minister of Israel, in the foreword to Har-Zion's book "Chapters from a Diary."

Meir Har-Zion, legendary hero of Unit 101 and the paratroopers, was known for his fearlessness. He was an outstanding figure in the reprisal raids conducted by the IDF across the borders in response to acts of murder and looting by infiltrators. In his book, Har-Zion revealed that he was often afraid but overcame his fear by force of will. In January 1954, on a freezing winter night, he led a group of four fighters on a raid on the town of Hebron, 21 kilometers inside enemy territory. On the way there, he was beset by hesitations. "Everything here is so alien," he wrote later in his diary. "We are so remote from anything safe, close, from people who care for us... I look at this small force. We're so small and weak! Suddenly I'm stricken with dread, appalling dread. I have the feeling that every tree and bush is staring at us, watching us, plotting against us. I feel small and weak, helpless against what faces me. I want to hide, to disappear, to be protected, but now, of all times, the light of the full moon seems so harsh, so hostile... I continue to march, clutching my tommy-gun. I must overcome this crisis, I know it will pass. We will get there!"

Meir Har-Zion was severely wounded in one of the reprisal raids and underwent surgery on the battlefield under enemy fire.

The famed Commando Unit 101. Ariel Sharon (right) with Meir Har-Zion

Are These Fellahin to Blame?

September 1953

Night-time near Kissufim. Tranquil moonlight spilling over the vast expanses which stretch in all directions. The lights of Jewish settlements are winking and glimmering on one side and the lights of the villages of the Gaza Strip are gleaming on the other. The monotonous roar of the waves is interrupted from time to time by the screech of a lone owl. We move ahead faster. Here is the border before us – a deep furrow in the ground. There is tension. A village lies ahead of us. The single file of ten men crouches down. Two go out to check and return, and we move on.

A wide, dry riverbed. We advance cautiously along it. Several houses are gleaming on the riverbank, dark bushes rustling in the wind. Three bright lights appear up ahead and the sound of a wailing Arabic melody rises from among the dark buildings. We split into three four-man units, two of them making for the south and the vast refugee camp and one for an isolated building on the plain north of Wadi Gaza. We advance. Our feet trample cultivated vegetable plots, sink into channels of flowing water. The quiet radiance of a full moon illuminates the scene. In a few minutes this peace will be disrupted and will turn into the roar of gunfire, the flash of explosions and the cries of those now sleeping peacefully in their homes.

We approach rapidly, slipping between the first houses. *Man hadh?* ("Who's there")?

We leap towards the voice. Two Arabs are standing by the wall of the building, frozen in terror. They try to escape; I shoot. There is a scream of pain. One falls, the other keeps running. Now we have to act, because there's no time. We speed between the buildings. Panic-stricken people are scuttling about the narrow alleyways. Short bursts of gunfire on all sides, mingling with bloodcurdling cries rising from among the houses. The submachine guns spit fire. We reach the main road of the refugee camp where more and more people are in flight. The second unit bursts through, grenades are exploding.

The order to withdraw is given. The operation is over. We return. Again the electric lights wink ahead of us and the oil-lamps gleam behind us. There are random bursts of machine-gun fire from the Egyptian positions. The night breeze cools our burning faces. Suddenly we are dejected. Is this the enemy? This screaming and wailing crowd; is it they who loot our property, threaten our lives? Are they the enemy? The sight of the tranquil vegetable plots is still fresh in my memory. Are these fellahin [Arab village farmers] to blame?

Yes, war is cruel, even the smallest of wars.

From Meir Har-Zion: "Chapters from a Diary," 1969.

The Gates of Gaza Weighed Too Heavily Upon Him

Moshe Dayan

At the height of the reprisal raids (1953-1956) the IDF chief-of-staff, Moshe Dayan, delivered this eulogy over the fresh grave of Ro'i Rothberg, security coordinator of Kibbutz Nahal Oz, who was killed by Egyptian soldiers.

Yesterday morning Ro'i was killed. The quiet of a spring morning dazzled him, and he failed to see those who lurked in wait for him behind the furrows. Let us not, today, hurl accusations at the killers. Why should we complain at their fierce hatred of us? For eight years they have been sitting in refugee camps in Gaza, and have watched as, before their very eyes, we transform the land and the villages where they and their forefathers dwelt into our home.

"It is not from the Arabs of Gaza, but among ourselves that we should seek Roi's blood. How could we have failed to look our fate in the eye, to see the destiny of our generation in all its brutality? Have we forgotten that this group of young people, living in Nahal Oz, bear on their shoulders the heavy gates of Gaza, gates beyond which are crowded hundreds of thousands of eyes and hands, praying for our weakness, so as to tear us to pieces – have we forgotten this? For we know that, in order for their hope of annihilating us to die away, it is incumbent on us – morning, noon and night – to be armed and ready. We are the generation of settlement, and without the steel helmet and the cannon's mouth we cannot plant a tree nor build a house.

Roi's blood cries out to us from his mangled body. Although we swore a thousand times that our blood would not be spilled in vain, yesterday we were beguiled once more; we listened and we believed. Let us conduct a reckoning with ourselves today. Let us not shrink from seeing the enmity, which attends and fills the lives of hundreds of thousands of Arabs, who dwell around us and await the moment when they can spill our blood. Let us not lower our gaze lest our arm be weakened. This is the decree of our generation. This is our only choice – to be ready and armed, hardy and unyielding, for if the sword slips from our hands – our lives will be cut short.

Ro'i Rothberg, the lean blond youth who left Tel Aviv to build a home at the gates of Gaza, to be a bulwark for us all; Ro'i – the light in his heart blinded his eyes, and he did not see the glint of the knife. The yearning for peace dulled his hearing, and he did not hear the sound of lurking murder. The gates of Gaza weighed too heavily upon him and crushed him.

Nahal Oz, 1956

Paratroopers at the Mitla Pass, the Sinai Campaign, October, 1956

Operation Kadesh – the Sinai Campaign

Order of the Day

Armored tank column, Sinai, 1956

Top Secret – for the recipient's eyes only
25 October, 1956
To: Head of Operations

Subject: Operational Instructions

Aim:

a. To create a military threat to the [Suez] canal by seizing targets adjacent to it

b. To conquer the Straits of Eilat

c. To interdict the Egyptian forces in Sinai and to cause their collapse

Method:

General: D-Day, Monday, 29.10.56

H-Hour: 17.00 hours

Stages:

First stage: Night of D-Day (29-30.10)

a. To seize by means of a paratrooper force the junction Sudar-el-Haitan on the route Nakhel-Suez

b. To capture Nakhel

c. To capture Kuntilla and Ras el-Nakeb

d. To secure the route Kusseima – Nakhel

e. To secure the route Kuntilla – Nakhel

f. To secure the route Ras el-Nakeb – Nakhel

g. Defensive readiness from dawn of 30.10 in the other [regional] commands

h. Full operational readiness in the air force and navy to carry out the following tasks: Defense of the country's skies, aid to the ground forces, attacking Egyptian airfields.

Second stage: Night of D-Day+1 (30-31.10)

a. To advance on axis Ras el-Nakeb – Sharm el-Sheikh so as to capture Sharm el-Sheikh

b. To be in readiness for a counter-attack on the Jordanian front

c. To capture Kusseima

d. Defensive readiness along the Syrian and Lebanese borders

Third stage: Night of D-Day+2 (31.10 – 1.11 and thereafter)

a. To capture the Straits of Eilat

b. To capture Rafiah, Abu-Aguila, and el-Arish

c. To form a defensive line parallel to the canal and not less than 15 kms to the east

d. To secure the route Sudar-el-Haitan via Bir Mor and al-Tur to Sharm el-Sheikh and securing the route from Abu Zneima to Dahab

Moshe Dayan, Lieut. Gen.
Commander-in-Chief

Lieut. Gen. Moshe Dayan, chief of general staff, reads a letter from Prime Minister David Ben-Gurion at a parade marking the termination of the Sinai Campaign. Right. Col. Avraham Yoffe, left: Maj.Gen. Assaf Simhoni, Sharm el-Sheikh, 1956

The Third Kingdom of Israel

David Ben-Gurion

The Sinai Campaign of 1956, also known as "Operation Kadesh," ended in total victory, and David Ben-Gurion sent an emotional message to the fighters of the 9th Brigade who captured the small Red Sea fortress of Sharm el-Sheikh. The next day the whole world – the great powers, the United Nations, Africa and Asia – were to force Israel, through threats and censuring resolutions, to withdraw from Sinai.

To the soldiers and commanders of the Ninth Brigade –

You have been afforded a unique historical privilege: you have brought to successful conclusion the greatest and most splendid military operation in the annals of our people, and one of the most splendid in human history. In less than seven days the whole of the Sinai Peninsula, including the Gaza Strip, was cleared of enemy forces from the Straits of Eilat to Rafiah, el-Arish, Qantara, and from Nitzana to the Red Sea in the south.

...Thanks to the coordinated mighty momentum of all the IDF forces - you have stretched out a hand to King Solomon who developed Eilat as the first Israeli port three thousand years ago and from there sent his ships to Tarshish.

Once again Eilat will be the Hebrew port of the south and the Red Sea straits will be opened to Israeli shipping; and Yotvat, known as the Isle of Tiran, which, until one thousand four hundred years ago, was an independent Hebrew state – will once again be part of the Third Kingdom of Israel.

All honor to the victorious Israel Defense Forces.

David Ben-Gurion, 6 November, 1956

At Mount Sinai

Yehiel Mohar

It is no legend, my friend,
And not a passing dream.
Because here at Mount Sinai
The bush is burning still.
And now our youth will sing
A melody of flame,
And at the city gates
Our Samson stands again.

Now the holy flame burns in our hearts once more
'Tis the holy flame - as all the engines roar.
Brothers, we'll tell this day's tale again,
How we returned to stand before Sinai.

It is no dream, my friend,
Nor a fleeting vision,
for from that time till now,
The bush remains in flame.
And still it's burning bright,
Within the minds and hearts
Of the youth of Zion
And the chariots of Israel.

"Sharm el-Sheikh – we have returned to you again..."
Prime Minister Levi Eshkol in the Straits of Tiran, following the Six-Day War, 1967

Jerusalem of Gold

Naomi Shemer

The song "Jerusalem of Gold" written and composed by Naomi Shemer, became the unofficial hymn of the Six-Day War of 1967 and subsequently has been sung in hundreds of versions and languages throughout the world.

The mountain air is clear as wine
The scent of pines around
Is carried on the breeze of twilight,
And tinkling bells resound.

The trees and stones there softly
slumber,
A dream enfolds them all.
So solitary lies the city,
And at its heart - a wall.

The wells ran dry of water,
Forlorn the market square,
The Temple Mount dark and deserted,
In the Old City there.

And in the caverns in the mountain,
The winds howl to and fro,
And no-one takes the Dead Sea
highway,
That leads through Jericho.

But as I sing to you, my city,
And you with crowns adorn,
I am the least of all your children,
Of all the poets born.

Your name will scorch my lips for
ever,
Like a seraph's kiss, I'm told,
If I forget thee, golden city,
Jerusalem of Gold.

The wells are filled again with water,
The square with joyous crowd,
On the Temple Mount within the City,
The shofar rings out loud.

Within the caverns in the mountains,
A thousand suns will glow,
We'll take the Dead Sea road together,
That runs through Jericho.

Jerusalem of gold and of light and of
bronze,
I am the lute for all your songs.
*Yerushalayim shel zahav veshel
nekhoshet veshel or
Halo lekhol shirayikh ani kinor*

Ammunition Hill

Yoram Teharlev

Yoram Teharlev turned the survivors' reports into a powerful description, in prose and verse, of the battle for Jerusalem's Ammunition Hill.

"It was the morning of the second day of the war, the eastern horizon was paling. It was the height of the battle for Ammunition Hill. We fought there for three hours. It was a fierce, bloody battle. The Jordanians fought stubbornly. Their positions were highly fortified. At a certain stage of the battle, only four soldiers were left beside me. We had started out with a force two companies strong. I didn't know where the others were because contact with Dodik the CO was cut off at the beginning of the battle. At that moment I thought that everyone had been killed.

Ammunition Hill,
surrounded by
trenches, bunkers and
firing positions, Six-Day
War, Jerusalem, 1967

At two p.m or half past two,
We came across the rocky
ground,
Onto a minefield full of fire
On Ammunition Hill.

Opposite the fortified
bunkers
And 120 mm. mortars
A hundred or so young guys
On Ammunition Hill.

The dawn had not yet risen,
And half the force was
steeped in blood,
But we were there, yes, we
were there,
On Ammunition Hill.

Between the fences and the
mines,
We left the medics in the rear,
And ran without a single
thought
To Ammunition Hill.

At that moment a grenade was hurled from outside. By some miracle we were not hit. I was afraid the Jordanians would throw more grenades. Someone had to run down to check. I had no time to ask who'd volunteer. I sent Eytan. Eytan didn't hesitate for a moment, ran and started to fire the sub-machine gun. Sometimes he ran ahead of me and I had at shout to him to stay in place. We advanced about 30 meters in that way. Eytan gave us covering fire as we cleaned out the bunkers, till he was hit in the head and fell in.

Jordanian communication trenches on Ammunition Hill

We went down into trenches deep,
Into the warrens and the paths,
And death was waiting in the tunnels
Of Ammunition Hill.

Those who fell were left behind
In case they held the others back,
Until the next in line was hit
On Ammunition Hill.

And no-one asked: Why go this way?
Those who went first were first to fall,
You needed quite a bit of luck
On Ammunition Hill.

Maybe we were lions there,
And those who wanted to survive,
Should not have been there on that day
On Ammunition Hill.

We decided to try to blow up their bunker with a bazooka. It only scratched the concrete. We decided to try explosives. I waited up above until the guy with the explosives came. He threw them to me parcel by parcel and I positioned them one by one at the entrance to the bunker. They had a method: first they hurled a grenade, then they fired a volley, then they rested. So, in the interval between volleys and grenades, I crawled over to the entrance to the bunker and set the explosives. I lit the fuse and moved as far back as I could. I had only four meters for maneuvering, because there were legionnaires behind me as well.

I don't know why they gave me a medal. All I wanted was to get home safe and sound.

At seven p.m or seven twenty,
At the Police Academy building
We gathered all those left alive
On Ammunition Hill.

Seven came back into the city,
And smoke was rising from the hill.
The sun was high up in the east
On Ammunition Hill.

Smoke was rising from the hill,
The sun was high up in the east.
And only seven of us returned
From Ammunition Hill.

On all the concrete bunkers there,
On all our dear comrades in arms,
Left behind, forever young,
On Ammunition Hill.

"The Temple Mount is in our Hands!"

Mordechai Gur

Mordechai (Motta) Gur (1930-1995), was Israel's chief-of-staff, a Knesset member and a government minister. In the Six-Day War he served, with the rank of colonel, as commander of a reserve paratrooper brigade. This is his address to the troops he commanded in the battle for the Temple Mount and the liberation of the Western Wall, delivered at a parade held on the Mount.

Left: Forward command group of the Parachute Brigade overlooking the Temple Mount from the Mount of Olives, Jerusalem
Below: Paratroopers break into the Old City through the Lion's Gate

Paratroopers, Conquerers of Jerusalem!

When the Temple Mount was captured by the Greeks, the Maccabees liberated it. The zealots and Bar Kochba fought against the destroyers of the Second Temple.

For 2000 years, Jews were barred from the Temple Mount until you, the paratroopers, came and restored it to the bosom of the nation. The Western Wall, for which every Jewish heart yearns, is in our hands once again.

Many Jews have risked their lives throughout our long history in order to find their way to Jerusalem and live here… In the War of Independence great efforts were invested in restoring the heart of the nation – the Old City and the Western Wall – to the people

You have been privileged to complete the circle, to give back to the people their eternal capital and their sacred core.

Many paratroopers, the oldest and finest of our comrades, fell in this bitter struggle. In that fierce and resolute battle, you fought as one, overcoming everything in your path, paying no heed to your own injuries.

You did not complain, you did not murmur, you did not answer back. You merely forged ahead – and conquered. Jerusalem is yours – for ever.

12 June, 1967

The Western Wall – in Jewish hands once again

Eulogy on the Dead of the Armored Corps

Shmuel Gonen

Col. Shmuel Gonen ("Gorodish" - 1930-1991) commanded the Seventh Brigade in the Six-Day War and was CO Southern Command in the Yom Kippur War of 1973.

You were the spearhead of the armored onslaught against the hard core of the Egyptian army, the largest and most assertive of enemy forces. In a cruel and bitter fight, marked by glory and heroism, we stormed through their fortified positions and broke through … destroying their armor at Khan Yunis, Rafiah, Sheikh Zuweid, Jiradi and el-Arish, at Bir Lahfan and Bir Hama and along the path of blood and fire leading to Ismailia. Wherever we passed, we left behind us the skeletons of tanks.

We stared death in the eye and it lowered its gaze. Because we fought as Jews, we fought for our lives. We fought with fury.

My warrior comrades, you yourselves did not know how splendid was your courage. And when I saw armored vehicles split open and burning, and you, the men inside them, continuing to fight, I knew that these men were made of steel – while the armor was mere metal…

Tanks advancing in Sinai, 1967

Sinai, 1967

The Sirens Wailed

Eitan Haber

Eitan Haber, journalist and writer, was director of the office of Prime Minister Yitzhak Rabin. In this article, he describes the surprise attack by Syria and Egypt against Israel in the Yom Kippur War.

Statisticians say that of almost seven million people living in Israel today, only some two million were here on that day, at that hour. The others were either not yet born or had not yet arrived in the country. So how can one describe to those who were not here what "surprise" means in a war, and who did not freeze to the spot when they heard the wail of the sirens. Where are the words, where are the writers to describe today, 30 years later even one moment, one or two minutes of that Yom Kippur noontime in 1973.

How can one describe a surprise attack?

Should one describe a country wrapped in prayer-shawls, the quiet which descended on the streets, the *Kol Nidrei* melody [The opening lament of the Yom Kippur prayers] wafting from the windows of the synagogues? Or perhaps we should write about David Nahlieli who fasted on Yom Kippur on the Mount Hermon fortified position and gazed from the height of the mountain at the quiet stretched out below him? Or Shlomo Ardinst, who was spending yet another holy day at the jetty position at the edge of the Suez Canal, and spied Egyptian soldiers preparing to wade across? Or perhaps one should describe how, in the early hours of the morning, the chief of staff, Dado Elazar, realized the gravity of the situation and from then on kept glancing at his watch, as if he knew that every moment that passed was one of the most fateful the State of Israel had ever known? Where were you on that Yom Kippur at 2 p.m.? The two million people in the State of Israel remember exactly where they were and will never forget.

Yediot Aharonot, 5 October, 2003

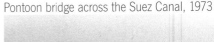
Pontoon bridge across the Suez Canal, 1973

The Oath

Michael Bar-Zohar

On the Eastern bank of the Suez Canal, 1973

On the night of October 15, 1973, at the height of the Yom Kippur War, we launched our long-delayed attempt to cross the Suez Canal. I had joined the paratrooper brigade entrusted with that mission. Some of our half-tracks were late in arriving at the paratroopers' camp, so we had to leave one battalion behind and set out on our way, a rather small unit of reserve paratroopers. I had been assigned a place on the command half-track, together with the brigade commander. Night had fallen as we crossed the front lines and started our journey toward the canal.

Our convoy sped westward on the desert road. A black strip it was, narrow, frail and ravaged by the winds and the sun, spearing through the wavy dunes. In the pale moonlight the desert glowed with a dull-grey hue. I sat silent in my corner, staring ahead, as strange thoughts and images ran through my mind. The road stretched like a ruler toward a blurred horizon, whose center pulsated in a red, evil incandescence. It looked like the fringe of a huge ball of fire, a red sun tearing the night, its smoky glow expanding and shrinking in unison with the approaching thunder of cannon. The battle was there. Seen from above, I thought our column must look like a convoy of damned souls heading to its doom.

…The entire operation was an act of folly. Seven hundred and sixty paratroopers, carrying small arms, machine guns, and mortars, had to cross six miles held by tens of thousands of Egyptians, reach the Suez Canal, cross it on their launches, and establish a bridgehead on its African bank. And because it was pure folly, it had a chance of success. No sane Egyptian general would ever believe the Israelis would be so suicidal.

…We kept progressing, past the charred carcasses of Israeli tanks and supply trucks. The vehicles had been destroyed during the desperate battles of the first two days of the war. Some bodies were lying on the sand, ten or maybe twelve, in two parallel lines. "Our boys," Ron said. "Captured, disarmed, then shot." I looked up, but Ron had retreated into the darkness. And from the dark came his low whisper. "We'll do the same to them. No prisoners." I found myself nodding back. No prisoners. No prisoners, I heard some paratroopers mutter hoarsely. And the grim slogan spread like lightning inside our half-track, mysteriously reaching the other vehicles.

…The oath of revenge burned in my heart all that night and the next day. The blazing menorah on the crossroads kept haunting me, as did the rows of rigid bodies lying cold and forlorn beside the road. I had seen so much death before, in Israel's former wars. I was seeing it again today, during the fierce fighting that started at dawn on the African bank of the canal; at the assault of the Purple compound, to the north of the bridgehead; at the desperate battle at Sarafeum railway station where our scout unit was attacked by throngs of Egyptian commandos; on the road to Ismailia.

But no death in battle, no pain for a fallen comrade, no feeling of helplessness under an air raid or a murderous artillery onslaught could be compared to the rage caused by the memory of the dead soldiers bathed by the cold moonlight. We had always gone to war to kill and be killed, to face an enemy in battle. But this was assassination. I felt that last night's grim discovery had released, deep in my soul, an unsuspected load of hatred and ugly determination. And only the certainty of the forthcoming revenge kept me going through this first day across the canal.

Sundown was near when Ron and I walked into a small enclosure a few hundred yards west of the bridgehead. It was surrounded by a half-ruined fence made of rough-hewn stones. About a dozen paratroopers were waiting inside, some of them lying on the ground, smoking, others leaning on the shoulder-high fence. In the far corner, behind two lengths of concertina wire, squatted about twenty Egyptian prisoners.

…Ron was beside me, cocking his weapon.

"Let's get it over with, boys," he said, his voice unusually loud. "No prisoners, remember?"

…Nobody fired. Ron stirred, irritated. "What are you waiting for?" he asked.

A redheaded lanky paratrooper cleared his throat. "Listen," he started, gauchely shifting his weight from one foot to the other.

"What now?" the body standing beside him said angrily.

"Listen," the redheaded soldier stammered. He seemed embarrassed, groping for words. "We should blow their heads off, I am all for it. Cut off their balls too. Only I…" He looked about him, searching for help. "I can't do it."

"What's wrong?" Ron hissed. "You chicken now? Afraid?"

The redhead spread his arms helplessly. "No, I mean, I approve of the decision and I'll share responsibility. If they throw you in jail, I'll go with you. But I can't do it, that's all. I've never killed somebody like that, in cold blood." He turned and walked to the opposite wall, trying to light a cigarette with unsteady fingers.

"You call that cold blood?" the Rumanian shouted at him. "After all that they did over there?"

"Leave him alone," Alex said. Somebody had told me Alex was a real killer; he had distinguished himself at the Battle of Jerusalem, in the Six-Day War. "The guy's right. We've never done it like that." He stepped forward and turned to face us. In the quickly fading twilight his features were blurred. The prostrated Egyptian raised his head. "Don't get me wrong," Alex said. "I am with you. You want to shoot them, go ahead. I agree. Only I can't do it. Never shot an unarmed soldier before."

"But they did," Ron grunted.

"Okay, so go ahead, what's stopping you?" Alex stepped aside and slung his submachine gun on his shoulder.

Nobody moved.

"Well," a frail birdlike fellow standing beside me quipped, "till you make up your minds, I'll give some water to that sonofabitch over there. He's wounded." Without waiting for approval, he crossed the yard, uncapping his canteen, and approached the wounded Egyptian.

"F… you!" Ron yelled after him. But the line had already broken, and a couple of others approached the prisoners. "Hey, Sabag, have you got any cigarettes?" somebody called and a voice answered "Sure."

"F… you all!" Ron muttered again, but his voice carried the ring of defeat. He turned and walked out of the yard.

Darkness was falling. Somebody pulled back the concertina wire around the prisoners. I couldn't see my comrades' faces anymore. A lump had formed in my throat and I swallowed painfully. All of a sudden I felt very proud. And very grateful to those boys, to the redhead, and to Alex and Sabag and the skinny one who had been next to me, for not trying to explain their behavior by some pompous nonsense about being Jewish and Israeli and humane and pure. Actually I was ready to bet that if asked, they wouldn't even be able to say why they couldn't pull the trigger. That's why I loved those clumsy, awkward, inarticulate boys and the land that made them. I wanted to hug the kid who had spoken first. Only in the dark they all looked the same.

Facing a Cruel Mirror, 1989

"Hey soldier – do you have any cigarettes?"
Egyptian prisoners of war

The Music Must Carry On

Oded Feldman

At a ceremony held after the Yom Kippur War to celebrate the return of Israeli pilots from Syrian captivity, the Air Force commanding officer, Maj. Gen.Benny Peled said, in his speech: "This melody must never stop. We must carry on with the music..." Lieut. Col. Oded Feldman, the Air Force chief education officer, turned these words into a song which became widely popular.

This melody must never stop,
This melody must never stop.
We must carry on the music,
We must carry on playing,
Because this melody must never stop.

Number 2 from Hardal squadron – gone.
Number 4 from Egoz squadron – gone.
Like a great harp with a thousand strings
Which plays on and on and on.

And from time to time a string snaps
Yet it continues to play with one string less,

And another string less
And some strings snap and never return,
But others return and continue to play
Because this melody must never stop
We must carry on playing.

Phantom fighter plane taking off

Col. Yoni Netanyahu, commander of the Entebbe rescue mission before setting out

Our Yoni

Ehud Barak

Ehud Barak has been chief of staff, cabinet minister and prime minister. As head of the elite General Staff Commando Unit, he was the commanding officer and personal friend of Yonatan ("Yoni") Netanyahu, who was killed in 1976 leading the Entebbe rescue operation. In that daring military raid, thousands of kilometers from home, paratroopers and commandos landed on the airfield of Entebbe in Uganda, East Africa, where a group of Arab and German terrorists were holding Jewish and Israeli hostages after the hijacking of an Air France aircraft. The plane was flown from airport to airport in Africa and eventually found a refuge in the country of dictator Idi Amin.

The Israeli troops landed on the airfield in several transport planes. They broke into the hall where the hostages were being held and took the hijackers by surprise. All the hijackers were killed and all but one of the hostages were saved. However, the planes which brought the survivors home also carried the body of the raid's commander, Yoni Netanyahu.

This is not a eulogy for Yoni; nor general remarks about him, only some thoughts about the way he fell – comrade, warrior, an officer whose commander I was privileged to be, a human being.

In synagogues throughout the centuries our forefathers used to recite the words:

"Know from whence you come, where you are going and before whom you will render an account. From whence - from a fetid drop, where – to dust and worms. And to whom you will render account – to the King of Kings, the Holy One blessed be He."

When one sees the random – though not unsymbolic – way in which death selects its victims on the battlefield – the way in which death chose our Yoni; when from time to time you face another corpse in a long line of graves of the best of your comrades- you cannot but wonder at the meaning of life between the beginning and the end and the meaning of that reckoning.

Perhaps that question has no complete answer and it certainly does not have a single answer...

If there can be any consolation for a life cut short at 30 – this is the consolation.

Our Yoni. We saw him torn again and again between the thirst for knowledge and the sense of mission and the satisfaction gained from military action. Yoni of books of history and of philosophy – Plato and Marx; Klausner and Raymond Aron.

Yoni observing Jewish history not as a collection of facts but as a source of individual exhortations to action.

Yoni who rehabilitated an armored battalion which had been decimated by the battle for the Golan Heights.

And the serene domestic Yoni, with his pipe and his records – without his uniform.

We saw him in his crowning moments of satisfaction and achievement and also when – in pain and with gritted teeth he took on the heavy burden of solitude as commander of the unit at whose head he was to fall – with courage, with wisdom and with unflinching spirit...

We cannot bring back Yoni the human being, but Yoni the heritage and the symbol – that undaunted spirit; that warm heart with its thirst for knowledge, that faith in the justice of his path and that readiness to sacrifice himself to the very end – all these we can – if we choose – adopt for ourselves, and bequeath to those who follow.

And if we can do all this – we will be building Yoni's monument, and there can be none more important, nor more beautiful.

Jerusalem, 1976

Embarking on the Entebbe mission

The released hostages disembarking in Israel after their rescue in Entebbe

Eretz

Ehud Manor

"Operation Peace for Galilee" the war in South Lebanon of 1991, caused a deep rift in the nation and bitter public dispute. Ehud Manor (1942-2005) was personally opposed to the military operations, but nevertheless penned these words which became a slogan for all Israelis from left or from right, who love their country.

I have no other country
Even though my land is blazing
Just a Hebrew word invading
My veins, my inner soul
A body hurt – a heart of thirst
Here is my home.

I will not rest, for my country's face has veered
I will not let her, I'll tell her
And I will sing here in her ear
Until her eyes become clear.

I have no other country
Until her days should reappear
Until her eyes become clear.

Translated by Chaya Evelyn Abel

To be Continued

Meir Wieseltier

With shocking prophetic insight, the poet Meir Wieseltier anticipated the war in Lebanon ("Operation Peace for Galilee") four years before it actually occurred.

War is the continuation of politics,
and South Lebanon is the continuation of Upper Galilee:
Therefore it's all too natural for a state
to wage war in Lebanon.

Youth is the continuation of childhood,
and South Lebanon is the continuation of Upper Galilee:
Therefore it's all too natural for boys and young men
to shoot at each other in Lebanon.

Grave-digging is the continuation of the rabbinate,
and South Lebanon is the continuation of Upper Galilee:
Therefore it's all too natural for the Army Rabbinical

Burial Corps to dig fresh graves in Lebanon.
The press is the continuation of idle blabber,
and South Lebanon is the continuation of Upper Galilee:
Therefore newspapers discuss with high solemnity
the achievements of the war in Lebanon.

Poetry is the opposite of statement
in South Lebanon as well as in the Upper Galilee.
Therefore what was stated is as good as unstated,
and again we'll wage war in Lebanon.

2 April, 1978

Translated by Shirley Kaufman with the author

Israeli forces withdraw from Lebanon after Operation "Peace for Galilee"

167

Jerusalem bus route no.14, 8.30 am, 22 February, 2004

Victory in the Profound Sense of the Word

Amnon Rubinstein

No, we are not the victors in the war of terror declared against us by the Palestinians. They have not surrendered and we are not celebrating our triumph over them. On the contrary – our fears at the thought of renewal of terror are great just as the prospects of ending the dispute are small. But there is a partial ceasefire and Israel has always known how to recover strength during ceasefires.

...No, we have not won but Arafat has failed in his dual scheme: to break our spirit in order to force us into flight as was the case in Southern Lebanon and to bring about the internationalization of the dispute and the dispatch of foreign forces to the region. Arafat has not received aid from Arab states in his struggle. Jordan and Egypt withdrew their ambassadors from Israel but did not rally to Arafat's side. In Europe, Israel's standing has been undermined in public opinion but the European Union did not propose sending troops. In the United States, Arafat is irrelevant, and Russia has not held out a hand.

No, we have not won, but Israeli society – to the surprise of many – has displayed magnificent resilience.

...Israeli society has passed another test, no less important: despite the terror, despite the aid extended by several Israeli Arabs to terrorists, despite the vicious provocation on the part of Arab Knesset members – Israel has not experienced riots of ethnic origin, of the type which occurred in northern Ireland or former Yugoslavia, nor have there been shocking incidents such as those which occurred in France – where, innocent Arab bystanders were murdered and their corpses thrown into the Seine or hurled out of a train. Moreover, although violence and terror usually generate a shift to the right, in Israel the opposite has occurred. In Belgium, in Austria, in France and in Holland, the right-wing parties gained strength because of the opposition to Moslem immigrants although those countries had not suffered from terror...in Israel the public voted massively for the Likud, but only after the prime minister announced his support for "painful concessions" and for the establishment of a Palestinian state. In which other democratic country did a similar process occur during times of war? Hence one might say that in the most profound sense of the word, Israel did in fact win, because during three years of continuous nightmare, it proved its robustness and political moderation.

Ha'aretz, 10 July, 2003

Shahida

Agi Mishol

Agi Mishol, one of Israel's leading poets, addresses her poem to a young Arab girl who became a suicide bomber.

You are only twenty
and your first pregnancy is an exploding bomb.
Under your broad skirt you are pregnant with dynamite
and metal shavings. This is how you walk in the market,
ticking among the people, you,
Andalib Takatkah.

Someone changed the workings in your head
and launched you towards the city;

even though you come from Bethlehem,
the Home of Bread, you chose a bakery.
And there you pulled the trigger inside yourself,
and together with the Sabbath loaves,
sesame and poppy seed,
you flung yourself into the sky.

Together with Rebecca Fink you flew up
with Yelena Konreeb from the Caucasus
and Nissim Cohen from Afghanistan
and Souhila Houshy from Iran

and two Chinese you swept along
to death.

Since then other matters
have obscured your story,
about which I speak all the time
without having anything to say.

Translated by Lisa Katz

168

Why are You Crying?

Haim Gouri

Sonia Levakov, known as "the old lady" had four sons. She is now about 85. I knew two of them, Zvi, who fell in 1948 and Haim (Haimke) Levakov, may he enjoy long life. I never met G., who served in the British Army in the Second World War. He was severely wounded, suffered a great deal and died a lingering death. Nor did I ever meet the fourth brother.

I know Haimke very well. He is one of the finest sons of Eretz Israel....I was told he had recently celebrated the marriage of his daughter, Zvia, who is named after Zvi.

A volunteer serves out refreshments to the troops, Yom Kippur War, October, 1973

People said it was a wonderful wedding. It was held, if I'm not mistaken, in the Circassian village of Kafr Kama in Lower Galilee, between Kfar Tabor and Yavne'el. There was singing and sword dancing and sheep were slaughtered. Zvia married Amit, a member of one of the kibbutzim in the Megiddo area. He was killed in battle in the Yom Kippur War.

Haimke went home to his village to tell his old mother about the death of his son-in-law. He found her standing at the kiosk, which was what he jokingly called her stall. Outside her house in the village, the old lady had set up a stall where she handed out free sandwiches and coffee and cookies to the soldiers who passed through. She also did their laundry. He told her that Amit had been killed, but she didn't budge from the stall. She said she had to continue to serve the soldiers on their way north. Everyone has to do their duty at such a time, she said, and so do I. The next day she came to the kibbutz where her granddaughter was sitting shiva [the Jewish seven days of mourning] with the parents of her dead husband and his family. She saw them weeping and was silent for a long time. When they continued to cry, the old lady raised her voice and asked: "Why are you crying?... Did he die in a pogrom?!"

Davar, 8 February, 1974

Memorial Prayer for the Fallen (*Yizkor*)

May the people of Israel remember their sons and daughters, loyal and courageous soldiers in the Israel Defence Forces, who laid down their lives in Israel's battles.

May Israel remember and take pride in their children, and mourn the radiant youth and bravery, the blessed will and dedication, which succumbed to the bitter fighting. May the victorious heroes of this generation be sealed in the hearts of Israel for ever and ever.

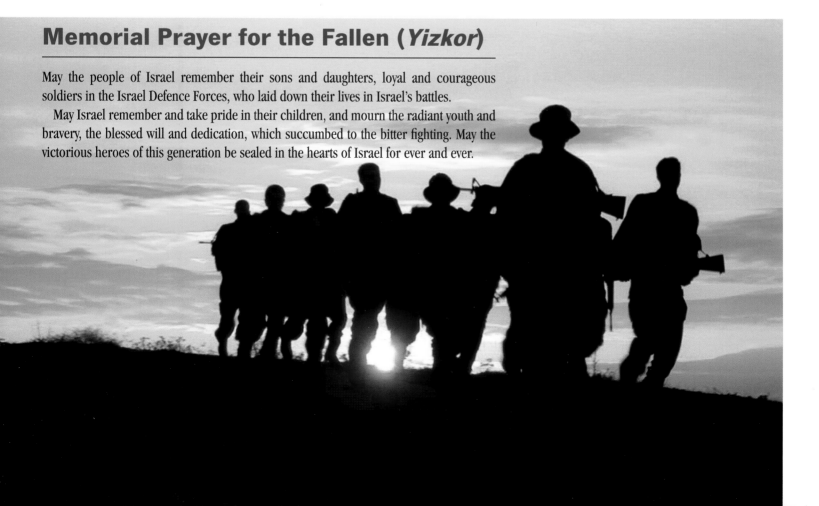

Chapter 9

The Independence Day Torch

I, Yelma Radai from Beersheba, am honored to kindle this torch on the 36th anniversary of the State of Israel.

In honor of my brothers and sisters who are returning with pride to their homeland.

In honor of those who were themselves once immigrants and who now welcome newer immigrants with endless love and devotion.

In honor of those who have volunteered to help their people and are participating in the release of their brothers and sisters from hardship.

And to the glory of Israel.

Eve of Independence Day, 1999

...FOR JEWISH IMMIGRATION AND THE INGATHERING OF THE EXILES

"Operation Solomon": Ethiopian immigrants landing in Israel, May, 1991
Background: Immigrants from Europe released from British displaced persons camps in Cyprus arrive in Israel, 1948

171

From the Four Corners of the Earth

Immigrants from the four corners of the earth flowed into the country following the establishment of the state. Hundreds of thousands arrived from Europe, Asia and Africa; from the United States and Australia, and together welded the people of Israel into one. Airborne missions such as "On Eagles' Wings" and "Magic Carpet" brought tens of thousands from Iraq and Yemen; from East Europe came waves of mass immigration, especially from Romania. Over the years the flood increased – from North Africa, South America, Ethiopia and the Former Soviet Union.

The pangs of absorption were not easy: there were those who fell by the wayside, bereft of their property, others could not become acclimatized to life in Israel, the unfamiliar culture or the constant tension gripping the Israeli society.

Many nations did not allow their Jewish citizens to emigrate, or forced them to abandon their property and leave with nothing. After the foundation of the state the struggle of many continued so as to force open the locked gates of Arab and African countries and the Soviet bloc. Jews were frequently incarcerated in prison and forced labor camps when their only crime was the desire to immigrate to Israel. Often the Jews had to flee from their land of birth and many paid with their lives for the dream of the return to Zion.

And Let our Eyes Behold thy Return to Zion

Sound the great horn for our freedom; raise the ensign to gather our exiles, and gather us from the four corners of the earth. Restore our judges as in former times...

And to Jerusalem thy city, return in mercy and dwell therein as thou hast spoken; rebuild it soon in our days as an everlasting building and speedily set up therein the throne of David. Blessed art thou O Lord who rebuildest Jerusalem...

And let our eyes behold thy return in mercy to Zion.

Sections of the 18 Benedictions (the *Amidah*) recited in the daily prayers

Poster to raise funds for bringing in immigrants

The Last Departure

David Levy

David Levy, himself Moroccan-born, is a long-time member of the Knesset and has served as a government minister in several Israeli cabinets.

"My heart is in the East and I am at the edge of the West" wrote Judah Halevi, the 12th century poet, during his sojourn in Toledo, Spain. If Toledo was at the edge of the West, how much more so were the neighboring Casablanca and Straits of Gibraltar which are located even further to the West. At this edge of the West, at the beginning of 1961, the bitter fate of 44 Jews was sealed; their hearts were certainly in the East, and they went in pursuit of their heart. These Jews, men, women and children – who were unable to emigrate to Israel openly and were forced to participate in a clandestine "illegal" operation – found their deaths in a disaster on the boat "Egoz". Brethren in fate, they shared the fate of other blockade runners during all the years of exile and yearning for Zion. They were all born in Morocco. Forty three of them were still subjects of King Mohammad the Fifth. One of them, a Frenchman, had been an Israeli citizen for ten years. Haim Zarfati was born in the city of Fez in 1933. When he reached the age of 18 in 1951, he immigrated to Israel following in his eldest brother's footsteps. He joined the Israel Defense Forces, passed an officers' course in communications, served with the air force and at one point during the Sinai Campaign, was among the communications officers attached to units of the French army occupying Port Said. Later on, Zarfarti found his way into the service of the Mossad. Rumor had it that this organization was involved in saving Jews, and Zarfarti very much wanted to play a part in saving the Jews in the land of his birth. This desire and his professional expertise secured Zarfati a job as a radio operator for the Mossad in Marseilles. Later, he was thrown into the lion's den and served in Morocco and Gibraltar, especially operating in the straits between the two. He was fanatic about secrecy. During the entire period of his work in Morocco he never met members of his family, the majority of whom still resided in Fez. On the one occasion when curiosity got the better of him, he approached his family's house and from a distance, photographed his mother, Pnina, who was sitting at the entrance to the house. More than this he did not dare to do.

The ill-fated immigrant boat "Egoz" in the port of al-Huseima, Morocco, 1961

In September 1960, when the Mossad purchased a small boat to smuggle Jews in secret across the straits dividing Africa from Europe, it was clear that only he, of all the agents in the field, would be suitable for maintaining radio communications from the boat when it would be at sea.

Zarfarti embarked on the Egoz 12 times, each time returning safely, although each time he did so with great trepidation... I'm afraid, he told one of his senior colleagues, that if a disaster happens to us, I will not succeed in reporting in time about our location and you will be unable to bring help fast enough. He worried about himself less. Everyone knew that he was an excellent swimmer, and one could assume that in time of a mishap he would be able to look after himself.

But fate decreed otherwise. The Egoz was called upon to make one more voyage of emigrants from Morocco and the last according to the plans.

… In the first eight years of the state, 92,000 Jews had emigrated from Morocco, the overwhelming majority doing so after Morocco won independence from France and the Jewish community's fears for its future increased.

… At the beginning of December 1960, a a main claiming to be a British businessman arrived in Casablanca, accompanied by his secretary who also was his mistress. They were actually the Israeli agent, Alex Gatmon, who had been appointed to the command of the clandestine network, and his wife, Carmit. Gatmon, a Holocaust survivor and partisan, started to plan carefully the Egoz's last voyages. His wife took upon herself the role of contacting the meteorological service prior to each journey to check "if the conditions were right to set out on her yacht," from the port of al-Huseimah.

The twelfth voyage of the Egoz was set for the 7th January; its passengers were 60 children aged between ten and 12 from Casablanca. After an exhausting journey of 800 kilometers, the caravan reached its planned destination, a bridge near al-Huseima. They alighted from the vehicles and made their way to the beach by foot, through a rock-strewn valley. "The mothers marched clutching their children wrapped in blankets" related Meir Knafo, who was in charge of the operation.

The Egoz sailed. The sea seemed calm, but suddenly a storm blew up that wrecked the light boat. Haim Zarfati broadcast emergency calls for a long time. His friends assumed that Haim would be able to save himself if he would disconnect his broadcasting equipment and swim a distance from the sinking boat, but Zarfati did nothing to save himself, even when water poured into the belly of the boat.

Various vessels, and the communications officer in Gibraltar - intercepted Zarfati's SOS, but the search started too late. After many hours they rescued the captain and two of his crew, and later discovered 22 more bodies floating in the water. All the other passengers of the Egoz were lost in the depths of the sea.

The bodies that were recovered were quickly buried in the Jewish cemetery of al-Huseima, where they stayed until being transferred to Israel in December, 1992. Moroccan police began a hunt for the members of the network and for relations of the drowned people, some of whom were subject to torture. Among them was "Marlene," Rahel Giladi, who despite torture, revealed none of the secrets of the expedition. On 9th February, 1961, a month after the sinking of the Egoz, Gatmon launched operation "Lightning." Members of the Zionist underground in Morocco distributed posters throughout the country proclaiming: "The hope of 2,000 years commands us to emigrate to Zion and Jerusalem, by any means and in any way. Do not despair, take heart and be strong! The struggle for our rights and our freedom continues!" And indeed, thus it was. After the sinking of the Egoz, more than 80,000 Jews emigrated from Morocco to Israel.

From " The Book of Valor," 1997

Above: coffins of the 22 drowned victims of the "Egoz" immigrant boat brought to rest in Israel, December, 1992
Left: Moroccan immigrants on the way to Israel

Zekharia Ben Ezra

Yaakov Orland

In Orland's poem, Zekharia Ben Ezra is a Yemenite immigrant, who is happy to be in the land of his ancestors, in spite of the hardships and the vicissitudes.

I am Zekharia Ben Ezra
And a poor man am I,
I live here in a *ma'abara**
With all my family

In winter it is bitter cold,
In summer blazing hot,
But I ask for nothing more,
Contented with my lot.

Oh, who could have dreamed,
Who could have hoped
That the redeemer would

remember us.
If what he promised came to pass,
And our Messiah arrived,
Then all's worthwhile,
Both bad and good,
Says Zekharia Ben Ezra.

One day an idea came to me,
I raised the standard of Zion.
And traveled down to Sde Boker
To visit Ben-Gurion.
Listen to me, sir, I said
Why are you filled with woe?

So long as there's a God up high,
Zekharia follows you.

Then I saw his face light up,
And so said Ben-Gurion,
Oh, Zekharia, blessed is the nation
With such a son like you.
Blessed the people and the state
Whose power and strength you are!

And thus, not in vain I came down here
And good was the move that I made.
It's all worthwhile
By the name of the Lord,
Said David Ben-Gurion.

*Transit camp for new immigrants

Immigrants from the 1950s – as Writers

A symposium with the participation of the authors Eli Amir, Ya'akov Besser, and Dan Tsalka. The interviewers were members of the editorial board of the literary magazine *Idan*: Mordechai Na'or, Shlomit Meshulam, David Amit and Zvi Zameret.

Eli Amir, why has it taken so long since you immigrated to Israel until we saw the fruits of your literary work? Was this a continuing process, or was the material hidden away?

Eli Amir: The material did not mature any earlier, even though the experience of the early years of absorption was profound, powerful, even traumatic; and I think that I have not yet finished the account. Which is to say, I have not yet completed everything I wanted to do. [My book] "Scapegoat" was an illegitimate child, because I began writing something else about the ma'abara [immigrants' camp] and for some reason this scapegoat sprang up and pushed other things aside.

Which ma'abara are we talking about?

I didn't mean any specific ma'abara, but rather a ma'abara in general . The delay in the writing came from problems that beset me. First, there was the problem of making a living and studies. Everything came to me late. I live all the time with a feeling that I am missing ten years. I lost ten years in the process of immigration to Israel, and I am still running after them. Then there was the problem of Hebrew. I started to write early on. But I saw that it didn't work for me. I didn't write what I wanted to. The things were either above or below – and not exactly what I wanted to say. The process of command of the Hebrew language was problematic There was another reason. The material that I wrote about the ma'abara was bitter and harsh. Extremely sour. I wasn't happy with it. Which is to say I wanted consciously to capture the hearts of those born in Israel – since it was clear to me that with my friends who had emigrated from Poland, Romania, Libya, and Morocco - I

Children in a ma'abara, early 1950s

New Year card on the theme of mass immigration to Israel

had no problem. My problems were all the time with the native-born Israelis, for whom we were completely alien. The question was: how to transmit to them our experience, with all our differences, and perhaps also how to transmit to them the sacrifice that we, too, just like their parents, had had to make in order to conquer this country. But, as I said, I wasn't comfortable writing these harsh things.

Ya'akov Besser: Eli Amir emigrated from Iraq in 1950, the same year in which you came from Poland. I understand that all of you entered by way of the same ma'abara gate – Camp Sha'ar Ha'Aliyah. Did you suffer from absorption pains?

Ya'akov Besser: With me, practically speaking, there were no problems of moving from place to place; since my early childhood I have been wandering all the time. I was born a few years before the outbreak of the Second World War, and I immediately moved to another place. Later I stole across the border of the Soviet Union. Then I returned to Poland and stayed there for a number of years until we immigrated to Israel. So the issue of moving from place to place was not the problem. Neither was it a traumatic experience to learn a language: there was the technical problem of acquiring a language and having a command over it, but it was not an emotional problem, since for all practical purposes, I did not have a mother tongue. I began to speak a certain language, actually two languages – Yiddish and Polish; after that I changed to Russian, and when I came to Israel I began to learn Hebrew, slowly, with many difficulties.

"We will pass your contribution to the mother and her children." Fund-raising poster in aid of ma'abara dwellers

A kiosk in Tel Aviv: a Tower of Babel of languages, 1950s

Did you emigrate with your family?

With my parents and brother. Sha'ar Ha'Aliyah was for us merely a transitory place. The initial problem there was connected to the food, since we had neither seen nor tasted anything remotely like it before. For the first time in my life I saw, for example, olives, and I didn't know how to eat them. Something else that surprised me was the fact that among the Jews, people were so different and strange. Until then the Jewish people I had seen were all of European origin, and I had never seen Jews from other countries, who looked so different from us.

Eli, you also reached Sha'ar Ha'Aliyah. Was your encounter with the country similar to that described by Ya'akov Besser?

Eli Amir: Not at all. Ya'akov says that he came to just another place of transit. For me it was terrible, as though I had fallen into a deep chasm from another world. Many of the Jews from Iraq, us among them, had come wearing suits and ties. More than 100,000 people left Iraq only after buying new clothes. Every man, even every boy, wore a new suit tailored from English tweed with stripes and a wide lapel, as was then fashionable, with two lines of buttons. Apart from this, I also had a felt hat, like Humphrey Bogart. And thus we came, 12 year-olds, dressed like that. The flight was short. Four and half hours, no more. At Lod airport my father suddenly saw that our three suitcases were being loaded on a truck. Everything the family possessed was in those three suitcases. And suddenly he sees them being loaded on a truck, and the truck is about to move. Then he says to me: "Fuad (this was my name then) my son, they are taking our suitcases. Jump up and guard them." I sprinted after the suitcases, jumped into the truck, they pulled down the tarpaulin, and the truck was on its way. The family stayed in Lod while I found myself alone among the pile of boxes and suitcases, until I reached Sha'ar Ha'Aliyah. I was unloaded into a huge storeroom for suitcases. And suddenly instead of a suitcase there came out a 12 and half year-old lad dressed in a suit. They all looked at me and asked: "What are

Lining up for the food tent,
Sha'ar Aliya ma'abara, 1949

you doing here, sonny?" I began to speak to them in English, a language I knew, and they allowed me to leave, but not before I had checked and found that our three suitcases were alright, and that I would be able to report to my father that they were all there.

I exited from the storeroom alone. I didn't know where to go and when my family would arrive. Suddenly to my left I saw the sea. I had never seen the sea before. In Baghdad there is a river, which also seemed huge. To my right were the Carmel mountains, I had never seen mountains either; Baghdad is in the middle of a plain... Suddenly before me I saw a blond couple – a beautiful girl in shorts, walking along and embracing a young man. Instinctively I covered my eyes. I thought I had seen something forbidden – both a girl in shorts and a couple embracing. I carried on walking forward and then I began to notice terrible smells coming from the sewage that flowed between the tents and the open lavatories. The wave of unpleasant odors also reached the nearby dining hall. In short, it was a complete shock. I was not used to such sights or the smells, and also the blow to my ethical standards at the time.

Dan Tsalka, you came some years after Eli and Ya'akov, how was your absorption?

Dan Tsalka: Like Ya'akov Besser, I, too came from Poland, although at a relatively older age. I was 21. The shock we had was that here they were not prepared for our arrival.

Where did they send you?

A neighborhood of [the town of] Yavneh, where there were huts made of plywood and planks on top of which was this asbestos roofing, and nearby were tin shacks where the Yemenites, who had emigrated earlier, lived. I remember that they had beautiful gardens with sunflowers. There were also people who had emigrated from Morocco.

How did you manage with the other communities?

My 13 year-old sister and her friends got on well with the Moroccan youth, less so with

Day of Independence poster marking 40 years of mass immigration, 1989 (Design: Asaf Berg)

the Yemenites, maybe because they were not city-dwellers. And they had a different way of entertainment. By contrast I preferred the old Yemenites, even though it was difficult for me to understand their Hebrew. I joined them in hard physical labor - pulling up weeds, harvesting peanuts and felling trees. Thus I spent the first months in Israel.

Eli Amir, your book "Scapegoat" dealt almost exclusively with that traumatic encounter between immigrants and the kibbutz children." Is that how it really was?

The real meeting with native-born Israeli children took place when we went to the kibbutz. The encounter was extremely tough and difficult. It included all the elements of indifference and humiliation. I could sometimes deal with the humiliation but with the indifference it was more difficult. This indifference was not only towards us, because we came from Iraq. I heard a similar story from other groups of youth who came from other countries.

Did you believe that you had a chance to cope with the struggle?

No. I felt that we were inferior to them. Rejected. We could never be their equals and there was no chance that we would succeed in drawing near to them or making contact with them. There was no chance that one of them would fall in love with you or that you would fall in love with her, or that one of them could become a friend. At one point, I went

to a course for Gadna ["Youth Battalions"] leaders. When I returned, my chest was filled with merit badges (on top of all my other problems, not only was I from the ma'abara, but I was also the best student in the course...) On returning to the kibbutz, they were supposed to give me command over a unit of kibbutz youngsters. So what did they give me? My own group from the ma'abara. I said: "No! Either I will be put in charge of a kibbutz group - or go to hell. – you and the Gadna." I was stubborn, and they gave me a kibbutz group. I instructed them once, twice. But it didn't work out; I don't know how it fell apart. But after a while I began to understand that we were not inferior to them. I began to examine my knowledge. In Baghdad I had studied in high school, I was good in many subjects – literature, art, theater. And suddenly the kibbutz also needed my talents. They were putting on a play and they needed a kid. Of all people they picked me. This was a great honor. It reinforced the feeling that I was in no way inferior to the kibbutz people. But they rejected me and my friends. That is, the problem was that I could not be accepted into the kibbutz community. I understood that the community would never accept me, and that I would be always on the margins. And I wasn't prepared to be on the margins.

"The thingamajig on the kettle." Immigrants from all over the world provided the popular entertainment group, Hagashash Hahiver ("The Pale Tracker") with material for many skits, some of them, like this one, on the Hebrew language

Dan, I understand that you, too, reached a kibbutz – Hazor in the south of the country – a short while after your immigration. How was the reception in your case?

In my case, the relationship was different. I was among the group that was in the ulpan [class for learning Hebrew.] Most of the group came from Poland, there were some from France. On the kibbutz they approached us with curiosity, in contrast to Eli Amir.

I too was involved with the problem of the "Children of the gods, the children of the princes" that is, the kibbutz youngsters. There was a tall boy there named Uzi. He worked well with the hoe, and this made a big impression on me. He worked like pioneers were meant to work, and according to what was written in the books. What I saw I liked – working and singing. The girls in shorts and all of them suntanned. I have to admit, I had problems of a different kind. When I came here, I was happy that I had left university and had all sorts of Tolstoyan ideas regarding manual labor. I loved physical work. The kibbutz men were excellent at this and I was pleased to imitate them. I sometimes asked

myself how did Ben-Gurion and those attached to him produce this wonder; how they succeeded in creating ideal people like these. This seems strange in a simplistic way. Yet, as I said, it pleased me.

Ya'akov, in contrast to Eli and Dan, you were never on a kibbutz, but went straight to Jaffa. When did you meet with native-born sabras?

I visited kibbutzim here and there; I met with native-born Israelis, but my first really serious encounter with them was in the army. Jaffa, the first city I lived in, was a mixed city. There were Romanians, Poles, Bulgarians, Iraqis, and others – from every community that was coming to Israel then.

... The first meeting with the sabra experience in the army was not simple. I arrived in Israel physically weak after a serious illness. I was weakly, yet despite this I strived to join a fighting unit… They sent me to the Givati Brigade. I went willingly, but the first encounter with the Israeli experience was really very tough. The sabras apparently could not understand a person who looked different from them, or did not express himself in their way, and didn't talk in accent-free Hebrew... I have no anger for the sabras. I understand them quite well. One of my friends – the journalist and poet, Moshe Dor, once said to me: "You have destroyed the country. We once had a beautiful country, homogenous, with our own way of life and language, we built here a culture. You came, you destroyed the language, you destroyed the behavior; you imported here a different ethos altogether."

Eli, we've heard here that the new immigrants made an impact not only on the country, but also on the culture and the literature. Do you agree?

Absolutely. First, more than half of this country are immigrants. Since the establishment of the state, 1,800,000 immigrants have come, and it is impossible to hide from them. Literature, poetry, which does not express this crucial fact becomes the literature for only a small group... I dare to say that what will interest our children and our grandchildren is our story as immigrants and refugees who struck roots in this land with both tears and joy. The "there" became a part of the "here" and in my opinion, it enriches our life with the wide range of differences and cultures, and forms an unusual foundation for a flowering of an Israeli culture that will be based on universal values, Jewish values and a range of cultures and traditions.

Mordechai Na'or (editor): "Immigrants and Ma'abarot 1948-1952," 1986

Immigrants arriving at their new homes

The Poverty Line

Ronny Someck

The poet Ronny Someck was born in Iraq and suffered the bitter hardships of immigrant absorption in the difficult days of the 1950s.

Poverty Line

As if one could draw a line and say: under it is poverty.
Here's the bread wearing cheap makeup turning black
and here are the olives on a small plate on the tablecloth.
In the air pigeons fly in salute to the clanging bell from the kerosene
vendor's red cart and there is the squishing sound of rubber boots landing in mud.
I was a child, in a house called a shack,
in a neighborhood called transit camp for immigrants.
The only line I saw was the horizon, and under it everything was poverty.

Translated by Barbara Goldberg with Moshe Dor

Blue and White

Israel Reshel

"Blue and White," (Kahol veLavan) became the unofficial anthem of Soviet Jewry as they fought for the right to immigrate to Israel.

Blue and white
those are my colors,
Blue and white
the colors of my land.

Blue and white
blue and white,
These are my colors as
long as I live.

Blue and white
like a song, like a dream,
Blue and white
the hope for peace.

Blue and white
– Hermon and Kinneret,
Blue and white
my heart sings out loud.

Blue and white
heavens and snow,
Blue and white
the wonder of wonders.

Blue and white
no other color for me.
Blue and white
I will return.

"Let My People Go!" Demonstration in support of Soviet Jews, Tel Aviv, 1971

"We Never Forgot Jerusalem"

A letter from 18 Jewish families from the Soviet republic of Georgia to the Commission for Human Rights at the United Nations

"The Jews of Silence" which the Soviet Union had tried to silence with threats, exiles, imprisonments and banishment – the Jews of Silence were not silent any more. Gradually the voice of the Jews who wished to emigrate was increasingly heard throughout the Soviet Union. At the price of stubbornness and personal danger, some 180,000 Jews succeeded in breaking through the iron curtain during the years 1968 -1979 and immigrating to Israel. Among those who helped pave the way was a group of 18 Jewish families from Georgia who were the first to make their cry heard in public: Let us leave for the land of our ancestors!

To the Commission for Human Rights, the United Nations Organization, New York, USA.

We, 18 religious Jewish families from the Republic of Georgia, request you to help us emigrate to Israel. Each one of us has been invited by a close relative in Israel. Each one of has received from the authorized Soviet institutions the required documents, and has filled them out. Each one of us has been given oral promises that no stumbling block will be put in front of his departure. Each of us waits day after day to receive an exit permit, has sold his possessions and left his place of work. But a number of months have past, in many cases, years, and the exit permits have still not been given. We have sent hundreds of letters and telegrams; they disappear like tears in the sand of the desert. We hear brief words of refusal, but we do not receive responses in writing; no one explains anything to us. Our fate does not disturb anybody. But we still wait, because we believe.

What therefore is our belief and our tradition? For many days the Roman Legions besieged Jerusalem. Yet despite the severity of the sufferings that are well-known under

Cartoon by Dosh. "There are no immigrants! What shall we do?" and then " There *are* immigrants! "*Now* what shall we do?!"

siege conditions – hunger, thirst, plague and so on – the Jews did not abandon their faith and were not subdued. Yet even human power is not limitless, and ultimately the barbarians broke into the holy city. Thus thousands of years ago, the Temple was destroyed and with it the Jewish state. But the people remained.

...Since then the Jews were forced to seek sustenance in strange lands, among enemies... Insulted and stained by libels, shamed and pursued, the Jews earned their bread with sweat and blood, and brought up their children. Their hands were calloused, their souls stained with blood, but the main thing is: it did not bring an end to the people – and what a people!

The Jews brought to the world faith and revolutionaries, theoreticians and scholars, men of wealth and men of understanding, geniuses with hearts of children and children with the wisdom of old men. There is no branch of knowledge, no field of literature or art, in which the Jews did not make their contribution, there is no land where Jews dwelt that did not benefit from the fruits of their labors. But what did the Jews receive in return? While everyone was living well, the Jews lived trembling, fearing that the times would change. And when things were bad for everyone the Jews knew that their end had come, and they hid or fled from the country.

We are 18 families, who have signed this letter. But it would be a mistake to think that we are only 18. The number of signatories could be much greater.

They say that there are 12 million Jews in the world... But it would be a mistake to think that we are only 12 million. For at the right side of those who pray for Israel stand hundreds of millions – those that did not reach this day and are no longer with us . They march shoulder to shoulder with us, undefeated, living for ever, nurturing us with devotion to the struggle and the faith.

We are believers: our prayers reach God.

We know: our cries will reach humankind.

Thus we do not demand much – just to allow us to leave for the land of our fathers.

18 Jewish families from Georgia, 6th August, 1969

Jews from the Former Soviet Union disembarking at Ben-Gurion Airport, May, 2000

Raise Your Voices for the Sake of Justice

Sylva Zalmanson

Sylva Zalmanson was aged 26 when, on 15 June, 1970, together with another ten Jews, she tried to hijack an airplane in Leningrad and fly to Israel. The hijackers were caught and Sylva Zalmanson was sentenced to ten years imprisonment in a forced labor camp. She did not cease her fight to leave the Soviet Union, and was supported by Jews and non-Jews around the world. In March, 1973, she wrote from her prison a memorandum to the Commission for Human Rights of the Unite Nations, an extract from which follows. Ultimately her struggle met with success and she immigrated to Israel in September, 1974.

The Soviet authorities have meted out to me years of physical and spiritual deprivation for my failed efforts to reach my homeland and my right to live in it. They have taken away from me my relatives, my friends, my house and my possibility of being a mother. They have placed on me a sign of a felon, and surrounded me with spies with orders to dictate my entire life and watch my every move. They have stolen husbands from their wives and fathers from their children and prevented my convicted comrades from doing any creative work. It places a veto on the sun, not to shine on us.

It is impossible to describe what a person feels each day or hour, from the moment his freedom is taken away from him. No calendar separates these hours from each other – they clash with each other like solid blocks, like grindstones. There are new suspicions and new limitations each day; each hour sees new schemes to "purify" you, and to accuse you of transgressing some new clause. These clauses, written and unwritten, multiply and proliferate... The goal of this method of illusory salvation is to release one mosquito after another – and to cause the soul to despair; to break into little pieces and be emptied of its contents.

I request that all the Jews who live in the Soviet Union will be permitted to find a homeland in Israel. And I call upon all righteous people who appreciate fundamental spiritual values and the simple human joys: raise your voices for the sake of justice!

Ma'ariv 3 July, 1974

Bearing the Flag

Nathan Sharansky

Nathan (Anatoly) Sharansky, born in 1948, was a fearless fighter in the Soviet Union for human rights and the right to immigrate to Israel. In March 1977, he was arrested, accused of treason and sentenced to 13 years in prison. Sharansky became a symbol of the struggle of the Jews of the Soviet Union. Only in 1986, was he released in an exchange deal between the West and East, and immigrated to Israel. Later, he was elected to the Knesset and has served as a cabinet minister in the Israel government. On his arrival in Israel in 1986, he gave his first speech – in Hebrew.

Prime Minister Yitzhak Shamir, Foreign Minister Shimon Peres and Nathan Sharansky welcome another noted Prisoner of Zion, Ida Nudel, on her arrival in Israel, 1987

It is difficult for me to speak, not only because of my Hebrew, which is poor, and it is still easier for me to express myself in English, but rather because there are in a person's life moments of excitement, which are impossible to convey in any language. My immigration to Israel was difficult, extremely long, like the duration of the Exile. The fact that this day has arrived proves how great and how consistent was the struggle. The struggle was successful. Now every Jew in the world knows that what happens to Jews in other countries affects them, too. What unites us all is our strong and independent country. We – activists for emigration from Russia, have nothing against the Soviet regime, but we have a spiritual connection to our homeland, and nothing can sever this link..

I am simply overwhelmed by the rain – in fact not rain but the hail – of compliments that have descended on my head and that of Avital [his wife]. These compliments should be distributed amongst all those who struggled – and continue to struggle – all those Jews who stand up against the regime of the Soviet Union and claim their right to emigrate to their homeland.

We have never conspired against the Soviet Union. Rather we wished to connect the whole people with its state, united around the homeland.

There are feelings that are impossible to express. There are moments that are impossible to describe in any language. I understand that the blessings we hear now relate not just to the two of us but rather to the many people all over the world, Jews and non-Jews, who struggled in order to make this day and this moment happen – the happiest in our lives.

Speech at Ben-Gurion Airport, 1986

My Lawful Right to Travel to the Jewish State

Tina Brodetsky

When the KGB discovered Zionist literature in the possession of Tina Brodetsky, a student of philology in Moscow, they condemned her to two years imprisonment in a work camp. Following the Six-Day War of 1967, the Soviet authorities rejected her request to immigrate to Israel, and she sent a moving letter to the President of the Supreme Soviet and the President of the Ministerial Committee of the Soviet Union.

In the Soviet Union I have no one. My mother's family is also attempting to immigrate to Israel, where the sole survivors of the family live. During the Second World War, my father, who had volunteered for the Soviet army, was killed; two of my mother's brothers and many of my relatives also died. At the outset of my childhood I moved with my mother – an army doctor – with the Soviet army from the Ukraine to Berlin. I saw the most awful places in the world: German concentration camps, the embalmed heads of Jewish commissars, soap on which was written "from Jewish fat." It is impossible to describe the trials and tribulations of the Jewish people. A small but courageous people with a unique, tragic fate, which has managed to maintain itself despite the threats of exile in various countries, and is now building a new life in its own homeland. I wish to join this great rebirth in the land of my people.

...I think of Israel as my national and spiritual homeland... In 1958, I was convicted for Zionist activities. My desire is unshakable. I am unable to walk calmly on the ground, or breathe its air while my people, my homeland, face destruction at every moment. Because of this I demand with all my might that my request for my lawful right to travel to the Jewish state be granted.

Ma'ariv, 19 November, 1969

Former Prisoners of Zion demonstrating for the release of their compatriots; on their clothes are their prison camp number, Jerusalem, 1970

Below: cartoon by Dosh, inspired by the huge wave of Soviet Jews who had suddenly been permitted to immigrate to Israel, "Come in!" On the trouser leg are the words "Soviet immigration." The broken leg of the bed is propped up on a Hebrew dictionary

To Live in the Historic Homeland

Yosef Bigun

Yosef Bigun paid a heavy price for his request, in 1971, to immigrate to Israel. He was dismissed from his position in a scientific institute, was accused of "parasitism" and imprisoned in a forced labor camp in Siberia. Yet from there, too, his calls to emigrate continued to be heard.

I call upon all Jews, wherever they may be, to all people of goodwill, to raise a voice in protest, and not to be reconciled with what is happening in the Soviet Union regarding the Jews; to seek a stop to persecution, and to grant the Jews the right to leave this country, in order to enable them to live among their people in their historic homeland; to live fully as Jews, to learn their language, and to enjoy the fruits of their culture.

...The historic path which our people has traveled is long, and filled with many trials, but it always found the right way – the way of struggle and fighting for its existence. The unity of Jews throughout the world will protect Soviet Jewry, which is a large part of the united Jewish people. The people of Israel lives forever!

Ma'ariv, 31 March, 1980

Journey to the Land of Israel

Haim Idisis

As it was in the snowy Russian steppes, the yearning for Eretz-Israel burned in the heart of Africa as well as among the Jews of Ethiopia. In two amazing operations; "Operation Moses" (1984) and "Operation Solomon" (1991) most of Ethiopia's Jews were airlifted to Israel. This moving song, sung by an Ethiopian children's choir, conveys the heroic saga of the Ethiopian immigration.

The moon watches from above.
I'm carrying my meager pack of food.
The desert's beneath me and endlessly ahead,
And my mother promises my little brothers:
  Soon, very soon.
  Lift up your feet.
  One last effort
  Before we reach Jerusalem.

Moonlight. Hold on, stay strong,
Our pack of food is lost on the way.
The desert never ends, jackals howl,
And my mother soothes my little brothers:
  Soon, very soon
  We will be saved.
  We will keep on walking
  To Eretz Israel.

The robbers attacked by night,
With knives and sharp swords.
Mother's blood on the sand, the moon is my witness,
And now I am the one who promises my little brothers:
  Soon, very soon,
  The dream will come true,
  Soon we will be there
  In Eretz Israel.

In the moon my mother's image
Gazes at me. Mother, don't go
If she were here beside me
She could persuade them
That I am a Jew.
  Soon, very soon,
  Lift up your feet,
  One last effort,
  Before we reach Jerusalem

Black Labor

Ehud Banai

In this poem, Ehud Banai describes, with compassion and brotherly love, the pain of the Ethiopian immigrants who are sometimes faced with discrimination and arrogance in Israel. "Black Labor" is a play on words in Hebrew; other than its literal meaning, it also implies hard manual labor.

Our dark-skinned brothers who come from Ethiopia
Bring with them a wondrous ancient tradition.
These lost sons, after the tribulations of their journey
Gradually discover this distant land.
They dreamed of it for years, and now comes reality
As they are told to immerse themselves and wash away their innocence.
And I saw a light in their eyes
And who knows, perhaps Abraham too was black.

Our dark-skinned brothers bare-foot at the roadside
Bear their insult with them into town
They stand facing the building, they face a heart of stone
Waiting for the door to open from inside.
They were loyal, yes, they awaited the message,
Now all that remains is black labor.

"Operation Solomon." Ethiopian Jews on the flight from Addis Abeba to Israel, 1991

184

Song of the Caravan

Ali Mohar

We spoke a hundred different languages,
We knew almost nothing about one
another,
And we set out from many places
But we loved and wanted only one place
Yes, we set out from many places
And to this land, to this land we came.

And the caravan goes on
For a hundred years and more.
Long ago those others traveled,
Farmers, pioneers and workers.
How they sweated, how they labored,
Never saw the goal they strove for.
Now we too are coming nearer,
Never quiet, never resting.
They can't go on there without us,
For this is the adventure of our lives.

Out of ghettoes, out of camps we came
To the swamps and to the desert land.
From Arabia, Russia and Poland
We brought light to Dimona and Degania.

And out of all the hundred exiles
And with all the many problems,
We created state and nation.
And a language that was sleeping
Woke again and can't stop talking
All around the storm is raging
All the hardship, all the sorrow,
But there's a reason to be happy,
We have strength and courage aplenty.

How Israel grows around us
She is stronger than all our shortcomings
And the Negev will burst into flower
And we will make sure that the Old Man*

Independence Day poster, 1991 (design: Raphael Abecassis)

will be happy.
And from all the exiles
And from all the problems
If the storm surrounds us
And the difficulties and miseries are great
There is still a reason for rejoicing
There is still courage, there is still strength.

And the caravan goes on
From the century that is past

The pioneers and the farmers
May be far behind
They worked and labored so hard
Without seeing the end of the road
And now it is we who pass by
We did not keep silent neither did we rest
They will not continue without us
For this is the adventure of our lives.

*David Ben-Gurion

Chapter 10

The Independence Day Torch

I, Eliezer Paran, son of Hinda and Yosef Furman, a founder of Kibbutz Kfar Szold, a graduate of the Palmach officers course, a fighter on the northern border during the War of Independence, a member of Kibbutz Ramat Yohanan, coordinator of volunteers at the center for victims of terrorism, am honored to kindle this torch to mark the 55th anniversary of the State of Israel.

In honor of all those who strive, with deep conviction, a merciful heart and a sympathetic ear, to help those among us in their most testing hours.

I, Yehuda Meshi-Zahav, scion of eleven generations in Jerusalem, son of Menahem and Sarah and member of a distinguished family, from early youth an activist in the haredi [ultra-orthodox] community, and its struggles in Jerusalem; eight years ago, I established the "Zaka" - Search and Rescue Organization, which serves as part of the Civil Guard, am honored to kindle this torch to mark the 55th anniversary of the State of Israel.

In honor of the volunteers in all the search and rescue operations who have taken upon themselves, having due regard for the sanctity of every human life, to face appalling scenes of horror, to arrive at the site of every catastrophe, and to render every aid possible.

And to the glory of Israel.

Eve of Independence Day, 2003

BASED ON FREEDOM, JUSTICE AND PEACE

Gustave Doré: **The Judgment of Solomon**. Background: the Supreme Court in session

One law and one ordinance shall be for you and for the stranger who sojourns among you.

Numbers 15:16

On Human Rights Day

Shulamit Aloni

Shulamit Aloni, lawyer, writer on current affairs and prominent human rights activist, was a member of the Palmach. She was leader of the Ratz political party, a long-time member of the Knesset and a cabinet minister.

...We seem to be moving further and further away from the ideas which essentially constitute the foundation of Zionist thought as expressed in the Declaration of Independence, and the foundation of Jewish thought as manifested for four thousand years... In the course of four millennia of culture, everything can be found. In years gone by we have been exposed in this chamber to the ugliest, most primitive, most racist ideas and some of them still lie ahead of us. But in four millennia of culture we have also encountered the most enlightened and sublime ideas.

The truth is that when we read the declaration issued by the United Nations 40 years ago, in which profound thought was invested by the Jewish jurist, René Cassin, working together with Eleanor Roosevelt; when we read the words, we find it hard to believe that they are not rooted in the culture of life in contemporary Israel.

The Declaration was adopted 40 years ago and later became a Charter. Israel never ratified the Declaration although a commission of jurists recommended that we do so. The Declaration opens with words that each and every one of us should take to heart:

"Whereas recognition of the inherent dignity and of the equal and inalienable rights of all members of the human family is the foundation of freedom, justice and peace in the world... and whereas disregard and contempt for human rights have resulted in barbarous acts which have outraged the conscience of mankind..." How profoundly did our people suffer from those barbarous acts, which cost us six million lives, including one and a half million children, although there are those among us who see this as retribution...

The Declaration goes on to proclaim that:

"All human beings are born free and equal in dignity and rights..." Who, if not we, a nation whose culture has established that man is created in God's image, that man is only slightly lower than God and that no man should be subjugated and deprived of his rights and all are equal; who, if not we should conduct ourselves in the light of that statement? And yet, nonetheless, this perception of man, Everyman, his value and his rights, is not anchored in the laws and customs of Israel.

"Everyone is entitled to all the rights and freedoms set forth in this Declaration, without distinction of any kind, such as race, color, sex, language, religion, political or other opinion; national or social origin, property, birth or other status..." Is this in fact true of our country? Do we not practice discrimination on the basis of origin, sex, race and religion? "No one shall be subject to arbitrary arrest, detention or exile." This is the essence of the rule of law. "Everyone is entitled in full equality to a fair and public hearing by an independent and impartial tribunal." This is the true meaning of the rule of law, since there were laws in Pinochet's regime as well, in Khomeini's; in North Korea and in South Africa.

The formulators of the
Declaration of Human
Rights visit Israel:
Above: Prime Minister
Golda Meir with Prof.
René Cassin. Right:
Eleanor Roosevelt, widow
of President F.D.Roosvelt,
Sheikh Suleiman and Col.
Michael Hanegbi, 1952

...I would like to call your attention, members of the Knesset, to a brief passage:
"Everyone has the right to freedom of thought, conscience and religion; this right includes
freedom to express his religion or belief, either alone or in community, with others and in
public or private... Everyone has the right to freedom of opinion and expression; this right
includes freedom to hold opinions without interference and to seek, receive and impart
information and ideas."

...The father of this nation, Abraham, chose God no less than God chose him, since he
could have worshipped wood and stone, and his duty to obey his father could have left him
a worshipper of wood and stone. But Abraham argued with God about one righteous man
in Sodom...He wanted law and he wanted justice...

From a speech in the Knesset, Jerusalem, 1988

"There are Judges in Jerusalem"

Menachem Begin

"There are judges in Jerusalem." This short declaration by Menachem Begin
expressed his deep confidence in the judicial system of Israel. Over the years the
law courts, and in particular the Supreme Court, adopted a series of courageous
and enlightened decisions designed to protect citizen's rights and thus determined
the basic elements of freedom and justice in the developing Israeli society. To a large
extent, it was such decisions that established the nature of Israeli democracy.

The Authorities are also Subject to the Rule of Law

The Supreme Court

Arabs in Jaffa, 1949

In the midst of the War of Independence, when Israel was fighting for its very existence and the Egyptian army was still positioned well within Israeli territory, the Supreme Court adopted one of its most important decisions. On 9 September, 1948, four months after the declaration of independence, the military authorities arrested Haj Ahmed Abu Laban, an Arab from Jaffa. His family discovered that he had been imprisoned without a court order. A friend, Ahmed Shuki el-Karbutli, turned to the Supreme Court. The Court studied the reasons for his arrest and it transpired that in accordance with ordinance no. 111 of the prevailing emergency regulations, the military authorities were entitled to confine a person in administrative detention without trial. However, the prisoner was entitled to appeal against his incarceration before a public advisory committee which would present its findings to the military commander. It subsequently transpired that such a Committee had not, in fact, actually been established. Although it was a time of emergency, the Court was not deterred and it determined that the authorities were governed by the rule of law just as was every citizen of the state. The decision was written by Justice Yitzhak Olshan.

בבית המשפט העליון בשבתו כבית-דין גבוה לצדק

בפני : מעלת כבוד השופט ד"ר מ. זמורה – נשיא
י. אולשן " " "
ד"ר מ. דונקלבלום " " "

המבקש : אחמד שאוקי אל כרבוטלי

נגד

1) שר הבטחון
2) ראש המטה הכללי של צבא ההגנה לישראל
3) המושל הצבאי של יפו.

המשיבים

בקשה. למתן צו מטרג הביאס קורפוס נגד שלושת המשיבים
הדורש מהם לבוא וליתן טעם מדוע לא יביאו את חג' אחמד אבו לבן
לפני בית-דין זה על מנת לשחררו.

צו על הנאשי (הביאס קורפוס)

על יסוד בקשה זו שהובאה היום הזה לפני בית-משפט זה
במעמד עורך-דין י. בנימיני ועורך-דין ד"ר לורך בשם המבקש, מצוה.
בית-משפט זה כי יצא מבית משפט זה צו חנאי (הביאס קורפוס)המכוון אל
המשיבים והדורש מהם לבוא וליתן טעם מדוע לא יביאו את חג' אחמד
אבו לבן לפני בית משפט זה על מנת לשחררו.

ועוד. מצוה בית המשפט כי על המשיבים להגיש את תשובתם,
אם ירצו בכך בתוך עשרה ימים מתאריך מסירת הצו הזה.

ניתן היום כ"ס תשרי תש"ס (1.11.48).

Writ of habeas corpus issued against the minister of defence, the chief of general staff of the IDF and the military governor of Jaffa, November, 1948

A prisoner is entitled to challenge the detention order but this right is very minor – in comparison with the extraordinary power vested in the military commander. It can be assumed that this right of defence was intended by the legislator to be preserved with the greatest stringency, so that there will be at least this one constraint protecting the person against the power he is facing; this is the critical rod of a public committee. This right is given from the moment the order for arrest is issued according to the correct procedure. Therefore the army commander is duty bound to inform the prisoner that he is being arrested under ordinance 111 in order to allow him – if he so wishes – to exercise this right immediately. On September 9th, before the committee was appointed, the government still did not have the power to enact the law; thus it was as if the order to arrest had never been given and that the incarceration was still proceeding without an order...

The government is bound by the law like every citizen of the state. The rule of law is one of the solid foundations of the state. There would be in this a terrible blow to both the public and the state, if the government uses the power given it, even if only temporarily, to utterly disregard the limitations placed by the legislator in the way this power is used. It is true that the security of the state, which finds it necessary to apprehend someone, is no less important than the need to protect the rights of the citizen, but in a place where it is possible to achieve both goals simultaneously, one must not be blind to either. The right of the prisoner is that his objection should be heard by a committee whose composition is in accordance with the law.

Therefore in the light of all the above, we order the release of Haj Ahmed Abu Laban, unless there is a substantive legal reason for incarcerating him.

The Supreme Court 7/48. Ahmed Shuki al-Karbutli vs. the minister of defense, the chief of general staff of the IDF and the military governor of Jaffa, before Chief Justice Zmora, and justices Olshan and Cheshin, 3 January 1949.

The Right to Freedom of Expression

The Supreme Court

"Kol Ha'Am" was the daily newspaper of the Israel communist party, which also published a newspaper in Arabic called "al-Itihad." Both papers were prone to attack vehemently the government of David Ben-Gurion whom they saw as an agent of American imperialism. The angry criticism sometimes verged on incitement and the government, represented by the minister of the interior, several times suspended publication of both newspapers for specific periods of time.

On 18 March, 1953, both "Kol Ha'Am" and "al-Itihad" published editorials which announced that they would "intensify the struggle against the Ben-Gurion administration which sheds the blood of Israeli youth." The minister of the interior issued a closure order for ten days against "Kol Ha'Am" and for 15 days against "al-Itihad." Both papers appealed to the Supreme Court. The Court's verdict was to become one of the most important in Israel's constitutional history.

From time to time, a case reaches this court which raises some fundamental problem, demanding the reconsideration of ancient and well-worn principles. We are called upon to define the relationship that exists between the right to freedom of the press on the one hand, and on the other, the power held by the authorities to place a limit on the use of that right. The principle of freedom of expression is closely bound up with the democratic process. In an autocratic regime, the ruler is looked upon as a superman and as one who knows, therefore, what is good and what is bad for his subjects. Accordingly, it is forbidden openly to criticize the political acts of the ruler, and whoever desires to draw his attention to some mistake has to do so by way of direct application to him.

In a state with a democratic regime – that is, government by the "will of the people" the rulers are looked upon as agents and representatives of the people who elected them. Democracy consists, first and foremost, of government by consent, the opposite of government maintained by the power of the mailed fist; and the democratic process, therefore, is one of selection of the common aims of the people and the means of achieving them, through the public form of negotiation and discussion, that is to say, by open debate and the free exchange of ideas on matters of public interest. Nevertheless, the right to freedom of expression does not mean that a person is entitled to proclaim, by word of mouth or in writing, in the ears and eyes of others, whatever he feels like saying. There is a difference between freedom and license…

To sum up: if we do not wish to put obstacles in the way of discussion and free investigation in the political sphere and in that way divest ourselves of all interest involved in the freedom of the press, and if we do not also desire utterly to depart from the test which requires that the negative effect of published matter on the public peace be regarded in the circumstances as at least probable, then we shall have no alternative but to decide that, in making the order for the suspension of the newspaper "Kol Ha'am", for a period of ten days, for having published the article referred to, the respondent gravely exceeded his jurisdiction.…

In the circumstances the orders of suspension was wrongly issued and is hereby set aside.

The Supreme Court cancelled the writ of closure.

Supreme Court judgment 73/53; "Kol Ha'Am" newspaper vs. minister of the interior; heard before Justices Agranat, Zussman, Landau; 16 October, 1953.

על הפרק

ילך אבא אבן להילחם לבד...

ממשלת בן־גוריון–ברנשטיין לא הגיעה בה כלל על הודעת אבא אבן על נכונותו להעמיד 200 אלף חיילים ישראליים למלחמה נגד ברית־המועצות. את השתיקה הרשמית אין לפרש אחרת אלא כהסכמה מלאה לדברי א. אבן. יותר מזאת, אין להניח שהשגריר של ממשלת בן־גוריון ברנשטיין הכריז את דבריו בשמו הפרטי ולא בשם הממשלה כולה.

ההכרזה של א. אבן היא יוצאת דופן אפילו במחנה האטלנטי. הרי כל ממשלה בתוך הגוש האטלנטי התוקפני, משתדלת בכל כוחה להעמיד כמה שאפשר פחות חיילים לרשות הגנרלים האמריקנים. עד עתה נתקלים האישורים של הסכמי המלחמה של בון ופאריס בקשיים גדולים. ארצות רבות באסיה ובאירופה וביניהן, בריטניה והודו, מבקרות קשה את המדיניות של אייזנהאור־דאלס.

נמצא, איפוא, שממשלת בן־גוריון נחלק לשורות הראשונות של מחנה מצ־תי המלחמה, היא מזדרזת יותר מכל ממשלה אחרת, אף בגוש האטלנטי התוקפני.

אילי ההון האמריקנים לא מוצאים לנחוץ להתחשב ב"מאמץ מלחמתי" של בן־גוריון, שרת ואבא אבן. כך מודיע העתון הלבנוני "אל זמן" מפי פקידים אמריקנים, שג'והן פוסטר דאלס, שר החוץ האמריקני ואנטוני אידן, הגיעו לעמדה משותפת, התובעת מישראל להסכים "לסיפוח הנגב לירדן, כדי שהצבא הבריטי החונה באיזור תעלת סואץ, יע־בור לנגב, וכן להסכים לחיתורים אח־רים כגון העברת נמל חיפה לידי המם־קדה האטלנטית וכו'.

ה"בית הלבן" משתדל בכל כוחו להגביר את מירוץ החימון במזרח התיכון וש־ליחח נשק אמריקאי בשווי של 1 מיליון דולר, אינו משאיר ספק בכך. יותר מזאת, ה"סטייט דיפרטמנט" הגיש אול־סימטום לממשלת בן־גוריון בדבר סילוק שטח הקולג' הערבי בירושלים. ממשלת בן־גוריון מילאה את האולטימטום מב־לי להוציא הגה מפיה.

המדיניות האנטי־סוביטית של ממ־שלת בן־גוריון־ברנשטיין, דומה למד־ניות של הריאקציונרים הפולנים־סק־ורידז־סמיגלי, שמתרך עמרון ושנאת אנטיקומוניסטית, הביאו אסון לאמי על ארצם.

למרות ההסתה האנטיסוביטית, ע־עים המוני העם בישראל, שהעם והממ־צות נאמנה. למדיניות של שלום, עמים ושלום. הנאומים של אבא אבן מאנקנ־ בריה ומולוטוב, אישרו זאת. דבר זה פי־ נוספת. באם אבא אבן אל מישמע את רוצה ללכת להילחם לצד הצבאות של האמריקאים, שילך, אך לבדד המק־ני העם רוצים בשלום, בעצמאות ולאומית ואינם מוכנים לוותר על עצמאותם ולהת־הצטרפות ל"פיקוד המזרח התיכון".

נגביר את מאבקנו נגד המדיניות האנטי־לאומית של ממשלת בן־גוריון המ־סכסרת בדם הנוער הישראלי.

נגביר את מאבקנו לשלום ולעצמאות ישראל.

מ. ק. ח.

The original article in "Kol Ha'Am" that led to the issue of a writ of closure against the paper

Defensive Democracy

The Supreme Court

"The Socialists' List" which submitted its candidature to the Knesset elections in 1965, was established by an Israeli-Arab organization known as "El-Ard," which had strong Palestinian and pan-Arab nationalistic leanings and was strongly opposed to the Israeli government. The organization itself had been declared illegal; the members of El Ard formed therefore "The Socialists' List," that attempted to run for the Knesset. The Central Elections Committee refused to sanction the list.

The leaders of "The Socialists' List," appealed the decision to the Supreme Court. Of the three judges who heard the appeal, Justice Haim Cohen supported allowing the list to be permitted. However, Judges Shimon Agranat and Yoel Sussman strongly argued that the decision banning the list should be upheld. As in the "Kol Ha'Am" case, Justice Agranat called upon the Declaration of Independence, but this time on the grounds that Israel had been created as a Jewish state. The Jewish character of the state, maintained Agranat, had become a basic constitutional fact and any group not accepting this was not entitled to run in the elections. Justice Sussman raised another argument which is central to Israeli law – that of "defensive democracy." In his reasoning, he wrote:

Members of the Supreme Court in consultation

...Just as a person is not obliged to agree to be killed, thus a state is under no obligation to agree to be decimated and wiped off the map. Its judges are not permitted to sit with folded hands and despair at the lack of positive legislation while a litigant demands of them that they stretch out their hand in order to help them bring an end to the state. Similarly no other body of the state should be used as a tool for someone whose goal is the destruction of the state, and who has – perhaps – no goal other than this.

Someone wishes to throw a bomb at the Knesset in order to kill members of the Knesset, but from the guests' gallery there is no way of carrying this out. He therefore presents a list of candidates for the elections to the Knesset. His clear goal is that, as a member of Knesset, benefiting from immunity, he could enter the Assembly Hall and give vent to his anger. This person puts forward a faultless list of candidates. Does this oblige the election committee ...to approve the list, and thus help him to commit a crime? Or, perhaps, the committee is allowed to declare that it was not for this goal that, in a democratic regime, a House of Representatives was set up, and that the use that such a person sought to make in the running of the regime was a misuse, with which the committee is under no obligation to reconcile itself. And if the committee has the authority to refuse to permit candidates that were presented in order to further a crime of murder, surely it has the authority to refuse to permit a list that was presented to betray the state?

Over and above the said legalities, the fundamental principles are not in essence relevant to our issue, but rather the right of a society organized as a state to defend itself. As for myself, regarding Israel, I am prepared to be satisfied with a "defensive democracy" and with the tools for the defense of the state that we have, even if these are not to be found in the wording of the election law.

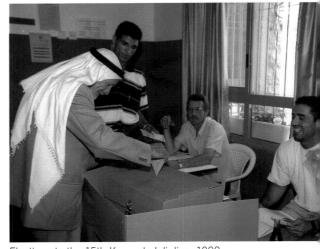
Elections to the 15th Knesset, Jaljuliya, 1999

The appeal lodged by "The Socialists' List" was dismissed and their list was not permitted to run for the Knesset elections.

56/1 Ya'akov Yardor against the chairman of the Central Election Committee for the Sixth Knesset. 23rd October, 1965.

Revoking the Right of Racist Lists to Run for the Knesset

The Supreme Court

The question of the right to elect and be elected in its widest sense which was denied to the Arab Socialists' List" arose again in 1988 when the Central Elections Committee disallowed the "Kach" list, headed by Rabbi Meir Kahana on the grounds of racism. Rabbi Kahana had been elected to the 11th Knesset in 1984, but in the meantime the Knesset passed a law banning racism. Because of this law Kahana's list was disqualified prior to the elections for the 12th Knesset. An appeal was lodged with the Supreme Court. The Court rejected the appeal by Kach; in his reasoning Justice Shamgar wrote:

...The history of the people of Israel provides the background as to why we saw the obligation of uprooting racism, to the extent of including an explicit ban on this issue, in our legal pronouncements ...in the words of the legislator it emerges that incitement to racism disqualifies a list from participating in the elections, even if the incitement is apparently motivated by the desire to keep the State of Israel uniquely as a state for the Jewish people. The desire to maintain the state cannot be used as a permit for racism.... the penal code also includes the definition of racism and this is how it appears in paragraph 149a of the penal code: "Racism – pursuing, humiliating, scorning, showing hatred, using violence, or inciting against a population or part of the population, on grounds of color, or creed or race."

...The national minority of another people is defined in Jewish law (*halacha*) as a "stranger and dweller" for whom the only condition is that he keep the "Seven Noahide Laws," which is to say, those elementary obligations for upholding law and order that every civilized nation takes upon itself. The ethnic minority merits all the civil and political rights of all the other state's citizens: "A stranger and dweller – who live among you" (*Leviticus 25:35*): "...that one treats the stranger dwelling among you with civility and kindness, as with Israel, because we are commanded to let them live." "And since you are commanded to let a stranger and dweller live ...you must heal him free of charge." (Maimonides: *Kings 10:12. Idolatry 10:2*).

Our sages further observed:

"The stranger and dweller should not be settled on the border, and not in a poor place, but rather in a beautiful location, in the middle of Eretz Israel. In a place where he can work at his trade, as it is written: "Your people shall dwell within you, in a choice place within one of your gates, and it should be good for him; do not exploit him." ("Treatise on Strangers" 3, 4 based on *Deuteronomy 23:17*)

In the exalted words of Maimonides, the essence of the basis of the halachic world regarding the issue in discussion is: "God is good to all and merciful to all his creatures. And it is said "Her ways are the ways of peace, and all her paths are pleasant." (Maimonides: *Kings 10:12*).

...Our clear conclusion is that by law the appellant's list is rightly denied by the Central Election Committee, since its advertisements, speeches, proposals and activities contain incitement to racism, as well as negating the democratic nature of the state.

1/88. Neuman and others vs. the chairman of the Central Election Committee for the 12th Knesset, 18th October, 1988.

Rabbi Meir Kahana, leader of the Kach ("Thus") Movement, Jerusalem, 1980

Despite the Great Anger

The Supreme Court

The issue of the right to elect and to be elected arose yet again in January, 2003. On the eve of the elections to the 15th Knesset, the Central Elections Committee rejected the list presented by a member of the Knesset, Dr Ahmed Tibi, and he also turned to the Supreme Court. The president, Justice Aharon Barak delivered the Court's judgment:

Member of Knesset Dr. Ahmed Tibi learns from Hizbullah's struggle

...The request to deny the participation of Knesset Member [Dr Ahmed] Tibi in the election was based on one argument according to which MK Tibi negated the principle of the Basic Law: Knesset, as formulated in paragraph 7a (a) (3 on the issue of excluding a candidate from presenting himself for election, because in his behavior he indicates support for an armed struggle by a foreign state or terrorist organization against the State of Israel. The proofs that were presented in relation to this issue were, in the main, excerpts from newspapers, minutes and other documents containing expressions = and, in some instances, actions = of MK Tibi. From these sources it emerges that a strong link exists between MK Tibi and the Chairman of the Palestinian Authority, Yasser Arafat. In the past, MK Tibi served as his consultant and when he completed this assignment, he remained in constant contact with him.

According to various sources, MK Tibi raises the standard for the struggle against the occupation. He supports the intifada and the struggle of the Palestinian people = "We offer real support for the intifada and the heroic Palestinian opposition to the occupation. This is not just the right to struggle against the occupation but an obligation." "We have learnt from you how to stand steadfast and the way of confrontation." MK Tibi warned also of a possible harm to Yasser Arafat: "It is forbidden to harm Yasser Arafat. He who harms Yasser Arafat shakes the entire foundations." (Speech in the Knesset, 10th December, 2001) and also "If Israel harms Yasser Arafat and one hair of his head falls, it will remove all the fences and barriers that there were up to now for a million of Arab citizens in Israel." (Ma'ariv, 9th December, 2001).

From the material presented it further emerged that MK Tibi expressed on more than one occasion support for various activists of the Palestinian Authority and organizations subservient to it (Marwan Barghouti, Tabeth Tabeth, Abed al-Rahim Maluah), even though it was claimed that they were engaged in acts of terror. He regards them as patriots (Speech in the Knesset, 12th December, 2002). MK Tibi was present at a meeting of activists in terrorist organizations in which it was decided to take up a comprehensive national and popular campaign supporting the opposition to Jewish settlements. MK Tibi harshly criticized the activities of the security forces directed against Palestinians. He termed the chief-of-general staff, Lieut. Gen. Shaul Mofaz as, "responsible for the murder of children." (Speech in the Knesset 15th May, 2002) and the prime minister, Ariel Sharon, "a child killer" (Speech in the Knesset 16th September, 2001.) MK Tibi referred to military actions of the Israel Defense Forces as "hideous crimes" (Yediot Aharonot, 9th May, 2001). In one instance, it is claimed that MK Tibi had been involved in an attempt to break through a road barrier of the Israel Defense Forces at the entrance to Jenin, and to have disregarded the order of the officer in charge. It was further claimed that MK Tibi is active in trying to free Palestinian prisoners who carried out acts of terror. From the words of terrorist activists who laud the actions of MK Tibi in the context of their struggle, one can learn of his support for their armed struggle.

From these words and actions = so it was claimed before the Committee for the

Ivan (John) Demjanjuk in court, Jerusalem, 1990

Election and before us = it emerges clearly that MK Tibi supports the armed struggle of a terrorist organization...

The chairman of the Central Election Committee, Judge Cheshin, objected to the opinion of the majority of the Committee to prevent MK Tibi's participation in the elections. He defined the actions and the utterances of MK Tibi as "brinkmanship. Some of his utterances were revolting and had caused a great deal of anger. By these utterances the candidate stumbled. However, the candidate is a son of the Arab people... He is an Arab and he shares the pain of the Arab people. This by itself does not invalidate him from offering his candidacy".

This being so, and despite hesitations, the chairman of the Central Election Committee determined that, "I have no doubt that the democratic right for a person to present himself in the elections is a decisive right." For these reasons the chairman of the Central Election Committee maintained that the candidate should be allowed to stand for election.

The State of Israel is a democracy, and as such is committed to guarantee that anyone interested in participating in the political life can realize the right to elect and to be elected... But this right is not absolute and a democratic state has the right to defend itself against those who would destroy and demolish it, even while using the tools that democracy provides them with...The effort to balance these two principles is not at all simple, but one always has to recall and repeat the original point = which is that one must allow for the utilization of the right to elect and be elected on the basis of equality and without discrimination.

Accordingly, we have unanimously decided not to ratify the decision of the Central Election Committee, according to which MK Tibi is prevented from participating in the elections for the 16th Knesset.

Land Day protest , Taibe, 1980

02/ 1128, 9th January, 2003

Demjanjuk Goes Free

The Supreme Court sitting as the Court of Criminal Appeal

The trial of Ivan (John) Demjanjuk, which took place in Israel in 1987 after his extradition from the USA, inflamed the Jewish people worldwide. Demjanjuk was accused of appalling war crimes against prisoners in the Treblinka death camp and was dubbed by his victims as "Ivan the Terrible." However, his defense attorney presented the court with evidence that cast doubt on his identity as Ivan the Terrible. After lengthy and difficult deliberations, the Court released Demjanjuk in 1993 on the grounds of "reasonable doubt." A deep feeling of unease was felt by many despite their appreciation for the moral honesty of the Israeli judges who had risen above their personal feelings and carried out their duty when their only criterion was absolute justice.

More than seven years ago Ivan Demjanjuk, the appellant, was legally extradited from the United States to Israel. There were apparently sufficient bases for the extradition decision. Before the courts of law in Israel, the district court and ourselves, proofs were brought that the appellant was one of a group of *Wachmanns* (Guards) from the Travniki unit that was established solely to "learn and teach" those in the group how to annihilate, to kill, to massacre, and to bring about the "Final Solution" to the "Jewish problem."

More proofs were presented that when the appellant received a Travniki certificate, he was posted in Sobibor, one of three death camps established by the German authorities of the Third Reich, in accordance with the Reinhardt plan of operations. It also emerged that

195

The Travniki document. A central item of evidence in the Demjanjuk trial, suspected to be a forgery

he served as an SS guard in the concentration camps of Flonburg and Regensberg.

The essence of the accusation against the appellant – identified as "Ivan the Terrible" – was that he was an operator of gas chambers in the death camp of Treblinka. Several of the survivors of the inferno of Treblinka identified the appellant as Ivan the Terrible, among the foremost murderers and sadistic torturers of the Jews that were brought to Treblinka on their way to being asphyxiated in the gas chambers. Thus the district court found him guilty. After concluding the hearing of the appeal, statements of various *Wachmanns* were brought before us, telling us of someone else who might have been Ivan the Terrible from Treblinka. We did not know how these statements came into being and who generated them; but we accepted them above and beyond the strict rule of law. Once they were presented to us, the doubt began to gnaw at our legal conscientiousness that maybe the appellant is not Ivan the Terrible from Treblinka. Because of the power of this gnawing doubt, whose nature we knew but not its solution, we restrained ourselves from finding the appellant guilty for the horrors of Treblinka.

347/88. Ivan (John) Demjanjuk vs. the State of Israel, appeal against the judgment of the Jerusalem district court in a specially constituted law court (for crimes calling for capital punishment). Judges D.Levin, Z.A.Tal, D.Dorner; since 25th April, 1988, Chief Justice M. Shamgar, deputy chief Justice M. Elon, Justice A. Barak, Justice E.Goldberg and Justice Y. Maltz. Advocate Y. Sheftel for the appellant; state attorney, Y.Blatman – for the respondent and others, July 1993.

This Unease, this Sorrow

Elie Wiesel

Why has a sudden feeling of unease invaded my heart, and why do I feel that something about this strange affair is wrong.

Nobody doubts Demjanjuk's guilt. Granted, maybe he was not in Treblinka, but he was certainly in Sobibor. And the guards at Sobibor were not known for their benevolence. So why does he deserve to go free?

On the other hand, the Supreme Court reached its decision and we must accept its ruling. As a Jew, I have complete faith in the Israeli legal system and its judges. To a certain extent, we may even feel proud that the Court was not afraid of hurting the feelings of the public and deciding that justice must be done, whatever the outcome.

Some will undoubtedly say that historically speaking, this ruling is to Israel's credit. But when one thinks of the survivors who testified at the trial, who identified the defendant, who placed their Jewish memory and their Jewish honor and their Jewish heart on the scales of justice, one cannot but share the pain of their disappointment. For their part, and that of many Holocaust survivors, what is the lesson to be drawn from this unfortunate trial? That they cannot rely fully on their memories, that a document uncovered in a Soviet archive is of greater value than their statements which are the essence of their lives; in other words: that what they have to relate cannot be depended upon.

This has grave implications. What if tomorrow all survivors are told that in the wake of the Demjanjuk trial – their memory too cannot be trusted? Do these survivors, these witnesses, these Jews, have anything more meaningful and vital than their memories?

Jurists will probably assert that, in the final analysis, it is the law that emerged as the victor. As for me, I do not know who prevailed, but I do know this, and I say it with profound pain: Jewish memory is the loser.

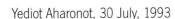

Elie Wiesel

Yediot Aharonot, 30 July, 1993

The Righteous Way

David Ben-Gurion stated that "The fate of Israel depends on two things: its strength and its righteousness." Indeed, Ben-Gurion deeply believed that Israel would be judged by the ethical stance that guided its footsteps and that the righteousness of its cause is no less important than its military prowess. Ethical principles must guide and direct the Israeli people, and instill in them the confidence that it is following the correct path.

That is how it was during the first 20 years of the state's existence. However, following the Six-Day War, the faith of many people in the righteousness of the cause became shaken. Within Israeli society a bitter argument developed which continues to this day.

Tanks in Gaza City, 1967

From a Culture of "The Besieged and the Righteous" to "Guilt and Remorse"
Haim Gouri

During the past few years, the ethos of "a besieged nation with right on its side" has been largely undermined; Hebrew poetry has been pervaded by the culture of "guilt and remorse;" by opposition and criticism to all that has hitherto been accepted and sacred. The massacre of the sacred cows has become very popular both in academe and in cultural spheres.

Whereas the 1950s were years when poetic taste was evolving and the status of the poet in Israeli society was changing, 1967 marked the beginning of a new and different historical-national era. The morning of June 5, 1967 was the turning point. Observe the Six-Day War and what it did to Hebrew literature. "It was not death that separated, but life," Nathan Alterman was to write later. Various cliques were disbanded and others were created with regard to the bitter dispute over the Land of Israel and the Arab question, which has been with us since the beginning of the return to Zion. The war that unified the territory between the Jordan and the Mediterranean, that breached the "Green Line," generated this passionate and ever-intensifying controversy… The issue of "the justice of our cause" is unsettling for a society split and divided between left and right, and the disquiet has been compounded by old-new disputes between the secular and the observant and between veterans and newcomers. We have also witnessed an upsurge of ethnic tension, which was

Then Satan Said
Nathan Alterman

This disturbing poem is one of the last that Alterman wrote. It concerns the worst danger threatening his beloved Israel.

Then Satan said, "this beleaguered soul
How can I subdue him?
He has courage and skill
and weapons and ingenuity and judgment.

And he said: I will not take his strength,
Nor fetter nor restrain him
I will not weaken his will
Nor dampen his spirit.
This will I do: Dull his brain
Until he forgets that justice is his.

And as Satan spoke
The sky paled in horror
As it saw him rise up
To perpetrate his scheme.

Yigal Tumarkin: Portrait of the playwright Hanoch Levin, whose plays caused constant controversy

197

פרקי
הקשבה
והתבוננות

שיח
לוחמים

בהוצאת
חברים צעירים
מהתנועה הקבוצית

The best-selling book *Siah Lohamim* ("Discussions Between Fighters") provided an introspective view of the Six-Day War and its aftermath

thought to have been eliminated in the melting-pot of Israeli society.

For many years, Hebrew poetry was the champion and guardian of Zionist achievement and stood at its helm. Outstanding poets regarded it as their obligation to take responsibility for Hebrew society and culture. This situation endured for many years but changed after the Six-Day War. It is illuminating to read the book *Siah Lohamim* ("Discussions Between Fighters") the journal *Shdemot*, and other publications which appeared mainly in the kibbutz movement. For the first time, we encounter the term *akeda* = ["binding" as in the near-sacrifice of Isaac], not in laments of fathers for their sons but as used by the sons who perceived themselves as the "generation of Isaac."

Very soon, oppositional literature begins to be published, in which the occupation is declared to be responsible for destroying the Israeli ethos. Personally, I find it hard to accept the term "occupation." The Jewish people are not conquerors in Eretz Israel, but it is true that we are maintaining a protracted, tough and futile rule over another people, with all that this implies for Israeli society, its spirit and its culture. What we have here is a bitter struggle between two national movements over the same territory. The *nakba* [Arab term for the "catastrophe"of 1948], the outcome of a concerted attack on us which gave us no alternative but to fight, casts a heavy burden of blame on Arab nationalism which refused to recognize the Hebrew nation, its existence and rights in this country, and rejected any form of compromise.

Some say that the origins of the fierce controversy over the "justice of our cause" lie in S. Yizhar's story *Hirbet Hiz'a*, [see page 152] which appeared after the War of Independence, before the smoke of the battlefield had cleared. It is in that, they claim, that the first crack was revealed in the ethos of the "a besieged nation with right on its side." It was there that we ceased to be the underdogs of history and became the victors with all that entailed, even though it was a war of self-defense, both fateful and just. Little Israel stood with its back to the sea facing the concerted might of Arab armies which attacked it on its first day of independence. Yizhar's story continues to breach and undermine the Israeli experience and cannot be silenced. The child crying "the tears of a helpless child" mentioned at the end of the story haunts us, as Yizar says: "when he grew to manhood [he] could be nothing but a viper." But the full intensity of the crisis was exposed after the Six-Day War in June, 1967, which unified all of the Land of Israel between the Jordan and the Mediterranean and yet tore the nation apart in an excruciatingly bitter dispute. What was to be done now that victory was ours with regard to our relations with the neighboring people who were now under our occupation? How were we to shape the new reality...?

Excerpts from an address delivered at Ben-Gurion University, May, 2002

Rally of the "Peace Now" movement, Jerusalem. The war that united the Land of Israel divided the People of Israel

The Silence of the Spirit

Aharon Megged

Yasser Arafat has been looking good lately. More than one hundred of his men were killed in the riots, several hundred were injured, but he is grinning from ear to ear. He stands amidst the crowd who are demonstrating their protest with stones and with Molotov cocktails – and smiles. He visits the wounded in hospital – and smiles. He picks up a child, kisses him, grins and declares, smiling broadly: "the struggle will not be over till one or our boys and girls raises our standard over the mosque of el-Aksa in al-Kuds [the Arab name for Jerusalem], the capital of Palestine. The spirit of our people is strong! strong! strong!"

....There is a mood of gloom, of lack of direction and of weakness among the Israelis. This frame of mind is now so commonplace, with no disgrace attached to it, that a certain travel agency recently published an advertisement which proclaimed, in blood-red letters: "There are places to escape to!" with offers of cheap "escapes" to India, Australia, New Zealand, Brazil and Argentina. It is not surprising that the national morale is low. Tufiq Tirawi, head of the Palestinian Authority's intelligence services, recently told an Israeli television interviewer: "There are two reasons why the Palestinians will prevail over your war machine – their faith in their homeland and in the justice of their cause, and their strength of purpose." And indeed, it must be admitted, with profound regret, that these two qualities, which characterized we Jews throughout a century of Zionist endeavor in Eretz Israel, and by force of which we overcame all those who conspired against us – both the Arabs and the British – have been eroded in the past few years and are now almost indiscernible.

How can one expect "faith in the homeland and in the justice of the cause" from readers of the Hebrew press when day by day, seven or eight out of every ten articles meticulously list all the sins we have committed against the Palestinians, not only during the present riots but since we first returned to this country? How can one have faith in the justice of one's cause, when distinguished professors harangue us and claim that Zionism is not only guilty of acts of injustice towards the Arabs, which, so they say, inspired the "el-Aksa Intifada" but is also to blame for the spread of anti-Semitism worldwide? How can one stand firm against adversaries when so many "men of goodwill" among us insist that we adopt a neutral and impartial stance towards the enemy; when anyone referring innocently and proudly, in Hebrew, to the "homeland" becomes the target of contempt and censure and is denoted a "nationalist"?

These statements are filling the Hebrew press, and reverberating in our media, morning, noon and night, at a time when the Palestinian media, on their part, are bombarding us with malicious and horrific propaganda and advocating the continuation of riots and terrorist attacks. There has surely been no previous example in history, in the course of a violent clash between two nations, of the attacked party relentlessly defending those who incite to massacre it.

Anti-Semitic and anti-Israel rally during the Durban Conference, South Africa, 2001

Yediot Aharonot, 2 November, 2000

Under This Blazing Light

Amos Oz

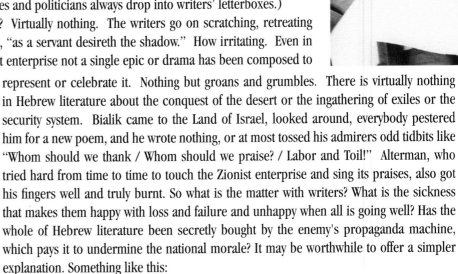

Amos Oz (b.1939) one of Israel's most renowned authors, published an article opposing the concentration of Israel's writers on "songs of praise to the great deeds" rather than dealing with painful and controversial topics.

This is the place for that old plea that is always heard from ideologues, reformers and idealists: hey, you there, poets, writers, come out of your holes and sing songs of praise for these great events. Momentous achievements are unfolding here, national restoration, building up the land, ingathering of exiles, social reform, wars and mighty deeds, and what are you doing? Sleeping! Scratching at old wounds! Writhing in dark dungeons! Come on out of there, wake up, sing up, plough up the fallow land, your mission is to observe, describe, represent, defend, infuse, plant, educate, exalt and praise, etc. (There is a fixed litany of verbs that ideologues and politicians always drop into writers' letterboxes.)

And what is the outcome? Virtually nothing. The writers go on scratching, retreating into their various dungeons, "as a servant desireth the shadow." How irritating. Even in the excitement of the Zionist enterprise not a single epic or drama has been composed to represent or celebrate it. Nothing but groans and grumbles. There is virtually nothing in Hebrew literature about the conquest of the desert or the ingathering of exiles or the security system. Bialik came to the Land of Israel, looked around, everybody pestered him for a new poem, and he wrote nothing, or at most tossed his admirers odd tidbits like "Whom should we thank / Whom should we praise? / Labor and Toil!" Alterman, who tried hard from time to time to touch the Zionist enterprise and sing its praises, also got his fingers well and truly burnt. So what is the matter with writers? What is the sickness that makes them happy with loss and failure and unhappy when all is going well? Has the whole of Hebrew literature been secretly bought by the enemy's propaganda machine, which pays it to undermine the national morale? It may be worthwhile to offer a simpler explanation. Something like this:

If you write a story or poem or a play about a successful undertaking, a dream that has come true, a struggle that has culminated in a resounding victory, it can never be as fine as the achievement itself. No poem about the act of heroism will ever be as splendid as the heroism itself. A poem about the ingathering of exiles or idealism or the delights of love cannot compete with life itself. A story about a railway bridge that has been well designed and well made and does its job well is nothing but a heap of redundant words beside the bridge itself.

A quartet of leading Israeli writers:
Standing: Amos Oz and A.B.Yehoshua;
seated: Aharon Appelfeld and Amalia Kahana-Carmon

By contrast – and here there is a mystery – it is possible to write a poem about loneliness, terrible, gloomy, ugly, ignoble loneliness, with eczema, gut-rot, and sticky self-abuse, and the poem can be touching and clean and even beautiful. Or to put characters on the stage so loathsome and tormented that nine out of ten of us would recoil from them in horror and disgust, yet on the stage they will also make us feel tender and compassionate and disgusted with ourselves for our own disgust.

It follows that when literature deals with the collapse either of an individual or of the relationship between two people, a father and son, a man and a woman, an individual and the party, or whatever, it has a chance of working a minor miracle. A transformation. To purge suffering, to make sense of senseless pain, to make collapse more beautiful than it is outside art, in "life." To be a kind of appeals court where monstrous characters and abominable events can demand a second hearing and get off almost scot-free. Think about it: how many murderers, how many madmen, walk free among the pages of what we call

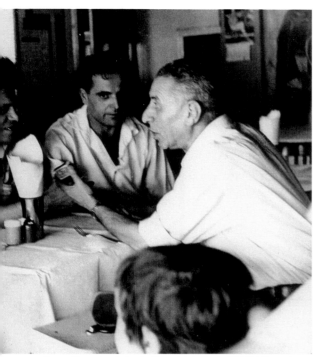

literary classics? And we put these murderers and madmen into our schools, to improve our children. Oedipus and Medea, Don Quixote, Hamlet, Macbeth, Othello, Raskolnikov and all four brothers Karamazov, Prince Mishkin and Kafka's heroes, they are all either murderers or madmen, or both.

If Shakespeare had written plays about, let us say, the expansion of the navy and improvements in transport and advances in agriculture in Elizabethan England, who would watch them today? After all, a new highway will always be more beautiful, more necessary, more self-evident than a poem about a new highway. But cruelty, suffering, madness, death – these are not self-evident. They call for some sort of justification or illumination or compassion…

Yes, I know we had no choice. Backs to the wall. "To conquer the mountain or die." A new land and a new chapter. I know all that. I'm just trying to explain, perhaps to apologize, and tell you why it is hard to make a story with depth here, one which, like any good story, works witchcraft and conjures up ghosts and spirits.

Maybe we ought to give up, do our best, and wait a couple of hundred years for a literature to emerge here that will be comparable to the Hebrew literature of the turn of the century, the great generations of Mendele, Berdyczewski, Bialik, Gnessin, Agnon, and the rest of them…

A meeting of minds: Left to right: Poets Uri Zvi Greenberg, Amir Gilboa, Haim Gouri, Nathan Alterman

Translated by Nicholas de Lange

From "Under this Blazing Light," 1980

We are not Alone

Ephraim Kishon

Every country has its own ally. It is as inevitable as marriage. For example, Saudi Arabia is the ally of the United States, Great Britain has signed a treaty with Jordan, Russia marches arm in arm with Egypt, and Justice marches with us. If truth be told, our situation was not always so good. For a very long time we were totally isolated in the international arena, until we discovered that Justice was on our side. We discovered that one day when the Israeli delegation went to attend an emergency meeting of the UN Assembly. Our representatives noticed on their way that Justice had joined them. They asked it:

"How come?" Justice replied: "I'm simply with you."

And it's a good feeling. We are no longer alone. If something happens, Heaven forbid, we can always rely on Justice. It is of course only a medium-sized power, but it is still better than nothing. Generally speaking, the following countries vote in the UN with Justice: Honduras and Peru (Cyprus abstains). Justice has a large fleet and its army is well-trained and equipped with modern weapons. If we are attacked, we can shout: "Justice, Justice!" and then Justice will come to our aid with its jet bombers and guided missiles.

Of course, there is no guarantee that Justice will arrive immediately, but it has given us its word that it will indeed come in the end. After all, in every generation there have been those who rose up against us to destroy us and we are still here. A smaller number of us, true, but still here. Because the villain always loses out in the end. All Israel's enemies have died in the course of history. Of course, it's true that they usually died at a ripe old age, some of them even at 120, but they did eventually die. Why? Because, as I've pointed out, Justice always triumphs in the end. If not now, at once, then in 38 years time, if not in 38 years time, then in 380 years. The main thing is: any plot against Justice is doomed to failure from the outset. And Justice is with us. We are no longer alone.

From "One of the People," 1963

Dosh: "Anyone home?" Israelik, the little Israeli boy, is standing on a mat marked "United Nations", knocking on a door marked "Justice"

201

Bella Belissima

Hadag Nahash and Sha'anan Street

This is a story that should be taught to children,
A worthy story.
Tuesday, 21st May, 1992
A woman walked out of her house in Jerusalem,
An ordinary day, nothing special, like all other days.
The street was full of children, (there was a teachers' strike).
At that very same moment a despicable terrorist
Drew a kitchen knife and stabbed two innocent boys.
Yet another crazy and cruel attack
Another nationalist incident.
He runs because the crowd is chasing him.
They catch him after a few minutes in a parking lot.
Dozens of people kick him, they want to vent their rage.
I'm not judging them, it's not a logical event,
It's an unreal situation, miserable, accursed, unclear.
But then the woman arrives and changes the end of the story.
Because she immediately throws herself on the terrorist, and shields him with her body,
The terrorist who's also a human being, and without her body = would be a corpse.
"I don't get it, weren't you afraid with the terrorist under you and the mob so close?
Wouldn't it have been easier to get up and go?"
She told the reporter she didn't have time to think.

Bella Bellissima, Bella Bellissima.

The story of that woman stuck in my mind.
Where did she get the strength to lie without moving, without fear?

I ask myself what I'd have done in her place,
If I'd happened to be around at that precise moment.
I know I wouldn't have kicked him
But, to be fair and tell the truth
It doesn't seem to me that I'd have done what she did.
It's much more likely that I'd have got up and run,
Or, at the most, tried to find a policeman.
But she lay there till her strength ran out.
For twenty minutes they kicked her.
Her children saw it all and didn't stop crying.

That woman didn't turn into a symbol
And her name has been erased from the public memory.
There's no postage stamp in her honor.
Perhaps because Israel's not yet mature enough
To adopt heroes
Whose heroism isn't warlike, heroes
Whose heroism isn't military, heroes
Whose heroism is only moral,
In this case a woman, and what's more, an ultra-orthodox woman.

I want you to know, dear lady, that I haven't forgotten
The story of your heroism, and I've promised myself
That it's a story that should be taught to children,
A worthy story.

Bella Belissima, Bella Belissima

Soldiers on active service, Ramallah, 2002

Our Magnificent Boys

Dana Prilutzky

Dana Prilutzky wrote this letter of appreciation to the armed forces, who were once described by Menachem Begin as "our magnificent boys" in protest against the contemptuous attitude of the media towards them.

Were it nor for "our magnificent boys," I would be standing now at the entrance to the mortuary in the Rambam Hospital in Haifa waiting to identify the torn body of my 19-year-old daughter. If I were one of the luckier parents, she would still be hovering between life and death and the newscaster would announce that the surgeons were fighting for her life, or perhaps she would be classified as merely seriously wounded and I would be sitting at her bedside, gazing at her burnt face and her seriously shattered body and offering silent thanks for her survival.

I have no idea which of our "magnificent boys" saved her = a kibbutznik, a Druze, a Tel Avivian, a fighter from a minority unit. I'm not sure I would have done the same thing in his/their place. I have never been put to the test. But a moment after the television newscaster announced that she had been rescued, I heard him mocking her rescuers, laughing at them, joking about their actions.

The radio continues to describe the catastrophe averted on Thursday evening, while the television reporter refers to other events which occurred this week and cynically mocks our "magnificent boys" who are engaged in blowing up abandoned houses and shooting at negligible targets. His comments are the culmination of a series of furious reproaches and accusations hurled at our "magnificent boys" who are charged with having committed acts of abuse and violations of human dignity, our cruel boys who, at best, are a gang of idiots, assaulting abandoned ruins.

I have no idea why our "magnificent boys" fought for the life of my beautiful and good daughter who went out on Thursday evening to a party at the City Hall club. They could have been there at the party with her, or buying real estate in Hungary, or at the very least, evading reserve duty or declaring themselves to be yeshiva students. Instead, they chose to patrol hostile territory (no power in the world could force me to do it), to run around loaded down with full military equipment between arid hills in the blazing heat, or to spend sleepless nights so that my daughter could go out clubbing. It is now Saturday morning. I gaze sleepily out of the window of my house on beautiful Mount Carmel. Instead of standing in the hospital mortuary, I am searching for the soap dish which my daughter needs because she is on furlough from army service and is going down to Eilat. Her twin brother, also a soldier, is not home yet from his girlfriend's house. I am very relaxed. Once again our "magnificent boys" have fought for my children's lives and prevailed.

And although I expressed myself differently, and although it is easier for me to employ my customary cynical left-wing style, I think I know why you "magnificent boys" fought for my daughter's life. And I hope that no spineless leadership, ineffective policy, fundamentalism of any kind whatsoever, self-hatred or the current fashion for promoting divisiveness and dispute among ourselves – will ever succeed in eradicating your will and your inner strength and your dedication and daring, the daring to remain human beings in the only place which is ours.

Ma'ariv, Letters to the Editor, 21 August, 2003

Gil'ad Harish who set up a country-wide organization of volunteers to help the needy, receives the President's Volunteering Award, from President Ezer Weizman and his wife, Reuma

To Give

Hamutal Ben-Ze'ev

Even at the height of the bitter controversy splitting Israeli society, and the stormy confrontation between left and right = the advocates of a Greater Israel and those who support the establishment of a Palestinian state = Israelis share a common moral ground. In times of internal and external threats, in the face of social or human injustice = we are united, and this unity is reflected in readiness to volunteer, to donate, to help others, even to take risks on their behalf. To give.

To give
To give your heart, to give your soul
To give
To give yourself, to give your all.

And how to find the perfect set
Between to give and what you get
Always learning ways to give.

Little secrets deeply hiding
Tangled inside, slowly finding
When your heart is touched with light
By every word, by every sight.

You are learning by the years
To build together, conquer fears
To live with changes as you sail
Embroider with her your story tale.

And to pass the hardest ways
Through the emotions, troubled days
Always know how to let go
The good taste keep and make it grow.

Inside the downfall you can see
Forgiveness is for you and me
You can always start and pray
Like usual, like a brand new day.

Translated by Hamutal Ben Ze'ev Efron

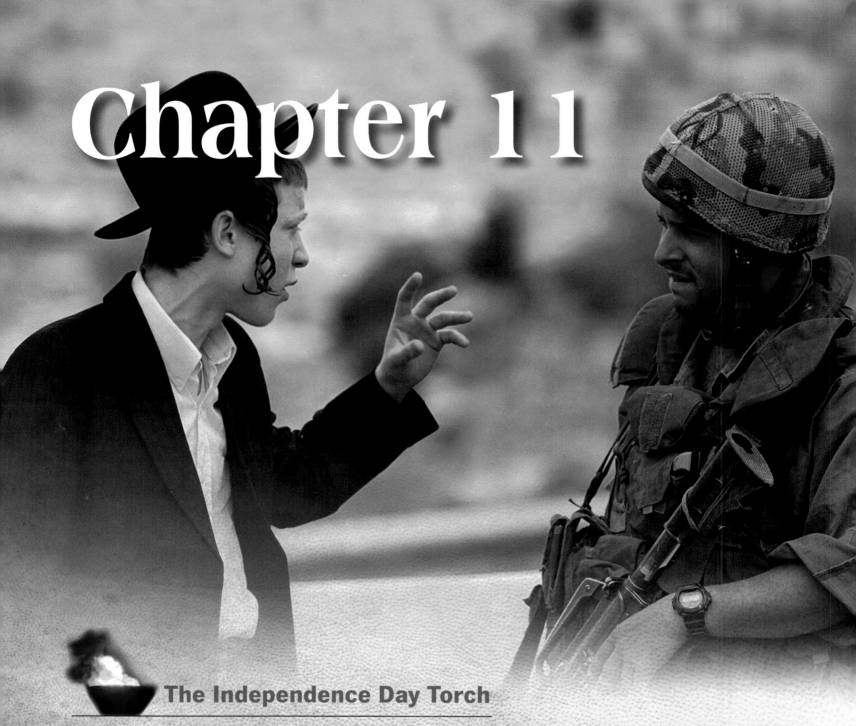

Chapter 11

The Independence Day Torch

I, Ali Yehia, from Kafr Kara' am honored to kindle this torch to mark the 36th anniversary of the State of Israel.

In honor of those working for the advancement of understanding between Arabs and Jews in Israel.

In honor of all the religions and communities living in this country who are seeking paths towards mutual coexistence.

In honor of friendship and tolerance between religions and communities.

And to the glory of Israel.

Eve of Independence Day, 1984

תשקוד על פיתוח הארץ לטובת כל תושביה, תהא מושתתה על יסודות החירות, הצדק והשלום לאור חזונם של נביאי ישראל, תקיים שויון זכויות חברתי ומדיני גמור לכל אזרחיה בלי הבדל דת, גזע ומין, תבטיח חופש דת, מצפון, לשון, חינוך ותרבות, תשמור על המקומות הקדושים של כל הדתות, ותהיה נאמנה לעקרונותיה של מגילת האומות המאוחדות.

מדינת ישראל תהא מוכנה לשתף פעולה עם המוסדות והנציגים של האומות המאוחדות בהגשמת החלטת העצרת מיום 29 בנובמבר 1947 ותפעל להקמת האחדות הכלכלית של ארץ-ישראל בשלמותה.

אנו קוראים לאומות המאוחדות לתת יד לעם היהודי בבנין

EQUALITY OF RIGHTS

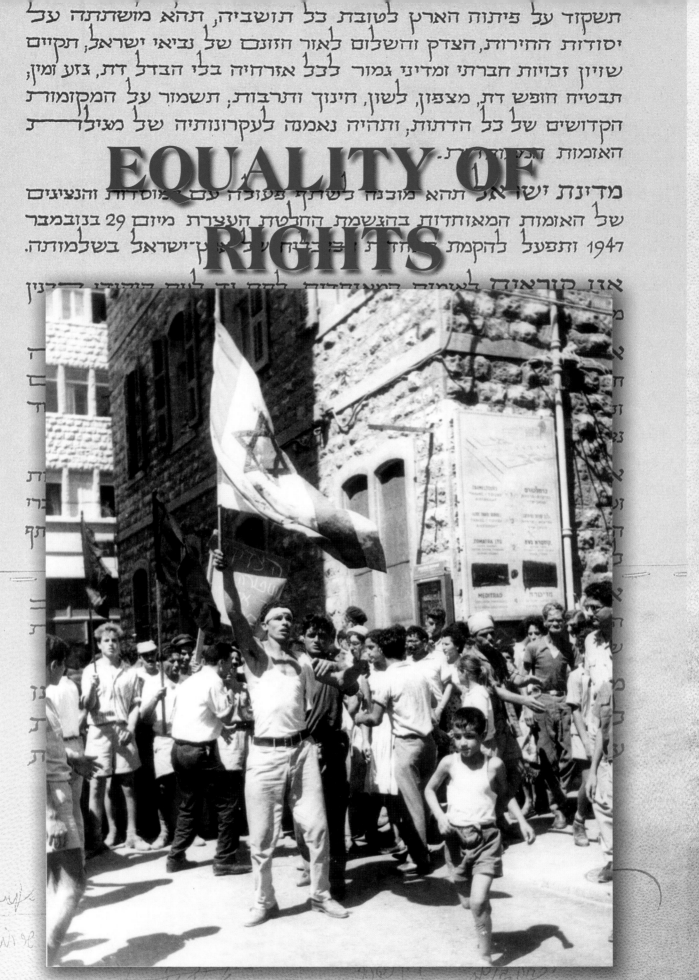

Demonstration in the Wadi Salib area of Haifa, 1959
Right: dialogue?

Of This

Nathan Alterman

Alterman published this poem at the height of the War of Independence, when he learned of the murder of Arab civilians by Israeli soldiers. Prime Minister Ben-Gurion immediately ordered that the poem be printed in thousands of copies and distributed in IDF camps.

He crossed the conquered city by jeep,
A young, armed boy – a young lion.
And in the conquered street an old man and a woman
Were pressed back against the wall.

The boy smiled with his milk-white teeth
"Let's try the machine-gun" and did.
And as the old man hid his face in his hands
His blood stained the wall.

It's a scene from the battle for freedom, my friends.
There are worse ones, as everyone knows.
Our war calls for poems and songs…
Then let's sing about this as well.

Let us also sing of "delicate matters"
A phrase which simply means murder.
Let us sing about hints for those in the know,
About smiles of acceptance and understanding,
Because those who bear arms, and we as well,
Whether by actions
Or by silent consent,
Slide, when we mutter of "necessity" and "revenge"
Into the realm of war criminals.

And to those who sing only of war's splendor
And bring it honeyed gifts
Could it but hand out penalties of steel!
Court martials in the field!

And the people's war, which, unflinchingly faced
The seven armies of the kings of the East.
Will not falter or cry "Tell it not in Gath!"
No, it is not as cowardly as that!

Davar, 19 November, 1948

IDF patrol in an Arab town, 1948

A Black Flag is Flown

With the outbreak of the Sinai Campaign on 29 October, 1956, a surprise curfew was imposed on the Arab villages of the "Triangle" area, adjoining the border with Jordan. The commander of a battalion of the Border Police, Major Shmuel Malinki, gave a command to his forces to kill any person, regardless of age or sex who would be found outside their homes after 5.00 p.m., even if unaware that a curfew had been announced. He issued the command after he had received a command to that effect from the brigade commander, Col. Issaschar Shadmi.

In the village of Kafr Kassem, the police arrested and shot to death 47 residents, among them, old people, women and children, who had returned to the village in the evening. In other villages in the Triangle area, the appalling command was not carried out, and the residents returned home safely. When the massacre was revealed, Israeli public opinion was horrified, and it was decided that the perpetrators would stand trial. Prime-Minister David Ben-Gurion announced in the Knesset that "Thou shall not murder is a supreme commandment that was handed down to us at Mount Sinai… the life of every person is sacred. That fundamental precept has been flouted in the most appalling way in this ghastly incident."

The Kafr Kassem trial was held before a military tribunal headed by Justice Benjamin Halevy. Eleven members of the Border Police maintained in their defense that they had carried out the command that they had been given, strictly according to the letter and that they, therefore, were not guilty. That was also the defense of Major Malinki who had received the order from Col. Shadmi.

In his verdict, Justice Halevy delivered a stinging indictment that has become since then a fundamental element of Israel's legal and moral code.

...There is no law in the world which sanctions the killing of "curfew violators" as such, and needless to say, the killing of people returning home who find themselves in a curfew area without any intention to violate the curfew [is prohibited]....no legislation has ever been enacted in Israel which grants a military commander in wartime excessive authority over citizens of the state...

...It is the rule that no soldier may...kill an unarmed individual who has given himself up to that soldier and has obeyed all the orders issued by that same soldier. How much more so when we are dealing with unarmed, non-combatant and totally helpless civilians even before they have "given themselves up to the army."

...A soldier is obliged to obey orders given by his commander and is exempt from criminal responsibility for the outcome. The exception to this rule is a manifestly illegal order, where the opposite is the case: a soldier is exempt from the duty to obey such an order and bears criminal responsibility for its execution. A manifestly illegal order is therefore null and void, and does not have the validity of an order, either negatively (obedience) or positively (justification).

The distinguishing mark of a manifestly illegal order is that above such an order should fly, like a black flag, a warning saying: 'Prohibited!' Not formal hidden or semi-hidden illegality, not illegality which is discernible only by legal experts; but rather overt and manifest violation of the law, definite and inevitable illegality of the order itself, the unmistakably criminal nature of the order or of the actions it specifies.

Military tribunal 3/57 The military prosecutor vs. Major Malinki and others. Colonel B. Halevi = presiding judge, Lt. Col Y. Divon, Major Y. Cohen, 16 October, 1958.
The military tribunal convicted those responsible for the massacre in Kafr Kassem.

"Sulha" = reconciliation meeting between Jews and Arabs, Kafr Kassem, November, 1957

The military tribunal, Kafr Kassem trial, 1958

and sentenced them to long terms of imprisonment. The Court of Military Appeals reduced the sentences of several of the defendants, but stated unequivocally:

The Kafr Kassem affair exposed the chasm yawning beneath us all. Intensive explanation and education are required in order to uproot this evil. It is not easy for a soldier, defending the borders of the state against an enemy seeking to destroy us, to comprehend that the compatriot of that enemy, who lives in Israel, is a citizen with equal rights. To grasp this fact and act accordingly calls for intellectual and emotional effort, but we cannot survive without that effort because therein lies the moral superiority over the enemies who surround us, which enables our state to exist: not only the spirit of sacrifice of our soldiers, not only our technical skills, but also – and perhaps mainly – the moral standards of the state, of its army and of all its citizens.

Rule of Law – Even in War Time

Judgment of the Supreme Court

One of a group of terrorists who barricaded themselves inside the Church of the Nativity, Bethlehem, is interrogated before deportation to Germany in the framework of an agreement reached in April, 2002

In quoting the well-known expression "When the guns roar, the muses fall silent," Aharon Barak, president of the Supreme Court, added "But when the guns roar, it is incumbent upon the military commander to obey the law. The strength of a society to face its enemies is based on the understanding that it is fighting on behalf of certain values that require defending: the rule of law is one of these values."

Therefore, even in the bitter struggle against terrorism in which Israel is engaged, the Supreme Court emphasized the obligation to obey the law. Contrary to every other country in the world, the Israeli Supreme Court has opened its doors to Palestinian Arabs in the occupied territories even though they are not Israeli citizens. Major nations that abide by the rule of law, such as the United States, the United Kingdom and France, have never granted access to citizens of conquered nations to their court system. The Israel Supreme Court became the watchdog of the rule of law in the country and has never hesitated to issue harsh and unpopular judgments.

In a judgment concerning the use of force against Palestinians being held by the General Security Service,[GSS] Chief Justice Barak said the following with regard to the interrogation methods of security prisoners and the degree of physical force permitted:

…In determining rules of interrogation, there is a clash of two values or concerns. On the one hand, there is the desire to reveal the truth and accordingly to realize the public interest in uncovering transgressions and their prevention. On the other hand, there is the desire to protect human dignity and freedom of the person under investigation. These values and concerns are not absolute. A freedom-loving democratic society cannot be prepared to allow its interrogators to use all methods in order to uncover the truth. "The investigative methods used by the police in certain regimes" noted Justice Landau, "are consistent with the very nature of those regimes as a whole."

…We shall now turn from the general to the particular. Clearly, "shaking" is a prohibited investigative method. It harms the suspect's body. It violates his dignity. It is a violent method which cannot form part of a legal investigation. It surpasses that which is necessary. Granting authority to the General Security Services to use physical force which infringes on human dignity and freedom during the interrogation of those suspected of hostile acts, gives rise to fundamental questions concerning law and society; of ethics and policy, of the rule of law and security. Such questions and the relevant answers need

to be determined by the legislative authority. We conclude, therefore, that according to the existing laws, neither the government nor the heads of the GSS have the authority to issue directives regarding the use of physical means during the interrogation of suspects suspected of hostile activities, beyond the general rules which can be inferred from the very concept of an interrogation itself. Similarly, the individual GSS investigator – like any police officer – does not possess the authority to employ physical means that infringe upon a suspect's rights during the interrogation… which must be both fair and reasonable.

…We are aware that our verdict does not make it any easier to deal with [the difficult security situation in which Israel finds itself.] That is the fate of democracy, that not all methods are permissible, and that not all the methods used by its enemies may be used by it. It so happens that democracy has to defend itself with one of its hands tied behind its back. Despite that, democracy retains the upper hand because regard for the rule of law and the understanding of individual rights are a major component in protecting its security.

…Arriving at decisions in the petitions before us was extremely difficult. In truth, from the legal point of view, our path was clear. But we are a part of Israeli society. We are fully aware of the difficulties and we live our country's history. We are not in an ivory tower. We live the life of the state. We are aware of the actuality of terrorism with which we sometimes have to contend. The thought that our verdict might prevent adequate dealing with saboteurs and terrorists worries us. But we are judges.

The Church of the Nativity, Bethlehem, is illuminated by IDF flares during occupation by terrorists, April, 2002

We must demand from our compatriots to act according to the law. That is also the demand we make of ourselves. When we pronounce judgment, we ourselves are judged. It is incumbent upon us to act according to our conscience and understanding of the law.

Consequently, it is decided that the order nisi be made absolute. The GSS does not have the authority to "shake" a man, hold him in the *shabach* position (which is particularly harsh and painful,) force him into a "frog crouch" position, or deprive him of sleep in a manner other than that which is inherently required by the interrogation.

Judgments of the Supreme Court 5100/94, and 4054/95: the Public Committee Against Torture in Israel, and other plaintiffs vs. the government of Israel, the General Security Services and others, 6 September, 1999.

Release of clergy held hostage by the terrorists, Church of the Nativity, Bethlehem, April, 2002

On March 29, 2002, the government decided to carry out a military operation – "Operation Defensive Wall" – against the Palestinian terror infrastructure in Judea and Samaria. The goal of the operation was to prevent the recurrence of the terror attacks which have plagued Israel. In the context of this operation, IDF forces entered Bethlehem on April 14, 2002. As IDF forces entered Bethlehem, approximately 30 to 40 wanted Palestinians terrorists broke into the Church of the Nativity, shooting as they entered. According to information in the hands of the security services, these men were responsible for the murder of Israeli civilians. Scores of armed Palestinian security services personnel also burst into the church compound. In addition, a number of civilians, unarmed and unconnected to the others, also entered the church. In total, approximately 200 Palestinians entered the compound. The armed Palestinians positioned themselves in the basilica of the church.

The IDF surrounded the church compound. Several times, the IDF requested that all Palestinians, especially the ill requiring medical care, exit the compound. The message was conveyed to those in the compound that those who were not involved in terror activity, and who were not wanted by Israel, were free to leave. The Supreme Court considered pleas that had been lodged by international organizations and others.

Justice Barak noted in his decision given on 24 April, 2004 that:

...Israel finds itself in the middle of a difficult battle against a furious wave of terrorism and is exercising its right of self-defense under the United Nations Charter. This combat is being carried out according to the rules of international law. The aphorism of Cicero that laws become muted in time of war is not relevant to modern reality.

The underlying principle of this statement [which states that an army is subject to the law] is an expression of the difference between a democratic state fighting for its very existence and terrorists trying to destroy it. The state fights in the name of the law and for its preservation. Terrorists fight against the law and disregard it. The war against terrorism is also the war of the law against those who would destroy it. Moreover, the State of Israel is a state governed by Jewish and democratic values. We have created here a state that abides by the law and which strives to achieve its national aims and the vision of generations. It does so by an appreciation and adherence to the rights of man in general and human dignity in particular...

...It is difficult to describe the seriousness of the seizing of a holy place by armed Palestinians, through desecration of the holiness of the site and by holding citizens as hostages. Negotiations are being held between the two parties in an attempt to find a solution to this difficult problem. It is incumbent upon these negotiations to find a satisfactory solution...

The petition is rejected.

Supreme Court Judgment 3451/02

Operation "Defensive Shield." An encounter in Bethlehem

IDF soldiers examine a Palestinian ambulance

The court also dealt with the difficult question – what were IDF soldiers supposed to do with regard to Palestinian ambulances when there was serious suspicion that they were transporting explosives and terrorists. Justice Dahlia Dorner stated:

...The state agrees that from an objective point of view, the situation with regard to treatment of casualties is not easy and in one instance shots were fired at a Palestinian ambulance. However, the state maintains that this resulted from the behavior of the Palestinians, who, on several occasions, used ambulances to transport explosives. At the same time, the state re-iterated that the IDF respects international law to which it is subject legally, ethically and practically. Moreover, the state declared that its fighting forces have been and are directed to follow these rules.

As to the crux of the matter, international law provides protection for medical stations and personnel against attack by combat forces. Article 19 of the Geneva Convention forbids, under all circumstances, attack on medical stations and mobile units of the medical services, that is to say, hospitals, medical warehouses, evacuation points for the wounded and sick, and ambulances. However, the medical services have the right to full protection only when they are exclusively engaged in the search, collection, transport and treatment of the wounded or sick... Moreover, Article 21 of the Geneva Convention provides that the protection of medical establishments shall cease if they are being "used to commit, outside their humanitarian duties, acts harmful to the enemy"...

We see fit to emphasize that our combat forces are required to abide by the rules of humanitarian law regarding the care of the wounded, the ill, and bodies of the deceased. The fact that medical personnel have abused their position in hospitals and in ambulances has made it necessary for the IDF to act in order to prevent such activities but does not, in and of itself, justify sweeping breaches of humanitarian rules.

Decision of the Supreme Court 2117/02, 28 April, 2002

The Death Penalty for Terrorists – an Injudicious Decision

Haim Zadok

Haim Zadok (1913-2002), one of Israel's most distinguished jurists, served as a member of the Knesset and a cabinet minister.

The instinctive reaction of many Israelis to barbaric terrorist acts, such as the murder of the Haran family (in Nahariya on 22 April, 1979) is that we must take revenge on the murderers, pay them back in kind, put them to death. But we must not permit such an emotional response to determine the decisions and actions of the government. It is incumbent on a government to take sober judicious action based on a thorough examination of all the implications.

Our fight against Arab terror is a life and death struggle. We not only have to defend ourselves against acts of sabotage and murder but also to seek out the terrorists and to strike at them whenever and wherever possible. In considering whether to impose death sentences on terrorists, the decisive question must be: is the death sentence effective in our war against terror?

If it could be proved, if there were good reasons to assume that the death penalty could deter terrorists from murderous acts, thereby saving lives, it might be feasible to ignore weighty arguments against imposing such sentences and to employ this weapon unhesitatingly in our struggle against terror. But historical experience of terrorist organizations inspired by ideological, national, social, religious or other motives – confirms that execution is not a deterrent. We are shocked by the actions of terrorists and we fight them unremittingly, but we must acknowledge that the terrorists who infiltrate Israel, though well-aware that they face almost certain death in battle, do not hesitate but continue to come. If one can indeed attribute rational considerations to a terrorist who is required to decide, in one split second, whether to surrender or die fighting – it is unlikely that fear of the death penalty will persuade him to surrender; it is more likely to impel him to fight to the bitter end and to inflict further casualties in the process of so doing.

One can understand the outrage of Israeli public opinion at the comparison drawn between today's Arab terrorists and Jewish freedom fighters under the British Mandate. To us the difference is evident. However, in order to gauge the impact of the introduction of death penalty for terrorists – we need to understand how their fellow-countrymen perceive them. They regard the terrorists as freedom fighters – and the greater the risks they take, the greater the aura of heroism that surrounds them. When a terrorist is sentenced to death – his trial, his statements and his conduct during the trial – all these will create the image of a hero, an ideal figure, an inspiration for young Arabs. Death penalties will not only fail to weaken the terrorist organizations but will actually reinforce and inspire them. And the deep chasm between Israel and the Arab community from which the condemned men come will grow ever wider.

And what will happen in the lengthy period between the capture of the terrorist and his execution – during the interrogation, the trial, the appeal? On the one hand, it may be assumed that the terrorist organizations will step up their activities, with the aim of taking hostages in Israel or abroad in order to provide a bargaining chip for the release of their comrade. They may also try, in advance, to accumulate a "reserve" of hostages. What will we do then? Will we release the condemned man in return for the lives of the hostages? Or will we harden our hearts, execute him and leave our hostages to their fate? This is the tragic dilemma that we could face. On the other hand, we will be inundated with appeals

Lest we Lose our Humanity

Dan Almagor

The fact that Dan Almagor's text was performed by the IDF Central Command entertainment troupe reflects the support of the army for the message implied in the words.

And God created Man
In his own image
In the image of God created He him.
And all human beings are created
In God's image.
All human beings.

All human beings are created
In God's image,
All human beings,
every one.
None are better than others
For all human beings are created in God's image,
In man's image.

Give us the strength never to lose the image,
The image of man.
Give us the strength
In these troubled times
Not to lose the image,
the image of man.
Not to lose the image,
Not to follow the path
Which is stained
with blood.

In these troubled times,
In these troubled times
Give us the strength
not to lose that image,
The image of man.

from organizations and public figures all over the world who will demand, request, beg us, for humanitarian reasons, not to execute the terrorist. The chorus will undoubtedly be joined by anti-Semites who will exploit the opportunity to depict us as blood-thirsty villains. But in some cases the appeal will be sincere and genuine and will often emanate from organizations and individuals on whose aid we rely on in our struggle to rescue Jews in distress. The attention of world public opinion will be distracted from the ferocity of the terrorist acts and will focus on Israel's "cruelty" in executing "freedom fighters."

...If judicious consideration prevails over emotion, if wisdom prevails over the desire for revenge, we can still ensure that there will be no capital punishment in Israel.

Ma'ariv, 4 May, 1979

Terrorists in the courtroom before trial

To be an Israeli Arab in the Next Generation

Anton Shammas

Anton Shammas is an Israeli-Arab writer, poet and lecturer.

Last Friday I traveled to the village of my birth in Galilee to accompany my Aunt Marie on her last journey. Word of her death had reached me before hazy daybreak that day, after a sleepless night during which I began to formulate what I am about to write here. The ring of the telephone which awoke me into her death interrupted a dream on which I am pondering now on my way to the village. In the banana plantations beside Shlomi junction, rain is splattering on the bunches of bananas enveloped in blue plastic bags, and I know that this is where Galilee begins.

...In the Israel of today there is no subject closer to science fiction than that of being an Arab in Israel in the next generation. Please note the phrasing of the headline, which excludes the possibility, however hypothetical, that in the 21st century, there will be no such thing as an "Israeli Arab." The status quo, it transpires, is not merely the domain of the ultra-Orthodox parties such as Agudat Israel, but it also applies to the gentiles dwelling among us. You are an Israeli Arab and you will remain one to the end of time, if at all.

...My theme is: what it will mean to be an Israeli Arab in the next generation?

If there are indeed Arabs in Israel in the next generation – and the cynical Cassandra-like prophet within me is proved wrong – I am not at all sure that this will be a country in which they will wish to live, and I am not at all confident that there will be another country in the region where they would want to live. I have no intention of dealing here with the issue of the Arabs of the West Bank (the Palestinians), and when I speak of Arabs in Israel in the next generation I am not referring to the Palestinians in any way. As for Israeli Arabs, and I permit myself to be blunt, they cannot live here in the long term while Israel fosters two axioms: 1) It is a Jewish state; and 2) It is a (Jewish) state lacking a constitution.

No national minority, and Israel's Arabs are defined as such, can exist for long in a country where their status is defined, for better or worse, by the degree of enlightenment

of the majority society among whom they live. No enlightened society is capable of, or is expected to protect the minority, and there is no need to dwell on the enlightened nature of Israeli society today, namely that sector of society which determines the tone, and not the society on the fringe, however wide the fringe.

...A minority group whose rights and obligations are not clearly spelled out will feel that they are suspended within an amorphous and ever-shifting situation, ever at the mercy of the whims and changing moods of the majority.

...The classic question that I am often asked in these neo-classical times is: if and when a Palestinian state arises, won't you want to live there? And to this I reply romantically: No, thank you, Sir; I want to live here, in the place where Aunt Marie is buried, And then we both have a problem. For me, to live here entails accepting the definition of the state as a Jewish state without a constitution, with all that implies. For the questioner, to live here means the perpetuation of the reality of equal minority rights in theory but not in practice. And that means, eventually, and according to the gloomiest predictions, evolvement into a state very like contemporary South Africa. Surely this was not the aim of the entire Zionist endeavor.

...The ceiling of my childhood home, in that Galilee village, rested on a wonderful arch which is no longer there. The existence of that arch depended on the keystone in the center which held up all the other stones. Once the keystone was removed – the arch collapsed. And in order to be an Israeli Arab in the next generation I need that missing keystone. Meanwhile I am traveling to Galilee and at the banana plantations at the Shlomi junction, I see a caravan of camels passing by:

The Arabs hear and are silent, the awe of Allah on their faces,
And pace quietly alongside their heavily laden beasts;
For a long while their robes gleam white from afar
The camels sway slowly as they disappear into the distance
As if they were bearing away yet another old legend.
And the silence creeps back as before to the desolate waste.

(Haim Nachman Bialik "The Dead of the Desert")

Jerusalem, 1983

Who is an Israeli? How Israelis Perceive Themselves

Emil Habibi

Emil Habibi (1922-1996), Israeli-Arab writer and politician, was a member of the Knesset and recipient of the Israel Prize for Arabic Literature.

I often recount the unremarkable story of an incident with a female student at an American university, the daughter of my niece. When Alex Haley's book, "Roots," appeared, members of ethnic minorities began to search for their own roots. My young great-niece sent me an electronic questionnaire about her family origins. One of the questions was: Why did you remain in Israel? I replied: Remaining in one's homeland is the natural thing to do. Ask your grandfather why he left the homeland. The Palestinian nation have no homeland apart from this one, they are unlike other peoples. They do not have West Germany or a biblical homeland. And we regard any regime which banishes some of its inhabitants from its territory – whether Turks from Bulgaria or Germans from the German Democratic Republic or Soviet Jews as reprehensible and tainted.

....It is time that the arbiters of Israeli public opinion realized that the State of Israel has no future in the Middle East unless it succeeds in establishing peaceful relations and ties of mutual respect with the Palestinian Arab people. Take note: the only public in the Arab world capable of and ready to live in peace with the State of Israel are the Palestinians. The Zionist nationalist view that the establishment of a Palestinian state side by side of the State of Israel would constitute a threat to Israel's very existence, is based on shameful ignorance of the history of the Middle East, and first and foremost, ignorance of the history of our country. The birth of Siamese twins may be an aberration but it is a fact that neither one of them can live without the continued survival of the other. No, the establishment of a Palestinian state by the State of Israel would not endanger the survival of Israel. The reverse is true: there can be no

Postage stamp in memory of the Israeli-Arab writer, Emil Habibi

guarantee of the continued existence of Israel in the historical future without the establishment of a Palestinian state by its side.

Am I an Israeli?

The trouble is, the problem is, that the leadership which has ruled Israel since it came into being is trying to exclude me from the realm of Israeli identity, from the realm of Israeli-hood.

...Give those Arabs who are Israeli citizens the same rights granted to other citizens who are involved in the struggle for the rights of their people. Why are we not permitted, if we so choose, also to shout aloud: Let my people go?" Why are we forbidden to raise our national standard beside the flag of our state, the Israeli flag? Why doesn't our state permit us, in practice, to acknowledge it as our state?

Am I an Israeli?

Direct that question, on my behalf, on behalf of my people in Israel, at the ruling establishment and intensify your struggle to gain a positive answer, in practice, with or without a human rights law. And do all this without making us feel that you are doing us a favor. Has it not been proved that one nation cannot survive without the continued life of the other? This is our common destiny. We have persuaded our own people that this destiny can be based on creative achievements and progress. Now persuade your people of the same thing. It is an unalterable fact that we share a common destiny.

Demonstration by Israeli Arabs during the deliberations of the Orr Commission, investigating charges of police brutality, September, 2002

Jerusalem, 1989

Postage stamp in honor of the *yeshivot hesder* (yeshivot whose students combine study with military service)

One Law for All

The Supreme Court on the issue of equality in Israeli society

Equality in Israeli society was not gained easily. To this day there are still major instances where it is ignored. As we have seen above, a lengthy and important struggle ensued on the granting of equal rights to the Arab citizens of the state. Within Israeli society at large, a number of struggles for equality have taken place concerning equality of rights and obligations, several of which have still not been resolved.

State Education Law, 1953

12 August, 1953

Purpose of State Education

The purpose of state education is to establish the foundations of education in the country on the cultural values of Israel, its scientific achievements, on love for the homeland and loyalty to the state and the Jewish people, on belief in agricultural work and labor, on pioneering training and on the aspiration to achieve a state based on freedom, equality, tolerance, mutual help and love of humanity.

State Education Law, 1954

Beginning in 1954 and thereafter, state education will take place in every official educational establishment. In official educational institutions which in 1953 were affiliated to the Mizrahi or the Agudat Israel [Orthodox and ultra-Orthodox] school systems, or within the workers' Orthodox school system, state religious education will be introduced.

One People, One Conscription

The Supreme Court

The question of the induction of yeshiva students into the IDF has occupied Israel society repeatedly and a satisfactory solution has still to be found. In 1948, when it was decided to release yeshiva students from military service, the issue concerned just a few hundred individuals, "brands saved from the flames" who would perpetuate the spark of Jewish learning after the great centers of Jewish study had been destroyed in the Holocaust. However, because of purely political considerations, successive governments breached all limits until the size of the problem became unconscionable: in 1987, there were 17,017 yeshiva students who did not serve in the IDF and ten years later the number had reached 28,772.

There were repeated appeals to the Supreme Court. In 1970, the first plea was lodged and in 1988, an additional plea was lodged by attorney Yehuda Ressler. The plea was dismissed, albeit with a great degree of discomfort. The Court decided that the minister of defense was entitled to reject the conscription of yeshiva students; nevertheless, Justice Aharon Barak said:

"In the final analysis, there is an importance to the number of yeshiva students who have not been inducted into the IDF. There is a limit which any reasonable minister of defense

Fighter in the *haredi* [ultra-Orthodox] unit of the Nahal Brigade

215

should not cross."

In 1997, Yehuda Ressler again turned to the Supreme Court together with two Knesset members, Chaim Oron and Amnon Rubinstein. This time, the court determined that the judgment of the Minister of Defense was not in accordance with the law. Justice Barak wrote:

"The present situation in which many do not endanger their lives in the cause of the security of the nation causes serious discrimination and a deep feeling of double standards."

The Supreme Court called for the situation to be resolved by legislation which would state that non-induction:

"Should be within the framework of a national decision to be adopted by the Knesset concerning the attitude of the State of Israel to the controversial social problem with regard to the conscription of yeshiva students, for whom 'Their Torah is their Occupation.'"

The situation has still not been resolved, and despite the establishment of various committees, such as the Tal Commission, charged with studying the problem and suggesting solutions, the issue of the induction of yeshiva students continues to inflame Israeli society.

Supreme Court judgments 3267/97 of 9 December, 1998, and 715/98 of 19 December, 2000

Morning service under field conditions

There is no Justification in Recognizing Refusal to Serve

The Supreme Court

The question of selective refusal to serve in the IDF was considered by Supreme Court justices, Aaron Barak, Dorit Beinish and Ayala Procaccia, in a case brought before the Court by eight army reserve soldiers who had refused to serve in the occupied territories. The president of the Court, Aaron Barak stated:

The eight petitioners before us serve in the IDF reserves. They were called to reserve duty for which they all reported... When they discovered that their service would be in the occupied territories, they informed their commanding officers of their objection to serving in those areas...As a result of their refusal they were brought to disciplinary trial on the charge of refusing to obey orders. They were sentenced to periods of detention ranging from 28 to 35 days.

...The question of the refusal to obey orders came up in Supreme Court judgment 470/80 Algazi vs. the minister of defense. The petitioner was in the army and requested not to serve in the occupied territories. The petition was denied. Justices M. Bejski and S. Levin noted in their judgment: "No military system can accept the existence of a general principle which allows such soldiers or others to dictate where they will serve, whether for economic or social reasons or for reasons of conscience."

This problem also arose in the case of Shane. In that instance, a soldier had refused to fulfill a reserve order which required him to serve in South Lebanon. He claimed that according to his "conscientious outlook, the IDF's presence in Lebanon was illegal and not in accordance with any fundamental justification of military activity." The court held that this argument was invalid. Justice M. Elon wrote: "This is a case of draft objection

which is based on ideological-political reasons not to serve in a particular location. This important, complicated issue of balancing the law with regard to the freedom of conscience – of balancing, on the one hand, the need to maintain military service in order to protect the sovereignty of the state and the safety of its residents against, on the other hand, the objection to participate in military activity for personal reasons of conscience – must take the particular circumstances of time and location into account. The phenomenon of selective refusal …raises the issue of distinction between "blood and blood." Moreover, in a pluralist society such as ours, recognition of selective conscientious refusal can bring about a weakening of the forces that link us as a nation. Yesterday the objection was to serving in South Lebanon, Today the objection may be to serve in Judea and Samaria. Tomorrow there might be an objection to dismantling illegal settlements in those areas. The army of the people might become an army of the peoples – made up of differing groups each of which might have its own ideas as to what its conscience allows them, and other areas where their conscience does not allow them to serve. The ability to distinguish between those claiming reasons of conscience in good faith, and those who object to the policies of the government or of the Knesset is less in the case of selective refusal because the border between political objections to that or another policy of the state, and conscientious refusal to carry out that policy is extremely thin, and sometimes even thinner than thin.

Justice Dorit Beinisch added:

I agree with the judgment and reasoning of my colleague, the President. ..Even if they are sincere, conscience and faith-based considerations do not stand alone. Against them stand considerations of preserving the security and the peace of Israeli society. Since its establishment, the State of Israel has been in a situation that requires military action. This has always been the position of the Israeli government regarding national security [The] petitioners themselves served in fighting units and participated in military activities. Their current objection is to serving in the occupied areas held by the IDF. This is in effect an objection to the steps being taken there during the military actions against terrorism. The questions which arise as the result

The number of volunteers for combat units is steadily rising

of those actions are at the heart of an intense political conflict. If this conflict is conducted within the army, it may substantially harm the Israel Defense Forces.

Judgment of the Supreme Court 7622/02, 23 October, 2002. The case of refusal to serve, before Justices A. Barak, D. Beinish, A.Procaccia, The petitioners: David Sonschein, Rami Caplan, Uri Fein, Romach Shacham, Maor Parsai, Dr Uri Toker-Maimon, Udi Elifantz, Yaniv Itzkovich, 23 October, 2002.

Youngsters working on their physical fitness prior to their induction into the IDF, Herzlia, 1999

Demonstration by unemployed seeking work

Vicky Knafo on a one-person march from her home town of Mitzpe Ramon to Jerusalem, in her struggle for rights for single-parent women

A Demonstration of Anger; a Demonstration of pain

Charlie Biton

Charlie Biton, one of the leaders of the "Black Panthers" protest movement in the 1970s, became a member of the Knesset. In 1979 he addressed the Knesset after the arrest of demonstrators who were protesting against the high cost of living and social deprivation.

Mr. Speaker, members of the Knesset.

I appeal to you from this rostrum and ask all members of the Knesset to join me in demanding the immediate release of all those arrested at the protest demonstration, the people detained in Jerusalem prisons, the people whose bones were broken and who received no medical aid. I ask you to join in the appeal for the release of all those arrested at the demonstration, a demonstration of anger and of pain.

…It appears, my fellow members of the Knesset, that the cry of the slum dwellers will not be heard. What was done will not help us. The Israeli government has deaf ears. The Knesset members have deaf ears. There is nobody listening today in Israel. I intend today, as a gesture of protest, to address my remarks to this wall in the Knesset.

Charlie Biton turns his back on the Knesset and talks to the wall behind him.

Yesterday, here, in this building, the Knesset, with the aid of its creaking coalition machine, confirmed its confidence in the government.

The Speaker, Benyamin Halevi: I am terminating this speech.

Charlie Biton: Nowhere is it written that I can't talk to the wall. Thousands of inhabitants of Jerusalem's poor neighborhoods expressed their non-confidence in the government and its policy which is leading to economic catastrophe on the backs of the poor and the weak.

Speaker: I am calling you to order.

Charlie Biton: I want it to be clear, it was not the demonstrators who started the violence. True, the demonstration was not legal, according to existing laws, but there was no justification for the conduct of the police.

Speaker: I am calling you to order.

Charlie Biton: How can one hold a legal demonstration when the police demand to know the date of the demonstration five days in advance?

Heckling from the floor of the House

Shoshana Arbeli-Almozlino: Talk to us. We are listening.

Minister Moshe Nissim: Mr. Speaker…

Charlie Biton: There has been resentment in the poor neighborhoods at the economic measures, at the pound of flesh taken from the weak. And what did you expect – that they would wait five days until the police gave them a licence?

Speaker: Members of the Knesset, on the basis of Paragraph 68 of the Knesset statutes, I am terminating this session.

Jerusalem, 1979

Demonstration against increasing unemployment
opposite the Prime Minister's Office, Jerusalem, 1997

Women's Equal Rights Law, 17 July, 1951

Equality in law

A man and a woman shall have equal status with regard to any legal proceeding; any provision of law which discriminates, with regard to any legal proceeding, against women as women, shall be of no effect.

Married women's property rights

A married woman shall be fully competent to own and deal with property as if she were unmarried; her rights in property acquired before her marriage shall not be affected by her marriage.

Equality of custody

(a) Both parents are the natural guardians of their children; where one parent dies, the survivor shall be the natural guardian.

(b) The provisions of subsection (a) shall not derogate from the power of a competent court or tribunal to deal with matters of custody over the persons or property of children with the interest of the children as the sole consideration.

Protection of women

This Law shall not derogate from any provision of law protecting women as women.

Graduating pilot officers,
Hatzerim Airbase, 2002

The Criminal Code Ordinance, 1936, shall be amended as follows:

Where the husband dissolves the marriage against the will of the wife without a judgment of a competent court or tribunal ordering the wife to dissolve the marriage, the husband is guilty of a felony and shall be liable to imprisonment for a term not exceeding five years.

"The Best Women to the Air Force"

The Supreme Court

The petition of Alice Miller against the minister of defence to allow her to participate in a pilots's course became a milestone in the struggle for women's rights.

In his verdict, Justice Eliahu Matza explained the background to the case. In November 1993, (more than one year before she was due to begin her military service) the petitioner informed the commander of the Academic Reserves of her wish to volunteer for service in aircrew and asked that she be invited to attend the examinations for suitability for pilot training. Her request was rejected. In a letter to the petitioner, the Academic Reserves officer wrote (15 December, 1993) that in accordance with instructions from the High Command, women could not serve in combat units and as flying was classified as a "combat unit," the IDF could not accept women for pilot training. The petitioner stated that she would appeal the legality of her rejection and detailed her arguments. Following that, she was invited to a meeting with the commander of the air force, however that meeting too, in December, 1993, brought no change. On 15 May, 1994, the IDF again informed her that, in the light of the written policy, according to which "women can not serve in combat units," there was no justification to invite her to an examination of her suitability for a pilots' course.

Justice Dahlia Dorner determined in her verdict:

Women are different from men. In general their physical strength is weaker than that of men. They are restricted by the necessity of their natural roles – pregnancy, childbirth and nursing. These differences were, apparently, the basis for the division of roles between the sexes in primitive human society, which gave birth to the patriarchal family. The man, who was both stronger and also free from the restrictions involved in childbirth, took charge of providing food and defending the family.

Compulsory military induction poster – for women too, 1949

"Yifat" the first woman to graduate as an IDF pilot, June 2002. (Publication of a pilot's full name is forbidden)

Alice Miller at the Supreme Court, 1995

All of this has changed greatly. In the State of Israel, as in other democratic states, the rule forbidding discrimination against women because of their sex is continually winning ground. In the declaration of the establishment of the State of Israel (the Declaration of Independence) it was stated that "the State of Israel will uphold complete equality of social and political rights for all its citizens irrespective of... sex." In the Women's Equal Rights Law, 5711-1951, section 1 provides that "There shall be one law for men and women for every legal act; and any provision of law that discriminates against women as women, for any legal act, shall not be followed."...

...The damage caused by closing the aviation course to women exceeds the benefit of the planning considerations. First, closing the aviation course to women violates their dignity and degrades them. It also, albeit unintentionally, provides support for the degrading slogan: "the best men for the air force, and the best women for its pilots."

Second, the potential of half the population is not utilized, and this damages society. "The best women for the air force" is also in the interests of society, and this was harmed by the respondents' decision. The policy of closing the doors also does not meet the accepted criteria in our law for violation of a basic right. In this respect the respondents needed to prove the existence of a near certainty that the integration of women in aviation would seriously harm national security. The respondents did not do this, nor do common sense and experience in themselves lead to a conclusion about the existence of such a near certainty.

For these reasons, I am convinced that the petition should be granted and the show cause order be made absolute.

Supreme Court judgment 4541/94 Miller vs. minister of defence and others,
8 November, 1995

Alice Miller did not succeed in completing the pilots' course. However, she was the trailblazer and other women managed to gain their pilot's wings. The first to do so was the grand-daughter of one of the heroes of the Warsaw Ghetto revolt

To be Captivated by You

Ehud Manor

To be born afresh each morning,
And die a little with each farewell
To bring sons and daughters into this world
In the land of milk, bitter herbs and honey.

To be captivated by you,
And breathe the scorching heat,
To dream of you under your skies
To bear your pain and fall in love again.

To bear a dream from birth, for generations,
To find comfort in your spring days,
To live upon and beneath
This terrible and beautiful land.

Women instructors in the Armored Corps School, June, 2002

Chapter 12

שלום

The Independence Day Torch

I, Raya Farhat, 16 years-old, from Haifa, a pupil in the Carmel Arab school.

I, Re'ut Ravhon-Spiegel, 15 and a half years old, from Kiryat Bialik, a pupil at the Re'ut School for the Arts.

Both of us together are honored to kindle this torch to mark the 47th anniversary of the State of Israel.

In honor of Arab and Jewish youth who meet together in peace and for the sake of peace.

In honor of the mutual exchange of youth delegations between Israel and Jordan as a sign of the peace between the two nations and in order to strengthen this peace.

In honor of our youth and the youth of the entire region who are growing up with the hope for a future of security and peace.

And to the Glory of Israel.

Eve of Independence Day, 1995

שנת השלושים

EXTENDING OUR HAND IN PEACE

50th anniversary celebrations of the State of Israel, Jerusalem, 1998
Background: Independence day poster, 1998 (Design: David Tartakover)

It shall come to pass in the latter days that the mountain
of the house of the Lord shall be established as the highest
of the mountains, and shall be raised above the hills;
and all the nations shall flow to it, and many peoples shall come and say:
"Come, let us go up to the mountain of the Lord,
to the house of the God of Jacob;
that he may teach us his ways and that we may walk in his paths."
For out of Zion shall go forth the law,
and the word of the Lord from Jerusalem.

He shall judge between the nations,
and shall decide for many peoples;
and they shall beat their swords into ploughshares,
and their spears into pruning hooks;
nation shall not lift up sword against nation,
neither shall they learn war any more.

Isaiah: 2:2-4

E.M.Lilien: Postage stamp with a design
of Jerusalem

He Who Would Make Peace – Turns Toward the Weak

The Maharal of Prague

Rabbi Yehuda Ben Bezalel Loewe flourished in the 16th century. He is known by the Hebrew acrostic of his name – Maharal

The name "shalom" indicates the importance of peace. For the name shalom begins with the letter "shin."

ש

The letter "shin" has three heads, one at each side and the third connecting the two. This is the essence of peace – the need for a third party to reconcile a conflict.

Notice how the middle head inclines toward the left side, for one who makes peace will lean towards the left, for the right side is the more dominant and if the middle were to turn toward it, the conflict would become more acute. Therefore it turns leftwards, as if it speaks on its behalf.

ל

Next is the letter "lamed." The lamed goes upward, for peace has a higher merit, and there is nothing higher than peace, for it is the culmination of everything.

ום

The action of peace is like the final "mem;" the written final mem is closed, surrounded by a border on each side. A wall on each side. This is to teach you that peace leads to a closure on each and every side, so that it cannot be overcome. That which is at peace is complete and has no breach in it.

In contrast the word for conflict – "Mahloket" – starts with an open mem for it contains an opening and a breach, which is the opposite of peace.

Ashkenaz, 16th cent.

224

First-day postage cover with drawing by Shmuel Bak, marking the peace treaty with Egypt, 28 March, 1979

Those Who Pursue Peace will Rule the World

Rabbi Eliahu HaCohen

Rabbi Eliahu HaCohen Ha'itamari from Izmir (1659-1729) gathered all his thoughts and commentaries into a book *Shevet Musar* ("The Rod of Ethics") which achieved wide circulation among speakers of Ladino.

Peace is one of the most fundamental elements in the striving for perfection, since it is the foundation and essence of the existence of all creation. The word *shalom* ("peace") in Hebrew, consists of four letters, that are like the letters at the root of the holy names.

Notice the greatness of peace through the letters. The word was given the four letters – *shin, lamed, vav* and final *mem* – all of which indicate elevated secrets. I will explain a small part of them.

ש

The "shin" has a greater head than any of the other 22 letters. For all the other letters have one or two heads – and the shin has three – indicating the most elevated places – as is known by the masters of hidden wisdom.

ל

It also consists of "lamed" – a flying tower in the air with a head raised above all the other letters, which is the image of a raised flag – to hint that peace is a tower of strength and that those who grasp it may raise a flag and have power over all.

ם ו

It also consists of the letter "vav'" a constituent letter in the ineffable name of God – which is the tree of life, that is to say: one who grasps peace – adds life to himself. Notice, too, the additional merit that included in the letters of the word *shalom* is the word *shalev* ("tranquility") hinting how peace covers every mistake and error. The letters of shalom also constitute the letters for the word *moshel* ("rule") which is to say that he who pursues peace possesses everything.

There is no more blessed vessel than that of peace.

The Jerusalem Talmud

To Our Arab Brethren

After the bloody attacks that the Arabs of Palestine launched against the Jewish community in 1920, the committee of the Yishuv issued an emotional appeal to "Our Arab brethren."

To the Arabs,

At this crucial moment in the history of the Jewish and the Arab peoples, we feel the need – after the events of the past few days – to address the following remarks to our Arab brethren:

Various people have hinted to you, and this is a fabrication on their part, that the Jews have come here to violate your rights and to banish you from your land.

It is a lie! We have not come here to oppress or to banish anyone – the truth is that we see Eretz Israel as our sole homeland, the land of our past and our future, to which we have returned to build our national home; but we have come, not to wage war, but in peace; not for stealing but for working and building. There is room in this country both for us and for you. We have come to establish a foothold and to settle here, to cultivate the land by the sweat of our brow, to revive its spirit and to develop its natural treasures, to bring it our energies, our knowledge, our material and spiritual forces.

For two thousand years, the ties between the Jewish people and the Land of Israel were not severed and in this generation you are witnessing the great endeavor we are developing before your eyes; you are not only witnesses but also beneficiaries together with us. The Jewish people, who suffered for two thousand years under the yoke of oppressors and tyrants will never deprive others of their rights or oppress and impoverish others.

We have no desire for wars and quarrels which can only cause harm and distress to both sides. We know how to defend our rights, our labor, the labor of peace and culture. There is no power which can halt our labors or deter us from attaining our goals.

For the renaissance and reconstruction of our country we are ready to work shoulder to shoulder with the Arab people who live here, with the masses, the farmers, the laborers, the workers whose hearts are not set on quarrels and rivalry but rather on joint labor in a spirit of peace and unity…

The Jewish and Arab peoples share a common destiny. Both our peoples were once material and spiritual rulers till historical circumstances subjugated us to others.

…We call on you to join us in peace and to work for your benefit, for our benefit and for the benefit of the country as a whole.

The Provisional Committee of the Jews of Eretz Israel.

Calling for peace. Above: a Palmach fighter pasting up peace proclamations in an Arab village, 1948. Left: meeting of Arab and Jewish youth prior to the War of Independence, 1947

The Days of the Messiah

Danny Litani

I walked down the street yesterday
And suddenly saw in the city square
A great crowd singing.
I asked: What's going on here?
And one of them answered:
It's a gathering of happy people.
I told him that couldn't be.
There's no such creature and certainly not here
In the twentieth century.

Ay, ay, how great I feel,
I just can't believe
That it's happening to me.
Ay, ay, maybe I've had too much to drink.
Or perhaps I'm just dreaming
And it's all my imagination.

So I switched on the radio,
And they announced on the news
That all over the world suddenly
The wars had stopped.
The ozone hole was closed,
And everyone had enough to eat
And peace would break out
Shortly after midnight.
And the Messiah's little white donkey
Was tethered outside the Diaspora Museum.
The sign had been given up above,
Miracles and wonders.

When Peace Will Come...

Golda Meir

Golda Meir (1898-1978) was one of the leaders of the Labor movement before the establishment of the state; following that, she was a member of the Knesset, a minister in several governments and prime minister from 1969-74.

"Peace will come when the Arabs love their children more than they hate us."

National Press Club, Washington, 1957

"When peace will come, we may be able to forgive the Arabs for killing our children, but it will be more difficult to forgive them for forcing us to kill their children."

Press conference, London, 1969

In a dramatic move which took the world by surprise, the president of Egypt, Anwar al-Sadat arrives in Israel, 21 November, 1977

Peace Treaty Between Egypt and Israel

The Government of the State of Israel and of the Arab Republic of Egypt… agree through the free exercise of their sovereignty to achieve the framework of a peace treaty on the following terms between the two nations.

I.

The state of war between the Parties will be terminated and peace will be established between them upon the exchange of instruments of ratification of this Treaty. Israel will withdraw all its armed forces and civilians from Sinai behind the international boundary between Egypt and Mandatory Palestine… and Egypt will resume the exercise of its full sovereignty over Sinai. Upon completion of the interim withdrawal, the parties will establish normal and friendly relations.

II.

The permanent boundary between Egypt and Israel is the recognized international boundary between Egypt and the former Mandatory territory of Palestine.

III.

The Parties will apply between them the provisions of the Charter of the United Nations and the principles of international law governing relations among states in times of peace. In particular: They recognize and will respect each other's sovereignty, territorial integrity and political independence; They recognize and will respect each other's right to live in peace within their secure and recognized boundaries; They will refrain from the threat or use of force, directly or indirectly, against each other and will settle all disputes between them by peaceful means… The Parties agree that the normal relationship established between them will include full recognition, diplomatic, economic and cultural relations, termination of economic boycotts and discriminatory barriers to the free movement of people and goods, and will guarantee the mutual enjoyment by all citizens of the due process of law.

Prime Minister Menachem Begin, President Sadat and the President of Israel, Prof. Ephraim Katzir, at Ben-Gurion Airport as the national anthems of the two countries are played

The Parties recognize a mutuality of interest in good neighborly relations and agree to consider means to promote such relations. The Parties will cooperate in promoting peace, stability and development in their region. Each agrees to consider proposals the other may wish to make to this end. The Parties shall seek to foster mutual understanding and tolerance and will, accordingly, abstain from hostile propaganda against each other.

Washington, 26 March, 1979

Left: Menachem Begin, Jimmy Carter, and Anwar al-Sadat during the Camp David talks, September, 1978
Above: Signing the peace agreement between Israel and Egypt, Washington, March, 1979

Peace is the Smile of a Child

Menachem Begin

Prime Minister Begin's speech at the ceremony of the signing of the peace agreement between Israel and Egypt: Menachem Begin and Anwar al-Sadat were awarded the Nobel Peace Prize.

I have come from the land of Israel, the land of Zion and Jerusalem and here I stand in humility and with pride, as a son of the Jewish people, as one of the generation of the Holocaust and redemption. The ancient Jewish people gave the world the vision of eternal peace, of universal disarmament, of abolishing the teaching and learning of war. Two prophets, Yeshayahu Ben Amotz and Micha Hamorashti, having foreseen the spiritual unity of man under God – with His word coming forth from Jerusalem – gave the nations of the world the following vision expressed in identical terms:

"And they shall beat their swords into ploughshares and their spears into pruning hooks. Nation shall not lift up sword against nation; neither shall they know war anymore."

…Despite the tragedies and disappointments of the past we must never forsake that vision, that human dream, that unshakeable faith. Peace is the beauty of life. It is sunshine. It is the smile of a child, the love of a mother, the joy of a father, the togetherness of a family. It is the advancement of man, the victory of a just cause, the triumph of truth.

It is a great day in the annals of two ancient nations, Egypt and Israel, whose sons met in our generation five times on the battlefield, fighting and falling. Let us turn our hearts to our heroes and pay tribute to their eternal memory; it is thanks to them that we have reached this day.

...However, let us not forget that in ancient times our two nations met also in alliance. Now we make peace, the cornerstone of cooperation and friendship.

...It is, of course, a great day in your life, Mr. President of the Arab Republic of Egypt. In the face of adversity and hostility you have demonstrated the human value that can change history: civil courage. A great field commander once said: civil courage is sometimes more difficult to show than military courage. You showed both. But now is the time, for all of us, to show civil courage in order to proclaim to our peoples, and to others: no more war, no more bloodshed, no more bereavement – peace unto you, Shalom, Salaam – forever.

...I have signed a treaty of peace with our neighbor, with Egypt. The heart is full and overflowing. God gave me the strength to survive the horrors of Nazism and of Stalin's concentration camps, to persevere, to endure, not to waiver in, or flinch from, my duty, to accept abuse from foreigners and, what is more painful, from my own people and from my close friends. This effort too bore some fruit.

Therefore it is the proper place, and appropriate time to bring back to memory the song and prayer of thanksgiving that I learned as a child in the home of father and mother, that does not exist anymore, because they were among the six million people, men, women and children, who sanctified the Lord's name with their sacred blood.

Washington, 26 March, 1979

Caricature by Ze'ev

229

What Have they Done to our Peace?

Yossi Sarid

Yossi Sarid is a Knesset member and a former cabinet minister. Speaking in the Knesset, he voiced his strong criticism of what he considered to be the decline of the peace initiative.

Mr. Speaker, members of the Knesset:

Look what they've done to our peace. What have they done to the Israeli peace? We remember November 1977, when Anwar al-Sadat came to Jerusalem; days that we viewed from the lofty, magnificent peak of the peace initiative; we remember September 1978, the time of the Camp David agreements, when peace was in full flood. And now we have reached the end of March 1979, the time of the signing of the treaty, a time without peaks and without crests. For months, slowly, the peace initiative has been falling from the heights onto the endless gray plains of regrets and misgivings, of pointless bargaining and barren legalese. Doubt, suspicion and petty-mindedness have gradually engulfed those flat arid plains. The tide has retreated, leaving behind it shallow murky pools; and peace, which was once borne on the crest of a mighty wave is now becalmed like a ship which has lost its direction in the dark…

Interruption from the Knesset floor: "Tell me, does it hurt you that we didn't give up more?"

Sarid continues:

What have they done to our peace? For months they tortured it, plucked it bare and battered it almost to death, but peace demonstrated that it is greater and stronger than its torturers. It can triumph over all the false prophets; it can triumph over all the Cassandras and the men of little faith; it can triumph over all the petty provocateurs; it can prevail over all the evildoers; none of them can defeat peace but they have succeeded in wearying it, wounding it, letting its blood till it can scarcely stand firm. They have not defeated it, but they have succeeded in fettering it like one of the Titans, like Prometheus. Now peace is tethered like an agonized giant, fighting for its ideals and for humanity while its political adversaries, like a flock of buzzards, hover over its head, swooping down on it from time to time to peck at its liver. Look what they have done to our peace, what they have done to the Israeli dream.

And now that this peace treaty has been signed, perhaps this hour is not as fine as it might have been, not the finest of all our hours, but we have been granted a unique opportunity to strengthen peace and to take it to our hearts, to heal its wounds, to set it on its feet again, firm and confident. We now have a unique opportunity to release peace, that tethered giant, from its fetters and to liberate it. From now on, from this time on, we will untie and tear open the bonds, rope by rope, raise peace from the dust. If we do not do so, its blood will continue to flow, and on our heads be it.

Speech in the Knesset, 1979

Song of Peace

Yaakov Rotblit

Let the sun rise up today,
Oh. let the morning dawn,
All your prayers and all your pleas
Won't give us life again.

Now our candle's flickered out,
Now we're turned to dust,
Bitter tears won't bring us back,
Or wake us from our rest.

You can never bring us back.
In the dark we lie,
No help for us from
All the songs of triumph you sing,
And the hymns of victory.

Just sing for peace, just shout it - shalom,
Don't murmur like a prayer,
Just sing to peace, just sing out loud
Let voices ring out here.

Let the sunshine filter in
Through the flowering wreaths,
Move ahead and don't look back
At those who lie beneath.

Raise your eyes in hope once more,
Don't gaze through rifle sights.
Sing a song to peace and love,
And not to war and fights.

Don't just say – the day is nigh,
Help to bring it near,
This is no dream now,
And in all the city streets
Just sing it loud and clear!

Yitzhak Rabin and Shimon Peres, recipients of the Nobel Prize for Peace, Oslo, 1994

As Young as his Dreams

Shimon Peres

Israel's President, the man who devoted his life to the security of Israel, created the military aircraft industries and the nuclear reactor and served twice as prime minister of Israel, received the approbation of the world, especially for launching the peace process with the Palestinians. Shimon Peres received, together with Yitzhak Rabin and Yasser Arafat, the Nobel Peace Prize when the Oslo accords were still in their infancy and wreathed with earnest hopes and naïve dreams for a meaningful peace. In the Nobel Prize ceremony, Peres gave voice to his dreams:

Foreign Minister Shimon Peres signing the Oslo Peace Accords at the White House, Washington. President Clinton stands behind. 13 September, 1993

From my earliest youth, I have known that while obliged to plan with care the stages of our journey, we are entitled to dream, and keep dreaming, of its destination. A man may feel as old as his years, yet as young as his dreams. The laws of biology do not apply to sanguine aspiration...

For two decades, in the ministry of defense, I was privileged to work closely with a man who was and remains, to my mind, the greatest Jew of our time. From him I learned that the vision of the future should shape the agenda for the present; that you can overcome obstacles by dint of faith; that you may feel disappointed – but never despair. And above all, I learned that the wisest consideration is the moral one. David Ben-Gurion has passed away, yet his vision continues to flourish: to be a chosen people, to live at peace with our neighbors. The wars we fought were forced upon us. Thanks to the Israel Defense Forces, we won them all, but we did not win the greatest victory that we aspired to: release from the need to win victories. We proved that aggressors do not necessarily emerge as the victors, but we learned that victors do not necessarily win peace. It is no wonder that war, as a method of conducting human affairs, is in its death throes, and that the time has come to bury it. The sword, as the Bible teaches us, consumes flesh, but it cannot provide

231

sustenance. It is not rifles but people who triumph, and the conclusion from all the wars is that we need better people, not better rifles – to avoid wars, to win peace…

Today as in my youth, I carry dreams. I would mention two: the future of the Jewish people and the future of the Middle East. In history, Judaism has been far more successful than the Jews themselves. The Jewish people remained small, but the spirit of Jerusalem -- the capital of Jewish life, the city holy and open to all religions – went from strength to strength. The Bible is to be found in hundreds of millions of homes. The moral majesty of the Book of Books has been undefeated by the ups and downs of history. Moreover, time and again, history has succumbed to the Bible's immortal ideas. The message that the one, invisible God created man in His image, and hence there are no higher and lower orders of man, has fused with the realization that morality is the highest form of wisdom and, perhaps, of beauty and courage, too. Slings, arrows, gas chambers can annihilate man, but they cannot destroy human values, the dignity and freedom of the human being.

Jewish history presents an encouraging lesson for mankind. For nearly four thousand years, a small nation carried a great message. Initially, the nation dwelt in its own land; later, it wandered in exile. This small nation swam against the tide and was repeatedly persecuted, banished, downtrodden. There is no other example in all history – neither among the great empires nor among their colonies and dependencies – of a nation, after so long a saga of tragedy and misfortune, rising up again, shaking itself free, gathering together its dispersed remnants, and setting out anew on its national adventure. Defeating doubters from within and enemies from without. Reviving its land and its language. Rebuilding its identity, and reaching toward new heights of distinction and excellence.The message of the Jewish people to mankind is that faith and moral vision can triumph over all adversity…

Ceremony of signing the peace agreement with the Palestinian Authority, Washington, 1993

In the five decades of Israel's existence, our efforts have focused on re-establishing our territorial center. In the future, we shall have to devote our main effort to strengthening our spiritual center. Judaism – or Jewishness – is a fusion of faith, history, land and language. Being Jewish means to belong to a people that is both unique and universal. My greatest hope is that our children, like our forefathers, will not make do with the transient and the substitute, but will continue to plough the historic Jewish furrow in the fields of human spirit, that Israel will become the center of our heritage, not merely a homeland for our people; that the Jewish people will be inspired by others, but at the same be to them a source of inspiration…

Israel's role in the Middle East should be to contribute to a great, sustained regional revival: a Middle East without wars, without enemies, without ballistic missiles...

A Middle East in which every believer will be free to pray in his own language – Arabic, Hebrew, Latin, or whatever language he chooses – and in which the prayers will reach their destination without censorship, without interference, and without offending anyone. A Middle East where young men and women can attain university education. A Middle East where waters flow to slake thirst, to make crops grow and deserts bloom, in which no hostile borders bring death, hunger, despair or shame. A Middle East of competition, not of domination. A Middle East in which men are each other's hosts, not hostages. A Middle East that is not a killing field, but a field of creativity and growth. A Middle East that so honors its history, that it strives to add to it new noble chapters. A Middle East which will serve as a spiritual and cultural focal point for the entire world...

Oslo, 10 December, 1994

"I, military ID number three-zero-seven-four-three..."

Yitzhak Rabin

The man who spent most of his life in uniform, from his early days in the Palmach to his appointment as commander-in-chief of the Israel Defense Forces in the Six-Day War, later become a "Soldier in the Army of Peace." Yitzhak Rabin (1922-1995) served twice as prime-minister, and in that capacity, he signed the controversial Oslo accords with the Palestine Liberation Organization and the peace treaty with Jordan.

Address by Prime Minister Yitzhak Rabin to the United States Congress

Soldier in the Army of Peace
Prime Minister Yitzhak Rabin, with King Hussein of Jordan on his right, addressing a joint session of Congress, Washington, July, 1994

Each year, on Memorial Day for the Fallen of Israel's Wars, I go to the military cemetery on Mount Herzl in Jerusalem. Facing me are the graves and headstones, the colorful flowers blooming on them – and thousands of pairs of weeping eyes. I stand there, in front of the large silent crowd – and read in their eyes the words of "The Young Dead Soldiers" – as the famous American poet Archibald MacLeish entitled the poem from which I take these lines:

"They say: Whether our lives and our deaths were for peace and a new hope, or for nothing, we cannot say; it is you who must say this."

I have come here from Jerusalem on behalf of those thousands of bereaved families – although I haven't asked their permission. I stand here on behalf of the parents who have buried their children; of the children who have no fathers; and of the sons and daughters who are gone, but return to us in our dreams. I stand here today on behalf of those youngsters who wanted to live, to love, to build a home.

I have come from Jerusalem in the name of our children, who began their lives with great hope – and are now names on graves and memorial stones; old pictures in albums; fading clothes in closets.

Each year as I stand before the parents whose lips are chanting *Kaddish* the Jewish memorial prayer, again ringing in my ears are the words of Archibald MacLeish, who echoes the plea of the young dead soldiers:

"They say: We leave you our deaths. Give them their meaning."

Let us give them meaning. Let us make an end to bloodshed. Let us make true peace. Let us today be victorious in ending war.

The debate goes on: Who shapes the face of history? – leaders or circumstances?

My answer to you is this: We all shape the face of history. We, the people.

We, the people; we shape the face of history.

And we, the leaders, hear the voices, and sense the deepest emotions and feelings of the thousands and the millions, and translate them into reality.

If my people did not desire peace so strongly, I would not be standing here today. And I am sure that if the children of Amman, and the soldiers of Irbid, the women of Salt and the citizens of Aqaba did not seek peace, our partner in this great quest, the King of Jordan, would not be here now, shaking hands, calling for peace.

Your Majesty, [King Hussein of Jordan was present at the occasion]

Beyond the ceremonies, after the festivities, we will move on to the negotiations. They will not be easy. But when they are completed, a wonderful, common future awaits us. The

Middle East, the cradle of the great monotheistic civilizations – Judaism, Christianity, and Islam; the Middle East, which was a valley of the shadow of death, will be a place where it is a pleasure to live.

We live on the same stretch of land. The same rain nourishes our soil; the same hot wind parches our fields. We find shade under the same fig tree. We savor the fruit of the same green vine. We drink from the same well. Only a 70-minute journey separates these cities Jerusalem and Amman and 46 years. And just as we have been enemies, so can we be good and friendly neighbors.

Your Majesty, we have both seen a lot in our lifetime, We have both seen too much suffering. What will you leave to your children? What will I leave to my grandchildren? I have only dreams to build a better world, a world of understanding and harmony, a world in which it is a joy to live. This is not asking too much…

Tomorrow I shall return to Jerusalem, the capital of the State of Israel and the heart of the Jewish people. Lining the road to Jerusalem are rusting hulks of metal; burnt-out, silent, cold. They are the remains of convoys which brought food and medicine to the war-torn and besieged city of Jerusalem 46 years ago.

For many of Israel's citizens, their story is one of heroism, part of our national legend. For me and for my comrades-in-arms, every scrap of cold metal lying there by the wayside is a bitter memory. I remember it as though it were yesterday.

I remember them. I was their commander in war. For them this ceremony has come too late. What endures are their children, their comrades, their legacy.

Allow me to make a personal note. I, military I.D. number three-zero-seven-four-three, retired general in the Israel Defense Forces in the past, consider myself to be a soldier in the army of peace today. I, who served my country for 27 years as a soldier, I say to you, Your Majesty, the King of Jordan, and I say to you, American friends:

Today we are embarking on a battle which has no dead and no wounded, no blood and no anguish. This is the only battle which is a pleasure to wage: the battle for peace.

Tomorrow, on the way up to Jerusalem, thousands of flowers will cover the remains of those rusting armored vehicles, the ones that never reached the city. Tomorrow, from those silent metal heaps, thousands of flowers will smile to us with a message of Peace: "Shalom."

In the Bible, our Book of Books, peace is mentioned, in its various idioms, 237 times. In the Bible, from which we draw our values and our strength, in the Book of Jeremiah, we find a lamentation for Rachel the Matriarch. It reads:

"Refrain your voice from weeping, and your eyes from tears: for their work shall be rewarded, says the Lord."

Let me conclude with the ancient Jewish blessing that has been with us in exile, and in Israel, for thousands of years:

"Blessed are You, 0 Lord, who has preserved us, and sustained us, and enabled us to reach this time".

God, Bless the Peace.

Washington, 26 July, 1994

A Dove with an Olive Branch

Talma Alyagon-Roz

I have a picture at home
Of a dove with an olive branch.
Above it the round sun blazes,
At its feet the debris of war.
It's the dove of peace,
Drawn by a master's hand,
A perfect picture,
A dream inside a frame.

Dove with an olive branch,
Step out of the picture!
Restore our belief
That peace will follow you.

I have a picture at home
Of a dove with an olive branch,
And my child gazes and asks:
What's that in its beak?
The dove of peace
It announces the end of war
A perfect dove
Of peace within a frame.

I have a picture at home
Of a dove with an olive branch.
It reminds me day and night
That outside on the cypress tree
lurks a raven.
The dove of peace
It never hurries anywhere
The dove is a tourist
Resting and staying.

There's a dove with an olive branch
Come out of the picture
Give back our hopes –
That peace will come in your wake.

There's a dove with an olive branch
In a picture I have at home.

Left: King Hussein, President Bill Clinton and Prime Minister Yitzhak Rabin: White House, July 1994

Below: Ceremony of signing the peace agreement with the Hashemite Kingdom of Jordan, Aqaba, 26 October, 1994

Peace Treaty Between the State of Israel and the Kingdom of Jordan

The Government of the State of Israel and the Government of the Hashemite Kingdom of Jordan:

Bearing in mind the Washington Declaration, signed by them on 25th July, 1994, and which they are both committed to honor;

Aiming at the achievement of a just, lasting and comprehensive peace in the Middle East based on Security Council resolutions 242 and 338 in all their aspects;

Bearing in mind the importance of maintaining and strengthening peace based on freedom, equality, justice and respect for fundamental human rights, thereby overcoming psychological barriers and promoting human dignity;

Reaffirming their faith in the purposes and principles of the Charter of the United Nations and recognizing their right and obligation to live in peace with each other as well as with all states, within secure and recognized boundaries;

Desiring to develop friendly relations and co-operation between them in accordance with the principles of international law governing international relations in time of peace; Desiring as well to ensure lasting security for both their states and in particular to avoid threats and the use of force between them;

Bearing in mind that in the Washington Declaration of 25th July, 1994, they declared the termination of the state of belligerency between them;

Deciding to establish peace between them in accordance with this Treaty of Peace;

Have agreed as follows:

I. Establishment of Peace

Peace is hereby established between the State of Israel and the Hashemite Kingdom of Jordan (the "Parties") effective from the exchange of the instruments of ratification of this Treaty.

II. General Principles

the principles of international law governing relations among states in times of peace.
In particular:

1. They recognize and will respect each other's sovereignty, territorial integrity and political independence;
2. They recognize and will respect each other's right to live in peace within secure and recognized boundaries;
3. They will develop good neighborly relations of co-operation between them to ensure lasting security, will refrain from the threat or use of force against each other and will settle all disputes between them by peaceful means;
4. They respect and recognize the sovereignty, territorial integrity and political independence of every state in the region;
5. They respect and recognize the pivotal role of human development and dignity in regional and bilateral relationships;
6. They further believe that within their control, involuntary movements of persons in such a way as to adversely prejudice the security of either party should not be permitted.

Done at the Arava/Araba Crossing Point this day 21 Heshvan, 5775; 21 Jumada Al-Ula, 1415 which corresponds to 26 October, 1994 in the Hebrew, English and Arabic languages, all texts being equally authentic. In case of divergence of interpretation the English text shall prevail.

For the State of Israel
Yitzhak Rabin, Prime Minister

Shimon Peres, Foreign Minister

For the Hashemite Kingdom of Jordan
Abdul Salam Majali, Prime Minister

Witnessed by: William J. Clinton
President of the United States of America

Kings of Israel Square, Tel Aviv (later renamed Rabin Square); the site of the assassination of the prime minister, the day after the shooting, 5 November, 1995

"Shalom Haver" – "Goodbye, Friend"

After the death of Prime Minister Yitzhak Rabin was confirmed, the director of the Prime Minister's Bureau, Eitan Haber, came out of Ichilov Hospital to the awaiting crowds and announced the shattering news:

"The Government of Israel announces in shock, in pain, and in deep grief, the death of Yitzhak Rabin, who was murdered by an assassin this evening in Tel Aviv. May his memory be blessed.

4 November, 1995

The Winter of Seventy-Three [After the Yom Kippur War]

Shmuel Hasfari

The poets of Israel did not only compose songs of praise to peace. They often voiced serious criticism that the striving for peace had not brought the long-awaited results: that a whole generation of Israeli children, whose parents had promised them a future of peace still found themselves in uniform and bearing weapons.

Leaving Sinai: "We have not retreated – we have withdrawn for the sake of peace"

We are the children
Of the winter of seventy three.
The first time you dreamed of us
Was at dawn, when the battle was over.
You, the bone-weary men,
Grateful for having survived.
You, the anxious young women,
So eager for love and for life.
And so you conceived us with love
In the winter of seventy three,
To replenish with your bodies
What war had taken away.

We were born into a country
That was wounded and sorrowful.
You gazed at us, held us close,
Seeking consolation.
When we were born, the old men
Gave blessing with tearful eyes.
They said - "Please God,
These children won't go to war".
Your faces in the old photograph
Prove that you meant it sincerely
When you promised to do your utmost for us
To transform enemies into friends.

Neither the firm attitude of Prime Minister Benjamin Netanyahu in the negotiations at Wye Plantation with Chairman Yasser Arafat, 1998, nor Prime Minister Ehud Barak's willingness to make serious concessions at Camp David, 2000, led to a breakthrough in the negotiations with the Palestinian leadership

You promised a dove and an olive branch,
You promised us peace - at home.
You promised us spring and blossoming-
You promised to keep promises!
You promised a dove –

We are the children
Of the winter of seventy three.
Now we too have grown up to be soldiers
With rifles and helmeted heads.
We too know how to make love,
To laugh and to cry.

We too are men,
We too are women,
We too dream of babies.
So we will not urge you –
So we will not demand –
And we will not utter threats.
When we were little,
You told us - promises must be kept!
If you need our strength,
We will give us unstintingly.
We just wanted to whisper:

We are the children
Of that winter – the winter of seventy three.

Let's Make a Small Peace

Leah Na'or

Let's make a small peace,
I with you, and you with me.
Let's make a small peace,
Real and true.
Let's make a small peace,
Not peace for all the world
Look, I'm making a small peace
With myself.

I'll never be angry – if I can manage it.
I won't make anyone else angry – anyone in particular.
I'll give in and you'll give in – more or less.
Let's make a small peace.
We won't shout or squabble.

We'll just sit together and talk - or listen.
Maybe it won't be a grand peace,
It'll be ordinary and simple,
But every peace has to start Somewhere.

237

A Palestinian State with Territorial Contiguity

Ariel Sharon

Ariel Sharon, Mahmud Abbas (Abu Mazen) and George W. Bush; the Aqaba Summit, 4 June 2003

Ariel Sharon, one of the most renowned of Israel's fighting soldiers and an ally of the settlement movement, assumed the post of prime-minister and reached the difficult and momentous decision that Israel had to vacate certain of the occupied lands of historical Eretz Israel and to accept the establishment of an independent Palestinian state. At the Aqaba summit meeting, together with the president of the United States, George W. Bush and the then prime-minister (now the Chairman) of the Palestinian Authority, Mahmud Abbas (Abu Mazen), Sharon spoke about the cessation of terrorism and the establishment of peace between Israel and the Palestinians.

As the Prime Minister of Israel, the land which is the cradle of the Jewish people, my paramount responsibility is the security of the people of Israel and of the State of Israel. There can be no compromise with terror, and Israel, together with all free nations, will continue fighting terrorism until its final defeat. Ultimately, permanent security requires peace and permanent peace can only be obtained through security; and there is now hope of a new opportunity for peace between Israelis and Palestinians.

Israel, like others, has lent its strong support for President Bush's vision, expressed on 24 June, 2002, of two states – Israel and a Palestinian state – living side by side in peace and security. The government and the people of Israel welcome the opportunity to renew direct negotiations according to the steps of the roadmap as adopted by the Israeli government to achieve this vision. It is in Israel's interest not to govern the Palestinians but for the Palestinians to govern themselves in their own state. A democratic Palestinian state fully at peace with Israel will promote the long-term security and well-being of Israel as a Jewish state.

There can be no peace, however, without the abandonment and elimination of terrorism, violence, and incitement. We will work alongside the Palestinians and other states to fight terrorism, violence and incitement of all kinds. As all parties perform their obligations, we will seek to restore normal Palestinian life, improve the humanitarian situation, rebuild trust, and promote progress toward the President's vision. We will act in a manner that respects the dignity as well as the human rights of all people.

We can also reassure our Palestinian partners that we understand the importance of territorial contiguity in the West Bank, for a viable Palestinian state. Israeli policy in the territories that are subject to direct negotiations with the Palestinians will reflect this fact. We accept the principle that no unilateral actions by any party can prejudge the outcome of our negotiations. In regard to the unauthorized outposts, I want to reiterate that Israel is a society governed by the rule of law. Thus, we will immediately begin to remove such outposts.

Israel seeks peace with all its Arab neighbors. Israel is prepared to negotiate in good faith wherever there are partners. As normal relations are established, I am confident that they will find in Israel a neighbor and a people committed to comprehensive peace and prosperity for all the peoples of the region.

Aqaba, 4 June 2003

Disengagement from the Gaza Strip, August 2005

"They shall never again be pulled up out of their land"

The biblical vision of David Ben-Gurion

Ben-Gurion selected and edited five biblical passages in which he saw the vision of Judaism and the testament they presented to the world and the Jewish people.

For thus says the Lord,
who created the heavens (he is God),
who formed the earth and made it
he did not create it a chaos
he formed it to be inhabited.
(Isaiah 45:18)

I am the Lord, I have called you in righteousness,
I have taken you by the hand and kept you,
I have given you as a covenant to the people,
a light unto the nations.
(Isaiah 42:6)

He shall judge between the nations,
and shall decide for many peoples;
and they shall beat their swords into ploughshares,
and their spears into pruning hooks,
nation shall not lift up sword unto nation,
neither shall they learn war anymore.
(Isaiah 2:4)

"I will restore the fortunes of my people Israel,
and they shall rebuild the ruined cities and inhabit them;
they shall plant vineyards and drink their wine,
and they shall make gardens and eat their fruit,
I will plant them upon their land,
and they shall never again be pulled up
out of the land
which I have given them." says the Lord your God.
(Amos 10:14-15)

When a stranger sojourns with you in your land,
you shall not do him wrong. The stranger who sojourns
with you shall be to you as the native among you,
and you shall love him as yourself,
for you were strangers in the land of Egypt.
(Leviticus 19:33-4)

A hand stretched out in peace:
Independence Day poster, 2002
(Design: Shiraz Wolman)

Illustrations

We have done our utmost to acquire permission from the various copyright holders of the photographs, art works and other illustrative material appearing in this book. Any omissions will be corrected in subsequent editions. We would like to express our thanks to all the photographers, artists and institutions who provided us with the illustrative material.

(Symbols after the page number: a – above; b – below, in brackets, the photographer.)

Bill Gross; Gross family collection: front endpaper, 13,14,18(b),21(a),22 (a), 23 (b),35, 39(a),46,49(b),50,51,52,54(a),55(b),64(a),6 5,85(b),224

Ilan Roth, Roth Collection, Herzlia www.jewishimages.com.: 18(a),61(a),67.68 (Walter Zadek),132(a),141 (no.8),144 (Nahum Gutman), 159(b),(Nahum Gutman),161(b) (Nahum Gutman),162(a) (Nahum Gutman),164 (Nahum Gutman),172, 175(b),178(b), (Nahum Gutman), 240

IDF Spokesman: 89(b) (Zvika Golan),95(a),(Zvika Golan),140 (no.3),143,(Zvika Golan),165(a) (Ro'i Tal),169 (b),208,210,212(a),215(b),216,217(a) Ro'i Tal

Haim Gouri: 201(a)

Kariel Gardosh (Dosh) family: 142,201(b)

Yaakov Farkash (Ze'ev) family: 180(b),183(b),229(b)

Batya and Ovadiah Hertzenstein: 74(a),75

Pnina Herzog: 43(a)

David Tartakover: 222

Geula Cohen: 118(a)

Avraham Katz-Oz: painting by Zionah Tagger 26-7(a),104-5

Yosef Tabor, son of the photographer Oscar Tauber: 205

Yigal Tumarkin: 197(b)

Tal Brody: 141(no.9)

Israel Airforce Industries: 140-1(no.2)

Iskar Blades, Industrial Park, Tefen: 141(no.7)

NASA: 138-9

Peter Schweitzer collection, New York: 15(a) (Beit Hatefutsot)

YIVO Archives, New York: 20(a), (Beit Hatefutsot)

Dr Uriel Federbush, New York: 21(a) (Beit Hatefutsot)

National and University Library, Jerusalem: 33

Jewish-American Historical Society,

Massachusetts, 62 (Beit Hatefutsot)

Library of the American Rabbinical Seminary, New York: 69 (Beit Hatefutsot)

Farkash Gallery, Old Jaffa: 84(b)

Shalom Seri: 79(b)

Amit Shabi: 218(b)

Michael Bar-Zohar: 5,74(b),96(a),160

Yehuda Salomon: 79(b),80(b)

Gilad Harish: 203 left

Yoram Sheftel: 196(a)

Yad Tabenkin Archives, Efal: 92(a) (Beit Hatefutsot)

Ben-Gurion Heritage Center, Ben Gurion College, Sde Boker: 128(b)

Alexandra Szyk-Bryce, Arthur Szyk Society, www.szyk.org: rear endpaper

Shamir Brothers Design: state emblem 128(a),posters 100(b),101(a)

***

Israel State Archives: Scroll of Independence Israel Government Press Office, Jerusalem: 17,2 8(b),29(b),37,41(b),42,47,49(a),61(b),81,88 ,90,91,93,94,95,97(b),98,99,100(a),103(b), 106(b),107(a),108,109(b),110,111,112,114 (a),115,120,122,123,124,126,128(a),129(b) ,131(a),135(b),136,137,140-1 (nos.1,5,6,10) ,145,146(a),147,148(a),150(b),151,152,158 9B0, 162(b), 167,168,169(a),170,171,174(a),177(a),180(a),181(a),182,184,187(a),188, 189,190(a),192-5,196(b),197(a),198(b),203 right,204,205,206,207(a),209,213,214(b),217 (b),218(a),219, 220(b),221(b),223,227,228, 229(a),231(a),232(b),234-6,237(b),238

Central Zionist Archives, Jerusalem: 19,24,27,3 2,48,54(b),64(b),70(a),72(b),76(b),77(a),8 2(a),83,134(a),174(b),176(a),220(a)

Jabotinsky Institute Archives, Tel Aviv: 114,130(a)

IDF Archives: 40(b),41(a),148(b),155(a),15 8(a),165(b)

Beit Hatefutsot Photographic Archives, Tel Aviv: 20-1(b),58-9(a),102(a),103(a)

Yad Vashem, photo and film division, Jerusalem: 86,89(a)

Lavon Institute for Research on the Labor Movement, Tel Aviv: 63,105,106(a),107(b),113

Israel Museum, Jerusalem: 34

Moshe Millner: 31,40-1(a),231(b),232(a),

Werner Braun: 207(b)

Dan Porges: 200

Flash 90: 186,220(b)

Associated Press: 199

Ofek Aerial Photography: 2-3,6-7,8-9,159

Albatross Aerial Photography: 30(b)

Jewish Heritage Museum, New York – gift of the Olera family. David Olera was deported from Drancy to Auschwitz on 2 March 1943; his number was 106144. Photograph by Peter Goldberg: 90 below right.

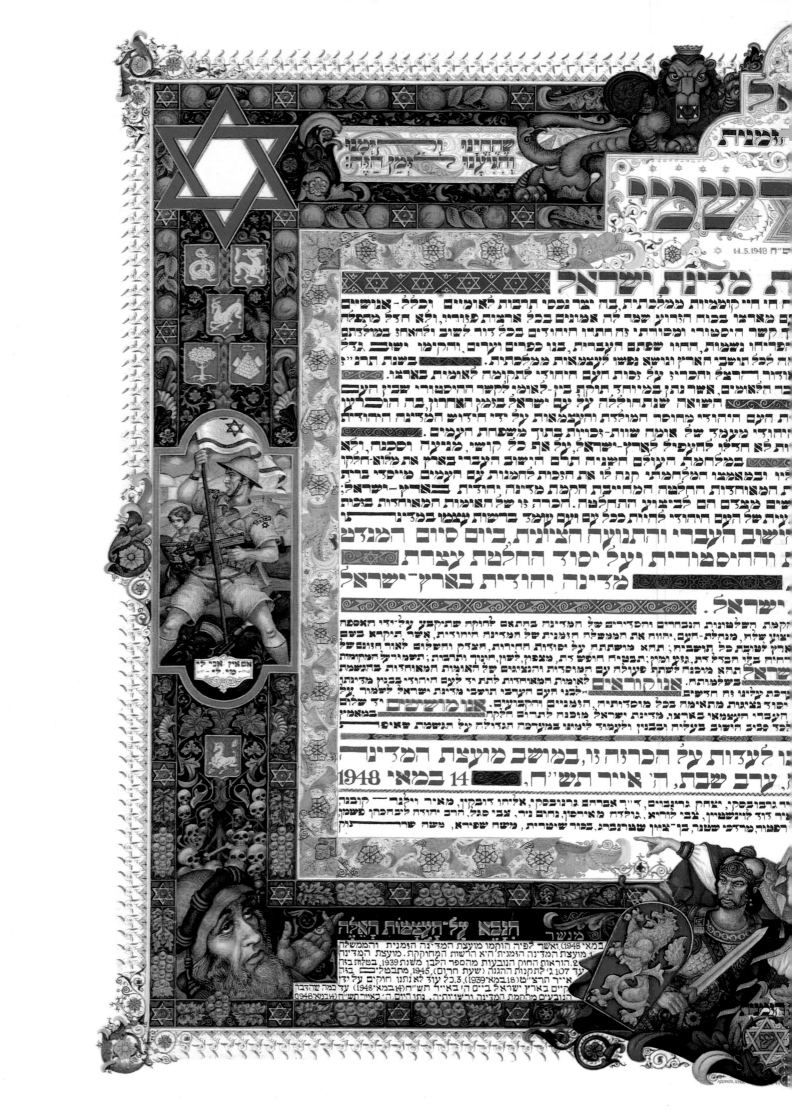